D0396461

A CABINET OF ROMAN CURIOSITIES

A CABINET OF ROMAN CURIOSITIES

STRANGE TALES
AND
SURPRISING FACTS
FROM THE
WORLD'S GREATEST EMPIRE

J. C. McKEOWN

UNIVERSITY PRESS
2010

OXFORD
UNIVERSITY PRESS

Oxford University Press, Inc., publishes works that further
Oxford University's objective of excellence
in research, scholarship, and education.

Oxford New York
Auckland Cape Town Dar es Salaam Hong Kong Karachi
Kuala Lumpur Madrid Melbourne Mexico City Nairobi
New Delhi Shanghai Taipei Toronto

With offices in
Argentina Austria Brazil Chile Czech Republic France Greece
Guatemala Hungary Italy Japan Poland Portugal Singapore
South Korea Switzerland Thailand Turkey Ukraine Vietnam

Published by Oxford University Press, Inc.
198 Madison Avenue, New York, New York 10016

www.oup.com

Library of Congress Cataloging-in-Publication Data
McKeown, J. C.
A cabinet of Roman curiosities : strange tales and surprising facts
from the world's greatest empire / J. C. McKeown.
p. cm.
ISBN 978-0-19-539375-0
1. Rome—Civilization—Miscellanea.
2. Rome—History—Miscellanea. I. Title.
DG77.M425 2010
937—dc22
2009043574

1 3 5 7 9 8 6 4 2

Printed in the United States of America
on acid-free paper

Any resemblance to actual persons, events, and institutions, long gone and often almost entirely forgotten, should be assessed by the reader on a case-by-case basis. Errors of fact are, for the most part, not attributable to the author. As Pliny the Elder wisely says, *nec tamen ego in plerisque eorum obstringam fidem meam potiusque ad auctores relegabo*: "I generally give no guarantee of the truth of what I say, preferring to leave that responsibility with the authors whom I quote" (*Natural History* 7.8).

For Mark and Matthew, Stevie and Annie

PREFACE

THE ROMANS have left us far more information about themselves than has any other Western society until much more recent times. Most books about ancient Rome sift and assess this material to present as coherent and accurate a picture of life and thought at that period as is possible at a distance of two thousand years. Extraordinary acumen and subtlety are required for such a task, since we so often have only an opaque and partial view of the broad context within which to judge this surviving evidence.

This is not such a book. Essentially, it is a collection of observations about ancient Rome, for the most part culled directly from Latin and Greek texts, which strike me as interesting, curious, or simply amusing, and which I hope will appeal to others in the same way. I am not an expert in ancient history and have rarely presumed to express an opinion on the validity, intention, or importance of statements made by the Roman and Greek writers quoted or cited in the book. As it happens, I personally find it hard to believe that a six-inch fish could have held back Mark Antony's flagship during the Battle of Actium, or that Milan was founded because a woolly pig was seen on the future site of the city, or that the phoenix appears every five hundred years, or that touching the nostrils of a she-mule with one's lips will stop sneezing and hiccups, or that fish sauce is an effective cure for crocodile bites, or that any Roman emperor was eight foot, six inches tall. I strongly suspect that goats do not breathe through their ears, and that there are no islands in the Baltic Sea inhabited by people whose ears are so enormous that they cover their bodies with them and do not need clothes. I do not myself wear a mouse's muzzle and ear tips as an amulet to ward off fever, nor do I know precisely how one might attach earrings to an eel.

Not all the material presented in this book is quite so bizarre. It seems worth noting that a gladiator could earn more by winning a single fight than most schoolteachers earned in a year; this may invite comparison with the disparate earnings of a football coach and a professor at the same college. When a dictator and his deputy were being appointed to deal with a national emergency, a shrew was heard to squeak, and this omen forced both of them to withdraw from their command; some readers may be struck by the difference from present-day methods of making senior military appointments. Cleopatra drank a priceless pearl to win a bet with Antony; this gesture may seem the more splendid when contrasted with the sad modern fad for gold leaf desserts and cocktails containing carefully appraised diamonds. After assassinating his younger brother, with whom he had ruled jointly, an emperor destroyed all images of him and removed his name from public records; is that not how the Orwellian Big Brother would attempt to control thought? This book does not often attempt to draw modern analogies of this sort.

The material has a superficial ordering (particular topics or people or historical periods), but this principle of arrangement is not observed consistently nor is it important. There is no argument being compiled as the book progresses; nearly every item in each section can be read in isolation. I am relying on classical precedent. As Aulus Gellius says in the preface to his *Attic Nights*, a miscellaneous collection of facts, anecdotes, and discussions ranging over a charmingly wide and unpredictable variety of topics, "I have presented the material in the same casual way as I gathered it; that is to say, whatever Greek or Latin book I took up to read or whatever I heard that was worth remembering, anything at all that caught my fancy, I noted it down without regard for system and order."

Our information about ancient Rome comes from material objects such as buildings, coins, pots and pans, and other such artifacts from everyday life, but also, and far more significantly, from written texts. Latin and Greek are the only two ancient European languages that are not only almost fully comprehensible but are also blessed with a wide spectrum of surviving written texts, ranging from poetry to history, from legal, medical, scientific, and other technical treatises to inscriptions and graffiti. Although the classical era of Greek literature was over before most Greeks had even heard of Rome, and although the Romans never came close to matching the Greeks in the quantity of their literary output, most surviving Greek texts were nevertheless written after the Roman conquest, and very many of them are more informative about life in the Roman world than they are about life in a Greek city-state. It will not therefore be surprising that Greek writers such as the historians Polybius, Plutarch, and Cassius Dio, the geographer Strabo, and the doctor Galen are cited so frequently in this book.

The same story has often been preserved in several different versions. I refer either to the best-known source, or to the most coherent, or simply to the passage in which I happened to note it. Frequently, to avoid cluttering the text and to ensure that the reader does not suppose that this book has academic pretensions, I do not cite sources at all. When ancient authorities are quoted directly, this is indicated either by italicization or by quotation marks. Such quotations should not, however, be assumed to be verbatim: details not relevant to the point being made are often omitted, and extra information is sometimes added to clarify the context.

The book started out as a serendipitous miscellany of short passages quoted directly from ancient authors, which were first collected to accompany the electronic exercises to *Classical Latin*, my introductory course in Latin (Hackett Publishing Company [2010]). Learning vocabulary and word forms is a necessary part of language acquisition, but it can sometimes be rather boring. To reward students for doing the online exercises, a new quotation appears every time a file is opened. This principle is sound and has a good classical model: the great Epicurean philosopher-poet Lucretius declares that he will try to make his difficult teachings more palatable by giving them a veneer of poetic charm, just as doctors trick children into drinking bitter medicine by smearing honey round the rim of the cup (*On the Nature of Things* 1.933–950). Unfortunately, however, as soon as the exercises were posted online, students told me that they preferred clicking through the quotations to doing the exercises. By making the quotations available in this book, I hope to have reduced this temptation.

The not-quite-so-great Epicurean philosopher-poet Horace famously says that, although the Romans conquered Greece, in intellectual terms it was the Greeks who conquered their unsophisticated conquerors and brought their arts to uncivilized Latium (*Graecia capta ferum victorem cepit, et artes/intulit agresti Latio* [*Epistles* 2.1.156f.]). The Romans did, however, have at least one fine literary tradition all but unknown among the Greeks: the custom of dedicating books to their sons (though hardly ever to their daughters). Cato, Cicero, Livy, the elder Seneca, Quintilian, Apuleius, Macrobius, and even St. Augustine all stand in this long and distinguished tradition, and nearly all express the typically Roman practical hope that the dedicatees will find the work improving and helpful in life. I aspire to a little originality in dedicating this book not only to my two sons, Mark and Matthew, but also to my two stepdaughters, Stevie and Annie, with the daringly un-Roman hope that they will be entertained by it.

Poets were never slow to imply their own greatness by humbly acknowledging the inspiration they had received from Apollo, the god of poetry, and from the Muses. (Ovid is a notable exception, declaring at the beginning of his *Art of Love*, a manual on seduction, that the poem is not divinely inspired, but is based on his own experience in love affairs.) On the other hand, Roman writers rarely thank by name the friends from whom they receive advice and criticism for the improvement of their work. This is remarkable, given that the *recitatio* was an important institution in Roman intellectual life; reciting their work to a group of friends provided an opportunity for authors to receive criticism before publication. There were many things wrong with Roman society, and such apparent discourtesy was hardly its most serious flaw, but no author nowadays would wish to emulate it. I cannot claim an epiphany by Apollo or by any of the Muses but, although I have not recited any part of this book to anyone, I am very happy to acknowledge my considerable debt to many friends for their advice and criticism. Linda Alston, William Aylward, Jeffrey Beneker, Sabine Gross, Danielle Kleijwegt, Arthur McKeown, Richard Miles,

Silvia Montiglio, David Potter, Alison Siddall, Richard Talbert, Andrew Wallace-Hadrill, and Sophie Zermuehlen have helped me greatly with their expert advice and opinions.

I am especially grateful to Debra Hershkowitz, not just for her many good-humored and patient suggestions for improving the presentation of the material, but also, and perhaps more significantly, for convincing me that numerous passages by ancient authors that I find fascinating are not likely to appeal to anyone else; I have reluctantly removed many such quotations and grudgingly grant that, as Ovid says in the epigram prefaced to the much reduced second edition of his *Amores*, "Even if there's no pleasure to be gained from reading the book, at least it will be less tedious now that so much has been taken away."

I owe a particular debt to my wife, Jo, who has not only helped me well beyond reasonable limits with the preparation of this book, but has also listened to interminable and indeterminate speculations on how soldiers could come face to face with bears in siege tunnels, or how members of one of Rome's leading families felt when their sacred coin refused to eat, or how Romans kept appointments when the whole city had only one sundial, known to be wrongly calibrated.

Finally, it is a great pleasure to acknowledge the unfailingly helpful and reassuring guidance I have received from Stefan Vranka, Deirdre Brady, and Christine Dahlin at Oxford University Press in preparing this rather odd *opusculum* for publication.

CONTENTS

A CABINET OF ROMAN CURIOSITIES

FAMILY LIFE

mater dicitur quod exinde efficiatur aliquid.
mater enim quasi materia
Mater means “mother” because it is the source from which things are produced, for *mater* (“mother”) is as it were the *materia* (“material”).

St. Isidore *Etymologies* 9.5.6

Romulus ensured that his city should be large and populous by requiring the inhabitants to rear all their male children and also their firstborn daughters. He forbade the killing of any child under the age of three years unless it was born crippled or with deformities. In such cases he did permit exposure, provided the parents had first shown the child to five neighbors and obtained their agreement (Dionysius of Halicarnassus *Roman Antiquities* 2.15.1).

Numa Pompilius, the second king of Rome, was praised for amending the law that allowed fathers to sell their sons into slavery. *He gave immunity to married sons, so long as the father of both bride and groom had approved the marriage, for he regarded it as unfair that a woman who married a man whom she thought to be free should find herself living with a slave* (Plutarch *Life of Numa* 17).

A marriage can be arranged even when the parties are absent. This is an everyday occurrence (Justinian's *Digest* 23.1.4). A proviso was later

The magnificent 5th-century B.C. Etruscan she-wolf, now on the Capitol. Romulus and Remus were added about two thousand years later. A replica of the group was given by Benito Mussolini in 1929 to the city of Rome, Georgia, and erected in front of its City Hall. For several years, to safeguard decorum when important civic events were scheduled, the she-wolf was draped, and the twins were diapered.

appended: *So long as the marriage is arranged with the knowledge of the absent parties, or they agree to it subsequently* (23.1.5).

❁

There is not the same strict age requirement for the contracting of an engagement as there is for an actual marriage. An engagement can therefore be arranged even at a very young age, provided that both parties understand what is happening: that is to say, they must not be less than seven years old (Justinian's *Digest* 23.1.14).

❁

Marriage is the joining together of a man and a woman in a lifelong partnership, in accordance with laws both human and divine (Justinian's

Digest 23.2.1). *It is on record that for almost five hundred years after the founding of Rome there were no lawsuits or other actions about dowries either in the city or in Latium, because there were no divorces* (Aulus Gellius *Attic Nights* 4.3.1). There is, however, a very considerable amount of space devoted in the legal texts to laws relating to divorce.

❁

Divorce was easy for a man to obtain if he was willing to return his wife's dowry. He simply had to recite the ancient formula *tuas res tibi habeto* ("Have your own things for yourself").

❁

If a man does not take a mistress and give regular payments to someone else's wife, all the married women regard him as pathetic, addicted to shameful practices, a chaser of slave girls. . . . No man gets married except by taking away another man's wife. . . . Can there be any disgrace in divorce, when no woman gets married except to retain her lover's interest? Sexual restraint is taken as proof of ugliness. What woman is so wretched, so ugly, as to be satisfied with only a pair of lovers? Any woman who doesn't know that having just one lover is called "marriage" is stupid and quaint (Seneca *On Benefits* 1.9, 3.16).

❁

As censor, with a responsibility to defend traditional morality, the elder Cato (234–149 B.C.), expelled a member of the Senate for kissing his own wife in broad daylight in front of his daughter. He claimed that he himself never embraced his wife except after a loud peal of thunder, adding that he was happy when it thundered (Plutarch *Cato the Elder* 17).

❁

The elder Cato praised a young man when he saw him leaving a brothel, since he felt that this would mean he would leave other men's wives alone. But, when he saw him leaving the brothel on other occasions also, he said to him, "Young man, I praised you for coming here from time to time, not for living here" (ancient commentators on Horace *Satires* 1.2.31).

❁

When a woman visited her and was showing off her jewels, the most beautiful in Rome at that time, Cornelia, the mother of the Gracchi, kept

A toy horseman.

her talking till her sons returned from school, and then she said, "These are my jewels" (Valerius Maximus *Memorable Deeds and Sayings* 4.4).

Do you not see how differently fathers and mothers treat their children? Fathers order them to be roused early to start their chores; even on holidays, they do not allow them to be idle, and draw sweat and sometimes tears from them. Mothers, however, cuddle their children in their lap, and try to keep them in the shade, away from sadness, tears, and hard work (Seneca *On Providence* 2).

The best slingers came from the Balearic islands, where mothers would not allow their young sons anything to eat unless they were able to hit the dish containing their food with a slingshot (Vegetius *Military Affairs* 1.16). The islands' name was associated with the Greek word βάλλειν (*ballein*, "to throw") (Diodorus Siculus *The Library* 5.17).

If ever we bumped into a rock when we were children, going along with our mouths gaping open, didn't our nurse smack the rock instead of scolding us? But what had the rock done wrong? Should it have moved out of the way because of our childish stupidity? (Epictetus *Discourses* 2.19.4).

The children of the wealthy were regularly given over to wet nurses. In the second book of his treatise *Gynecology*, written in the second century A.D., Soranus makes the following recommendations:

- *A wet nurse should be between twenty and forty years old and have had two or three children of her own.*

- *She should be self-controlled, sympathetic and even-tempered, Greek, tidy.*
- *She must not be superstitious.*
- *She must not allow the diaper to get smelly.*
- *She should not drink, because the psychological and physical damage done to her by wine spoils her milk; she may lapse into a stupor, and then neglect or fall over the child; the wine's characteristics are passed into the milk, and this can make the child slow and drowsy, sometimes even apoplectic, just as sucking piglets become slow and drowsy if the sow has eaten plants with narcotic qualities.*

Putting goat dung in their diapers soothes hyperactive children, especially girls (Pliny *Natural History* 28.259).

The elder Seneca records a simple but ingenious law by which the fair division of an inheritance within the family was ensured: *maior frater dividat patrimonium, minor eligat* ("Let the elder brother

One of the hundreds of half-burned wooden writing tablets excavated at the remote Roman fort at Vindolanda, near Chesterholm, south of Hadrian's Wall in northern England. It is an invitation to a birthday party, and it contains the postscript *I will be hoping* [*to see*] *you, sister. Farewell, sister, my dearest soul, as I hope to flourish, and greetings,* the earliest Latin identified with certainty as written by a woman (*Vindolanda Tablet* 291). For more about these tablets, written in the early second century A.D., visit vindolanda.csad.ox.ac.uk.

divide the patrimony, and let the younger one choose") (*Controversies* 6.3).

They say that, when the few survivors straggled back to Rome after the massacre at Cannae in 216 B.C., one woman died at the very gate of the city in the arms of her son who had returned safely; another, who had been told erroneously that her son was dead, was sitting sadly at home and died of joy as soon as she saw him coming back (Livy *History of Rome* 22.7).

Aristocratic families kept death masks of their ancestors on display in the atrium of their houses. These images were paraded at funerals: Sulla's cortège in 78 B.C. is said to have been accompanied by six thousand such masks, and that of Marcus Claudius Marcellus in 23 B.C. by six hundred (Servius's commentary on Vergil *Aeneid* 6.862).

HIC IACET CORPVS PVERI NOMINANDI: *Here lies the body of a child whose name is to be added* (*L'Année Epigraphique* [1931] no. 112; the stonemason has absentmindedly copied the general rubric onto a tombstone instead of adding the dead child's actual name).

It was a cliché that stepmothers (but not stepfathers) were cruel:

- *If parents treat their children unjustly in their will, their action should not be condoned. People usually pass a harsh judgment like this on their flesh and blood when they have been corrupted by the wheedling and urging of a stepmother* (Justinian's *Digest* 5.2.4).
- *If you marry a man who has children by a former wife, no matter how gentle you may be, all the comic plays and all the mime writers and all the commonplaces of the orators will present you as a very savage stepmother* (St. Jerome *Letters* 54.15).
- *A young man studied medicine after his father disowned him. When his father fell ill, and the doctors said he could not be cured, he cured him. His father took him back into the family. Subsequently, his stepmother fell ill, and the doctors despaired of saving her. The father begged his son to cure his stepmother and disowned him again when he refused* (Seneca *Controversies* 4.6).

Scenes from childhood on a child's sarcophagus.

- In soldiers' slang, a military camp pitched on disadvantageously uneven ground was called a "stepmother" (*noverca*).
- Marcus Aurelius was said to have declined to marry again after the death of his wife, the younger Faustina, *so as not to inflict a stepmother on so many children* [they had at least twelve children, and perhaps as many as fifteen] (*Historia Augusta* Life of Marcus Aurelius 29).

pater . . . nam tum esse conceptum, patet, inde cum exit quod oritur
A father (*pater*) is so called because, at the birth of a child, it is evident (*patet*) that conception has taken place.

Varro *On the Latin Language* 5.65

· II ·

WOMEN

utinam lex esset eadem quae uxori est viro!
I wish there was the same law for husbands as
there is for wives!
Plautus *The Merchant* 823

Our ancestors wanted all women to be under the control of guardians because of their feeble powers of judgment (Cicero *In Defense of Murena* 27). The supposed inferiority of women is not a peculiarly Roman prejudice. It was, if anything, even more entrenched among the Greeks. Aristotle, for example, says that *a woman is a kind of imperfect man*, and that *it is through a disability that the female is female* (*On the Generation of Animals* 728*a* and 737*a*).

Livy reports that about 170 women from leading families were convicted in 331 B.C. of poisoning their husbands (*History of Rome* 8.18). Other sources give even larger numbers.

A senator took his son to a meeting of the Senate but made him promise not to tell anyone what he heard discussed. That evening, the boy's mother kept asking him to tell her. To stop her cajoling him, he pretended that the Senate had discussed whether every man should have two wives, or every woman two husbands. She promised to tell no one, but next morning the Senate house was surrounded by women tearfully begging that women should have two husbands.

The senators thought that their wives had gone mad (Aulus Gellius *Attic Nights* 1.23). About three hundred years before Gellius, Polybius had dismissed this well-known tale as no better than the silly gossip one hears in a barber's shop (*Histories* 3.20).

Plutarch tells a similar story about a senator "whose wife was in all other respects a sensible woman, but a woman all the same." She asked her husband what the Senate had been debating. To put an end to her questioning, he pretended that they had been trying to determine whether it was a good or a bad omen that a lark had been seen flying around with a golden helmet and a spear. As he was leaving for the Forum, he told her to say nothing about it, but when he reached the Forum, he was met by someone who asked if he had heard about the lark that had been seen flying around with a golden helmet and a spear (*On Talkativeness* 11).

Aemilia Tertia, the wife of the elder Publius Cornelius Scipio Africanus and the mother of Cornelia, who was to be the mother of the Gracchi brothers, the great reformers, was a woman of great gentleness and tolerance. Although she was aware that her husband was attracted to one of her own slave girls, she pretended not to know so that she, a woman, should not charge Africanus, the conqueror of the world, with lack of self-control. Revenge was so far from her mind that, after Africanus's death, she freed the slave girl and gave her in marriage to one of her freedmen (Valerius Maximus *Memorable Deeds and Sayings* 6.7).

Citizens, if we could live without wives, we would all do without that trouble. But since nature has so arranged that we can neither live comfortably with them nor manage without them, we should consider the long-term advantage rather than the pleasant convenience of the moment (Metellus Numidicus, one of the censors in 102 B.C., attempting to increase the birthrate by urging men to marry, as quoted by Aulus Gellius at *Attic Nights* 1.6).

Mark Antony's wife, Fulvia, totally ignored the traditional wifely activities of spinning and housekeeping, and she thought it beneath her dignity to control an ordinary man: she wanted to rule a ruler and command a commander. So Cleopatra owed her a teacher's fee, for she had taught Antony how to be ruled by a woman, and Cleopatra took him over when he was thoroughly broken in, trained right from the start in obeying a woman (Plutarch *Life of Antony* 10). This observation will perhaps not have seemed so satirical from an Egyptian perspective; *in Egypt, the queen traditionally enjoys greater power and honor than does the king, and among private citizens the wife is lord over the husband, for, by the terms of the marriage contract, he undertakes to obey her in all matters* (Diodorus Siculus *The Library* 1.27).

❁

Fulvia stabbed Cicero's tongue with her hairpins in retaliation for what he had uttered against Mark Antony. (She already had reason to dislike Cicero, for he had also opposed her first husband, the rabble-rousing Clodius.) Fulvia was a strong character, described by Velleius Paterculus as "a woman in body alone" (*Histories* 2.74). Pomponia, the widow of Cicero's brother, who was also killed in the proscriptions, was perhaps no gentler. According to one account, when Antony sent her the freedman who had betrayed Cicero, she forced him to cut strips off his own body, then cook and eat them (Plutarch *Life of Cicero* 49).

❁

When Quintus Lucretius was proscribed by the Triumvirs, his wife, Turia, hid him in a little room between the ceiling and the roof. Only a slave girl knew about it. Turia kept him safe from imminent death, not without great risk to herself. Whereas the rest of those proscribed had difficulty in escaping and faced extreme tortures, both physical and mental, in unfamiliar and hostile surroundings, Lucretius was safe in his own bedroom, in his wife's bosom (Valerius Maximus *Memorable Deeds and Sayings* 6.7.2).

❁

The Julian Law on adultery of 18 B.C. decreed that a woman caught in the act of adultery could be killed by her father, provided that her lover was also killed. Her husband did not have the same authority. There was never any corresponding legislation on the adulterous behavior of husbands.

The Germanic custom of cutting and surrendering one's hair as a token of submission seems to have made blonde wigs fashionable among Roman women after the conquest of the Sygambri, a German tribe, in the Augustan period (Ovid *Amores* 1.14.45ff.). Ovid recalls the embarrassment for all concerned when a girl he unexpectedly visited hurriedly put her wig on back to front (*The Art of Love* 3.246). Faustina, the wife of the emperor Marcus Aurelius, was said to have had a collection of several hundred wigs. Justinian's *Digest* mentions a tax on wigs imported from India (39.4.16.7), along with similar luxury taxes on eunuchs, lions, and leopards.

Galen cites several concoctions intended to counter hair loss from a book on cosmetics supposedly written by Cleopatra. One involves pulverized mouse heads, another smearing the bald spot with an ointment based on mouse droppings (*On the Composition of Medicines by Place* 12.403). Ovid also wrote a surprisingly humorless poem on the subject, "Cosmetics for the Female Face" (*Medicamina Faciei Femineae*), of which only the first hundred lines survive.

A jar of Roman face cream was found intact in London in 2004. It is a mixture of animal fat, starch, and tin.

In A.D. 20, the Senate debated a proposal that provincial governors should be forbidden to take their wives with them to their provinces. It was argued that women were weak and unequal to the difficulties of travel. Given the chance, they would

A perfume jar in the shape of a mouse.

be cruel, ambitious, and greedy for power. Governors' wives were responsible for most charges of extortion, their demands were unreasonable and arbitrary, and they already ruled at home, in the courts, and even in the army. The proposal was rejected, but not on overly commendable grounds. Women, it was decided, were naturally feeble and should not be left at home, exposed to temptation and the lusts of other men. If husbands struggled to keep their marriage safe even when they were present, what did they imagine would happen if they were absent for several years? (Tacitus *Annals* 3.33–34).

Women were required to sit in the back rows at the theater, but there was no such segregation at the circus or in the amphitheater.

A woman urged her husband to commit suicide when she found that he had been suffering for a long time from putrescent ulcers of the groin, beyond hope of a cure. To make it easier for him, she tied herself to him and jumped out of a window into a lake (Pliny *Letters* 6.24).

There seems to be almost no valid and persuasive reason why adult women should have guardians. The common opinion, that they tend to be deceived because of their light-mindedness, seems superficially plausible rather than true. Some adult women do conduct their affairs personally, and, in many cases, a guardian gives his consent purely as a matter of form (Gaius *Institutes* 1.190).

Sometimes we can refute a statement by pretending to agree with it. When Fabia, Dolabella's wife, claimed to be thirty, Cicero said, "That's true, for I've heard her say it for the last twenty years" (Quintilian *Education of the Orator* 6.3.73).

When a Spanish woman gives birth, her husband lies in bed, and she looks after him (Strabo *Geography* 3.4.17).

VESTAL VIRGINS

The vestal virgins were responsible for maintaining the temple of Vesta and performing the rites of the goddess. They ensured that her holy flame, said to have been brought from Troy, was not extinguished. The vestal virgins had considerable privileges not enjoyed any other women in Rome:

- They were maintained in luxury at public expense.
- They were free from paternal authority.
- Wills and treaties were in their keeping, and they themselves could make a will.
- They could conduct business in their own name.
- They could give evidence in court without taking an oath.
- They were allowed to ride through Rome in wheeled carriages.
- Even the highest magistrates had to give way to them.
- If they accidentally met a criminal on his way to execution, he was spared.

For a vestal virgin to be convicted of sexual misconduct was a rare but momentous event. Such occurrences are recorded particularly often at times of military crisis, and the punishment of the vestal(s) concerned was part of a ritualistic purification of the state. Because a vestal's person was sacrosanct, she could not be executed. Instead, she was entombed in an underground chamber with a bed, a lamp, and some food and water, and left to die. Male accomplices were publicly flogged to death.

Pliny relates without further comment the well-known story that, when charged with sexual misconduct, a vestal virgin named Tuccia established her innocence by carrying water in a sieve to the temple of Vesta from the Tiber. He is skeptical, however, about the vestals' supposed power to fix runaway slaves to the spot by prayer, provided they have not yet left the city (*Natural History* 28.12–13).

Augustus rather paradoxically granted to vestal virgins legal privileges normally reserved for women who had borne three children.

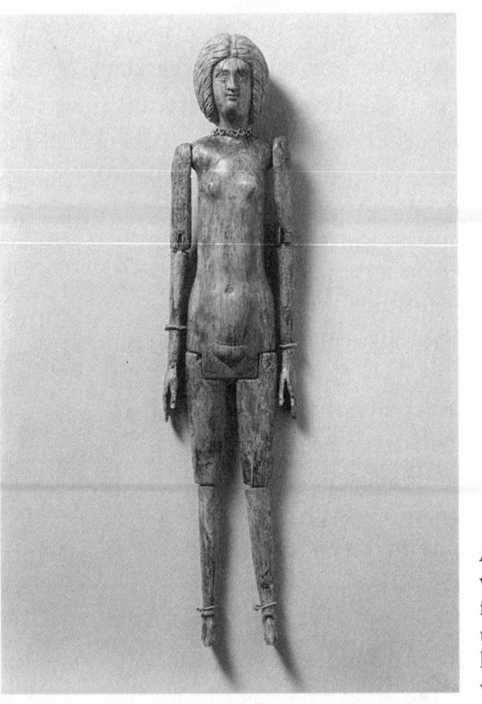

A doll carved from ivory, with a gold necklace, found at Tivoli in the tomb of Cossinia, who had served as a vestal virgin for sixty-six years.

Conversely, but just as paradoxically, Caligula made all three of his sisters, who were all married, honorary vestal virgins.

Elagabalus (ruled A.D. 218–222) greatly offended public opinion, first by marrying the vestal virgin Aquilia Severa, then by divorcing her, and then by marrying her again, an outrage that led to his assassination (Cassius Dio *Roman History* 79.9).

Vestal virgins had privileged seats at public spectacles. It is perhaps a little difficult to reconcile their staid and sober demeanor with the rabid fanaticism known to have been displayed by spectators at horse races and gladiatorial shows. Prudentius, a Christian poet at the end of the 4th century, notes this paradox in describing a vestal's ringside reaction to a gladiatorial bout:

She jumps up when the blows strike home and every time the winner sticks his sword in his opponent's neck. The modest virgin calls him her darling, and with a turn of her thumb she commands that the sprawling man's chest be ripped open, lest any part of his life should lurk in his inmost vital organs, while the gladiator quivers as he presses his sword in deeper (*Against Symmachus* 2.1096–1101).

❁

antiquum poetam audivi scripsisse in tragoedia,
mulieres duas peiores esse quam unam:
res ita est
I've heard that a poet long ago wrote in a
tragedy that two women are worse than one:
and so they are.
Plautus ***Curculio*** **591**

· III ·

NAMES

nisi nomen scieris, cognitio rerum perit
If you don't know what to call things, you
lose your awareness of them.
St. Isidore *Etymologies* 2.7.1

A male Roman citizen typically had three names, a *praenomen*, *nomen*, and *cognomen*: a personal name that precedes (*prae*) the family name (e.g., *Marcus*), then the family name (e.g., *Tullius*), and then the name that comes with (*cum/cog-*) the family name and either specified the particular branch of the family or was a nickname peculiar to that one person (e.g., *Cicero*). The praenomen was used by family and close friends; in public contexts, either the nomen or cognomen might be used, or both together. More formally, the names of his father and his tribe might be added (e.g., *Marcus Tullius Marci filius Cornelia tribu Cicero*, "Marcus Tullius Cicero, son of Marcus, from the Cornelian tribe").

By the end of the Republic, only eighteen praenomina were current, though nearly forty more are known from earlier times. Roman praenomina may seem very restricted to us, but a Roman would find our use of initials overly vague. Without further guidance, he could not fully identify M. Monroe, M. Mouse, M. Poppins, or M. Proust, whereas M. Tullius Cicero is unambiguous, since M. can stand only for Marcus.

Praenomina do not quite correspond to our first names. If that were so, Augustus would probably not have adopted the praenomen *Imperator* ("Commander").

Nothing illustrates the low public status of women so vividly as do their names:

- They were usually known simply by the feminine form of the family nomen; hence the daughters of *Gaius Iulius Caesar* and *Marcus Tullius Cicero* were called *Iulia* and *Tullia*, respectively.
- Not even the daughters of the grandest families had a praenomen, though *Maior, Minor, Tertia, Quarta*, and so on ("Elder," "Younger," "Third," "Fourth") would be used to distinguish between sisters, or between nieces and aunts.
- In the late Republic, it became frequent for women to be known by the feminine form of the family nomen and by the cognomen in the genitive case—the form of the name denoting possession; hence *Tullia Ciceronis* ("the Tullia of Cicero"). In modern Greece, an unmarried woman's surname is the family name in the genitive case, and most Slavic countries have a comparable system.
- Roman women generally did not change their name when they married. Many married women referred to in inscriptions do have the same name as their husbands, but this is presumably because they had both been slaves in the same household, or because freedmen and -women had married their former owners.

Curious forms such as *Gaipor, Lucipor, Marcipor* (= *Gaii puer, Lucii puer, Marci puer*; literally, "the boy of Gaius," "the boy of Lucius," "the boy of Marcus") attest that in early times slaves had little personal identity. Later, they had a single name, but their owner's name might be appended—as, for example, *Felix Antonii* (*servus*), "Felix, the slave of Antonius." There was a broad range of slave names, a large proportion of which were Greek. If a slave was freed, he typically took the praenomen and nomen of his ex-master, but retained his slave name as his cognomen.

Modern convention in referring to Roman names is unsystematic:

- Less familiar figures are generally denoted by their nomen and cognomen. Certain famous men are known by their nomen (e.g., Titus Lucretius Carus as *Lucretius*, Gaius Suetonius Tranquillus as *Suetonius*) or by an Anglicized version of it (e.g., Publius Vergilius Maro as *Vergil*, Quintus Horatius Flaccus as *Horace*), others by their cognomen, either without change (e.g., Gaius Valerius Catullus as *Catullus*, Marcus Tullius Cicero as *Cicero*) or with slight change (e.g., Lucius Sergius Catilina as *Catiline*, Marcus Annaeus Lucanus as *Lucan*).
- Praenomina are almost never used, although notable exceptions are made to distinguish between the *Gracchi* brothers (*Tiberius* and *Gaius*) and to denote *Sextus Pompeius*, the son of *Pompey* (Gnaeus Pompeius Magnus; to confuse matters, he adopted the name *Magnus Pompeius Magni filius* ["son of Magnus"] *Pius*). The Anglicized form *Mark Antony* is probably influenced by Shakespeare.

❁

The choice between the various combinations of praenomina, nomina, and cognomina seems arbitrary, but is adhered to fairly rigidly in individual cases:

- The playwright *Terence* (*Publius Terentius Afer*) is never called *Terentius* or *Afer* or *Terentius Afer*, whereas the great scholar *Varro* (*Marcus Terentius Varro*) is never called *Terence*, though he is occasionally *Terentius Varro*.
- To refer to *Ovid* (*Publius Ovidius Naso*) as *Naso* or to *Vergil* (*Publius Vergilius Maro*) as *Maro* is antiquated.
- To call *Cicero* (*Marcus Tullius Cicero*) *Tully* has long gone out of fashion, while *Sallust* (*Gaius Sallustius Crispus*) has never been known as *Crispy*, and *Marcus Porcius Cato* has always been known as *Cato*.

◎

There was no limit to the number of cognomina an individual might possess, but no one else comes close to having as many as did *Quintus Pompeius Senecio Roscius Murena Coelius Sextus Iulius Frontinus Silius Decianus Gaius Iulius Eurycles Herculanus Lucius Vibullius*

Pius Augustanus Alpinus Bellicius Sollers Iulius Aper Ducenius Proculus Rutilianus Rufinus Silius Valens Valerius Niger Claudius Fuscus Saxa Amyntianus Sosius Priscus, consul in A.D. 169, whose thirty-six cognomina are known from a commemorative inscription found at Tivoli, a few miles east of Rome (*Corpus of Latin Inscriptions* 14.3609). That *Iulius* is used three times, and *Silius* twice, will have made it that much easier for him to remember who he was.

SOME PROHIBITED NAMES

- Marcus Manlius Capitolinus saved the Capitol from the Gauls in the early 4th century B.C. when he was alerted to their approach by the cackling of Juno's sacred geese. Subsequently, however, he was convicted of aspiring to kingship and thrown from the Tarpeian rock on the Capitol. His family decided never again to use the praenomen *Marcus* (Livy *History of Rome* 6.20).
- The Claudians similarly stopped using the praenomen *Lucius* after two members of the family so named were convicted of highway robbery and murder, respectively (Suetonius *Life of Tiberius* 1).
- The Senate decreed that no Antonius after Mark Antony should be called *Marcus* (Plutarch *Life of Cicero* 49) and that the Scribonii should not use the cognomen *Drusus* after Marcus Scribonius Libo Drusus was convicted of attempting to assassinate Tiberius (Tacitus *Annals* 2.32).
- XVII, XVIII, and XIX, the numbers of the legions lost in the Teutoburg massacre of A.D. 9, were never again given to legions.
- Gnaeus Calpurnius Piso was condemned in A.D. 20 for the murder of Germanicus, grandson of Augustus's wife, Livia, on the paternal side, of Mark Antony on the maternal, and father of Caligula. His name was struck from the consular records, and his son Gnaeus was allowed to retain half of his inheritance only on condition that he changed his praenomen.

❁

Unwanted children could be left to die. The names *Proiectus* and *Proiecticus* mean "thrown out," and *Stercorius* indicates more specifically "left on a dung heap." One Flavius Stercorius was a military administrator in the Danube region in A.D. 369 (*Select Latin Inscriptions* 770).

Roma was the state's political name, but it had also another name, to be used only in mystery rites: the palindromic *Amor* ("Love"). In the Republican period, a tribune of the *plebs* named Valerius Soranus was executed, perhaps by crucifixion, a punishment usually reserved for slaves and noncitizens, for divulging this secret alternative name (Servius on Vergil *Aeneid* 1.277, Joannes Lydus *On the Months* 4.73).

Varro reports that Rome was originally called *Septimontium* ("Seven Hills"). The hills usually reckoned in this group are the Aventine, Caelian, Capitoline, Esquiline, Palatine, Quirinal, and Viminal, but there was no canonical list of seven in the classical period, largely because of the claims for inclusion of the two hills on the other side of the Tiber, the Vatican and the Janiculum, and of the Pincian to the north. Place names in Rome beginning with Monte (e.g., Montecitorio, Montevecchio, Monte Cenci, and, of course, Monte Testaccio) (see p. 176) are all man-made, originating from the ruin of large buildings or the accumulation of rubbish dumps.

Several explanations of *Palatium*, the name of the Palatine hill, were proposed in antiquity. It may have been so called after Pallas, the grandfather of Evander, a Greek settler who was living on the site in the time of Aeneas. Other derivations suggest the Romans' origins as a pastoral people: either from *balatus* ("bleating"), or from *pasco*, which means the same as, and is related to, the English word "pasture."

Augustus was at pains to avoid all suspicion that he wished to be king, so it is ironic that our word "palace" is derived from *Palatium*, after the relatively modest home which he built for himself on that hill. By a similar irony, the English word "prince" is derived from the title *princeps* ("first man"), which Augustus adopted because of its reminiscence of the traditional Republican title *princeps senatus* ("leader of the Senate").

One of the derivations suggested in antiquity for the name of the Vatican hill linked it with *vates* "priest"—a striking coincidence, given its modern function.

Byzantium had been founded c. 660 B.C. by colonists from the Greek city of Megara supposedly led by one Byzas. In A.D. 196, Septimius Severus renamed it Augusta Antonina in honor of his son, Marcus Aurelius Antoninus (Caracalla). In 330, Constantine established his capital there, renaming it Roma Nova, and subsequently Constantinople. The modern name, Istanbul, a corruption of the Greek phrase εἰς τὴν πόλιν (*eis ten polin* "into the city"), was not officially adopted until 1930, but it can be traced back to the 13th century.

Caracalla [ruled A.D. 211–217] *called himself* Germanicus *after victories over the Germans, and it was said that he was mad enough and stupid enough to say that, had he conquered Lucania* [a region in southern Italy], *he would have claimed the title* Lucanicus [which means not only "Lucanian" but also "sausage"] (*Historia Augusta* Life of Caracalla 5).

The Sicilian town of Segesta seems to have been founded by Aeneas; Egestus, whom he put in charge of it, called it Egesta. But the letter S was put at the front to prevent it from being called by an ill-omened name [*egestas* means "poverty" in Latin]. *Such changes have been made also to the names of the cities of Maleventum* [suggesting "turning out badly"] *and Epidamnus* [suggesting "loss," "damnation"], *respectively, to Beneventum* [suggesting "turning out well"] *and Dyrrachium* [after Dyrrachus, the son of Neptune and founder of the city] (Festus *On the Meaning of Words* p. 458). The town of Narnia (now Narni) in Umbria was once known as Nequinum, which has connotations of "worthless" (*nequam*). If Italians concerned themselves with such things nowadays, Milan's main airport, Malpensa ("bad thought"), would have been renamed.

The Romans named the five known planets *Mercurius*, *Venus*, *Mars*, *Iuppiter*, and *Saturnus*. The corresponding Greek names *Stilbon* ("Shining"), *Phosphoros* ("Light-Bringer"), *Pyroeis* ("Fiery"), *Phaethon* ("Shining"), and *Phaenon* ("Shining") are not so distinctive.

❁

The word for "sky" and "heaven," *caelum* (which is the origin of our word "ceiling"), was sometimes thought to be derived from the verb *caelare*, meaning "to engrave." All the stars were believed to be fixed in the vault of the sky equidistant from the earth.

❁

The Romans and Greeks thought that Saturn was close to the outer limit of the universe. Uranus, named after the Greek word for "sky" and "heaven," is the closest of the planets that are invisible to the naked eye and were therefore unknown in antiquity. When William Herschel discovered it in 1781, he wanted to call it *George*, in honor of George III of England.

❁

Rome's greatest poet was Publius Vergilius Maro, but the incorrect form "Virgil," first attested in the 5th century, is the commoner spelling in English, and the intrusive *i* is often found in other languages also. Vergil's cognomen, *Maro*, is an anagram of both *Roma* and *Amor*, but neither he nor any other ancient writer seems to make anything of this coincidence.

❁

The first member of the Cicero family to be so called was said to have a slight dent at the end of his nose, like the split in a chickpea (in Latin, *cicer*). When Cicero himself entered public life, his friends urged him to change his rather droll name. He is said to have replied that he would do his best to make it more distinguished than any of the great names in Rome. When he was dedicating a piece of silver plate to the gods, he had the engraver inscribe the names *Marcus* and *Tullius*, and then complete the sequence with a representation of a chickpea (Plutarch *Life of Cicero* 1).

❁

Greeks also could have what seem to us rather peculiar names. The Spartans Sauras ("Lizard") and Batrachos ("Frog") built the temples in the Portico of Octavia in Rome. Since they were not allowed to inscribe their actual names on the buildings, they had a lizard and a frog carved on the spirals of the columns (Pliny *Natural History* 36.42).

There are several lizards and frogs lurking in the foliage on the lower frieze on the outer screen surrounding the *Ara Pacis* (the Altar of Augustan Peace).

One of the many tombs that line the Via Appia is that of Publius Decimius Philomusus. *Philomusus* means "Lover of the Muses," but an alternative meaning, "Lover of Mice," is playfully suggested by the engraving of two mice nibbling at a cake.

The Latin word *musculus* means both "little mouse" and "muscle," since muscles rippling under the skin were compared to little mice. In the same fanciful way, St. Isidore of Seville (c. A.D. 560–636) says that the *lacertus* ("upper arm") is named after "little animals that lurk underground" (i.e., *lacertae*, "lizards") (*Etymologies* 11.1.117).

Publius Clodius Pulcher created a scandal by dressing as a woman to attend the festival of the Good Goddess (*Bona Dea*) in 62 B.C., allegedly to carry on an affair with Caesar's wife. He was actually born into the aristocratic family of the Claudii, but, to further his career as a populist politician, he changed the spelling of his name to its less distinguished form and had himself adopted into a plebeian family in which his adoptive father was younger than he was (Suetonius *Life of Tiberius* 2).

It was customary for an influential man to be accompanied by a *nomenclator*, a slave whose duty it was to remind him of the names of people he met:

- *Augustus used to complain about his* nomenclator*'s forgetfulness, and once, when the slave was going to the Forum, he said, "Take this letter of introduction, for you don't know anyone there"* (Macrobius *Saturnalia* 2.4.15).
- Seneca mentions senile *nomenclatores* who have to invent names for people whom their masters meet (*Letters* 27.5).
- The Persian king Cyrus could remember the names of all his soldiers. A member of the Scipio family could call every Roman citizen by his name. And Cineas, sent as an ambassador by King Pyrrhus, had memorized the names of all the senators and knights just one day after arriving in Rome (Pliny *Natural History* 7.88).
- *Hadrian often corrected his own* nomenclatores, *for he was able to remember a person's name even after hearing it only once and along with many others* (*Historia Augusta* Life of Hadrian 20).

A front-rank centurion angered the emperor Gaius by calling him Caligula ("Little Army-Boot"). *Since he was born in camp and had been brought up among soldiers, this is what he used to be called, and he was never so well known to the soldiers by any other name, but once he started to wear big boots he considered* Caligula *an insult and a disgrace* (Seneca *On Firmness* 18).

A pair of greyhounds.

Galba, the first emperor who was not a member of the Julio-Claudian dynasty, adopted *Caesar* as a cognomen. This practice extended throughout the Holy Roman Empire, producing the German *Kaiser* and the Russian *tsar*. In modern texts, when "Caesar" appears without further definition, the reference is usually to Julius Caesar.

⊕

So that each dog may hear quickly and accurately when it is called, they should not be given long names, nor names shorter than two syllables. For example, Greek names such as Skylax ["Puppy"] *and* Lakon ["Spartan"], *Latin ones such as* Ferox ["Fierce"] *and* Celer ["Swift"]; *for bitches, Greek names such as Spoudé* ["Haste"], *Alké* ["Vigor"], *Romé* ["Strength"], *Latin names such as* Lupa ["She-wolf"], Cerva ["Deer"], Tigris ["Tigress"] (Columella *On Farming* 7.12.13). Columella is influenced by Xenophon, who gives a list of forty-seven names for dogs at *Hunting with Dogs* 5.7. They all have two syllables.

WHAT'S IN A NAME?

The everyday names of many flowers retain interesting associations from antiquity:

- *alyssum*: ἀ and λύσσα (*a* and *lussa*, "not madness"). *Drinking a concoction made from alyssum prevents those bitten by a dog from contracting rabies* (Pliny *Natural History* 24.95).
- *delphinium*: δελφίς (*delphis*, "dolphin"). *Its seeds or flowers are shaped like a dolphin* (Pseudo-Dioscorides *On Female Herbs* 57).
- *gentian*: Gentius, the last king (ruled 180–168 B.C.) of the Illyrians (in the western Balkans) discovered its pharmaceutical properties (Pliny *Natural History* 25.71).
- *geranium*: γερανός (*geranos*, "crane," from the similarity of its flower to a crane's bill). The name *pelargonium*, from πελαργός (*pelargos*, "stork"), was given in antiquity to a variety of geranium, not to the closely related flower now so named.
- *gladiolus*: "little sword" (*gladius*), *from the shape of its leaves* (Palladius *On Farming* 1.37).
- *hyacinth*: the flower was said to have sprung from the blood of Hyacinthus, a Spartan boy accidentally killed by his lover Apollo with a discus (Ovid *Metamorphoses* 10.209ff.).
- *iris*: the flower is named after Iris, the Greek goddess of the rainbow, because it has many different colors (Pliny *Natural History* 21.41).

- *lily*: not all varieties of lily cultivated in antiquity were white, but St. Isidore associates them with *lac* ("milk"): lilia ("lilies") *are a plant with a milky* (lactei) *color, as if their name was really* liclia (*Etymologies* 17.18).
- *lupin(e)s* were not associated with wolves (*lupi*). *By their bitterness they make the face of anyone who tastes them sad* (St. Isidore *Etymologies* 17.4, alluding to a link with λύπη [*lupe*, "pain"] and suggesting that Vergil plays with this derivation in the phrase *tristes lupini* ["sad lupins"] at *Georgics* 1.75).
- *narcissus*: as punishment for spurning the love of the nymph Echo, Narcissus was made to fall in love with his own reflection. He lay gazing in the spring so long that he eventually took root and was transformed into the flower (according to one of the most brilliant narratives in Ovid's *Metamorphoses*, 3.407ff.). Pliny (*Natural History* 21.128) more prosaically supposes that the flower is so named because eating it causes numbness (*νάρκη*, *narce*).
- *nasturtium*: the sharp taste of nasturtiums causes us to twist our nose (*nasum torquere*) when we eat them (Varro *Fragments of Roman Grammar* 224.95).
- *onopordon acanthium*: cotton thistle, the emblem of Scotland, derives its name from *ὄνος* (*onos*, "donkey") and *πέρδομαι* (*perdomai*, "pass gas"). *As for Onopordon, they say if Asses eat thereof, they will fall a fizling and farting* (Pliny *Natural History* 27.110, in the translation of Philemon Holland [1601]).
- *orchid*: ὀρχίς (*orchis*, "testicle"). *The orchid has a twin root, like testicles* (Pliny *Natural History* 26.95). A variety of olive was also known in antiquity as the orchid, from the shape of its fruit.
- *ranunculus*: literally, "little frog" (*rana*), for no obvious reason the name of a large family of flowers, including buttercups, crowfoots, and the lesser celandine.
- *rhododendron*: *ῥόδον*, *δένδρον* (*rhodon*, *dendron*, "rose," "tree"). *As is obvious from its name, the rhododendron comes from the Greeks* (Pliny *Natural History* 16.79).
- *rose*: the varieties of rose cultivated in antiquity were almost exclusively red. Writing at about the end of the 6th century, St. Isidore could still suggest that *rosé wine is so called from its redness, for roses are red* (*Etymologies* 20.3, linking *rosa* rather imaginatively with *rubere*, "to be red").

- *rosemary* is derived from *ros marinus* ("sea-dew"), from the plant's liking for coastal regions. The first element has been falsely assimilated to "rose," the second to "(the Virgin) Mary."
- *saxifrage*: from *saxum* ("rock") and *frango* ("break"). *It has the marvelous quality of driving out and breaking pebbles* [i.e., gallstones], *especially black ones; I prefer this to the usual etymology, that it grows among rocks* (Pliny *Natural History* 22.64).
- *viola* (violet): *The violet has been given its name on account of its strong scent* (i.e., *vi olet*, "it smells strongly") (St. Isidore *Etymologies* 17.19).

❁

nomen atque omen
A name and an omen.
Plautus *Persa* 625

· IV ·

EDUCATION

caedi discentes, quamvis id receptum sit,
minime velim
Although it is usual to flog pupils, I really do
not approve the practice.
Quintilian *Education of the Orator* 1.3.14

The study of grammar in Rome was said to have started in the middle of the 2nd century B.C., when Crates of Mallos came to Rome as an ambassador from the king of Pergamum (in western Turkey). He had to open a school to make a living after he broke his leg by falling into the *Cloaca Maxima* (Main Drain) near the Palatine hill.

Porcius Latro, a distinguished teacher of rhetoric in the Augustan period, had a pale complexion, caused by incessant study. His students drank a mixture based on cumin to induce pallor, as a way of showing their devotion to him (Pliny *Natural History* 20.160). Latro was the rhetorician whom Ovid particularly admired (Seneca *Controversies* 2.2.8); it is tempting to suppose that the great author of the *Metamorphoses* was one of these adoring students.

The poet Horace was taught by Lucius Orbilius Pupillus [literally, "Student," a fine cognomen for a famous teacher], *who published a book titled* On Stupidity, *in which he complains about the injustices suffered by teachers because of parents' negligence or interference. He was*

The boy now arriving at school is carrying his writing tablets, not his lunchbox.

nasty not only to his critics, whom he savaged at every opportunity, but also to his students: Horace calls him a "flogger" [plagosus], *and Domitius Marsus* [a minor poet] *writes of "those whom Orbilius has struck with a cane or a strap"* (Suetonius *On Teachers of Grammar and Rhetoric* 9).

❁

Quintilian felt it necessary to argue at length against the widely accepted practice of flogging students (*Education of the Orator* 1.3), and Plutarch thought it noteworthy that Sarpedon, the tutor of Cato the Younger, was more likely to reason with his students than to thrash them (*Life of Cato the Younger* 1). Orbilius once appeared in court as a witness against someone whom the father of the future emperor Galba was defending. Galba, who was a hunchback, tried to unsettle him and deflate his self-importance by asking what his profession was, but Orbilius replied, "I massage hunchbacks in the sunlight" (Macrobius *Saturnalia* 2.6.4). The verb meaning "massage" here, *fricare*, probably bears also the sense "thrash."

❁

In the late 2nd century A.D., a senatorial decree allowed for the granting of a bonus of five hundred *sestertii* to a victorious gladiator if he was a free man, and of four hundred if he was a slave (*Select Latin Inscriptions* 5163.29ff.), the amount that a schoolteacher might make in a year (Juvenal *Satires* 7.242). Since the purpose of the decree was to limit the costs of gladiatorial games, we may infer that such bonuses were usually rather more generous.

❁

Payment of five hundred *denarii* (DENARIOS QVINGENTOS) to fighters for every leopard killed. This was a generous prize; Diocletian's price edict of A.D. 301, promulgated not long after this mosaic was created, set the daily wage for a farm worker at twenty-five *denarii*.

"One and one, two; two and two, four [*unum et unum duo; duo et duo quattuor*] was a loathsome chant to me" (St. Augustine *Confessions* 1.13.22, in one of his many outbursts of disgust at his schooldays).

A boy should begin his education with the Greek language, since he will in any case absorb Latin, the language which most people use. Another reason for starting with Greek is that Latin studies are derived from Greek. He should not, however, spend too long exclusively on Greek, since that will cause faults in expression and accent in his Latin (Quintilian *Education of the Orator* 1.1.12).

A graffito from Pompeii lists the letters alternately forward and backward, *AXBVCT* and so on (*Corpus of Latin Inscriptions* 4.9272; *U*,

W, *Y*, and *Z* are not in the original Latin alphabet), suggesting that students were expected to display considerable agility in learning the alphabet.

Quintilian recommends that very young children be given ivory letters as toys to encourage them to learn their alphabet. *Then, as soon as a child recognizes the shapes of the letters, it is useful to have them carefully carved on a board, so that the pen can be drawn along that furrow; this prevents the mistakes which a child makes on a wax tablet* (*Education of the Orator* 1.1.26).

The Ostrogoth Theodoric the Great, who ruled Italy from A.D. 493 to 526, was almost illiterate and such a slow learner that for the first ten years of his rule he could endorse documents only by tracing the word *LEGI* ("I have read [it]") through a stencil in a block of wood (*Excerpta Valesiana* 79). The Byzantine emperor Justin (ruled A.D. 518–527) was similarly said to have traced the letters of the word *FIAT* ("let it be so") (Procopius *Secret History* 6).

Wax tablets are more user-friendly, for it is very easy to erase writing . . . whereas the frequent need to dip the pen in ink delays the hand and interrupts the thought process when one is writing on parchment (Quintilian *Education of the Orator* 10.3.31).

occidit miseros crambe repetita magistros
Rehashed cabbage is the death of wretched teachers.

Juvenal *Satires* 7.154, criticizing the repetitive dullness of the highly conservative and unimaginative school curriculum

• V •

THE ARMY

bellum, hoc est minime bellum
War, that is to say not at all nice.
Donatus *Grammar* 4.402.4

Lucius Siccius Dentatus, a semilegendary icon of Roman bravery, fought in one hundred and twenty battles in the 5th century B.C. He received forty-five wounds on his chest but none on his back, and he won enough decorations for a legion, not just for one soldier (Valerius Maximus *Memorable Deeds and Sayings* 3.2.24).

Being an agricultural people, the Romans originally fought their wars only in the summer, between sowing and harvest, since winter makes troop movement difficult. Warfare was first continued into the winter during the siege of the Etruscan city of Veii in the early 4th century B.C. This innovation was hotly debated:

> *If a war is not finished in the summer, our soldiers must learn to wait through the winter and not, like summer birds, look around for shelter as soon as autumn comes. The pleasure of hunting carries men off through snow and frost to the mountains and the woods: Should we not apply to the demands of war the same endurance as is elicited by sport and pleasure?* (Livy *History of Rome* 5.6)

King Pyrrhus (319–272 B.C.) of Epirus defeated the Romans in two battles in 280 and 279, but at great cost. When he saw the corpses of the Roman soldiers, with all their wounds on the front and with savage expressions on their faces, he is said to have raised his hands to heaven and declared that he could have conquered the whole world if he had been lucky enough to have such soldiers (Eutropius *Breviarium* 2.11). Ever since then, the term "Pyrrhic victory" has meant a success won at too high a price.

An earthquake occurred at Lake Trasimene in 217 B.C. while the Romans and Carthaginians were fighting there. Despite its severity, neither the Romans nor the Carthaginians noticed it (Pliny *Natural History* 2.200).

The great-grandfather of Lucius Sergius Catilina, who attempted to overthrow the government in 63 B.C., was a hero in the Second Punic War. He was twice captured by Hannibal and kept in chains for twenty months, but twice he escaped. He had a prosthetic right arm made of iron so that he could continue fighting, and twice his horse was killed under him (Pliny *Natural History* 7.104–105).

When Scipio decided that enough of his troops were in the city, he unleashed the majority of them against the citizens, according to Roman practice, with orders to kill without mercy anyone they came upon and not to turn to plundering till the signal was given. The reason for this policy is, I think, to inspire terror. This is why, when the Romans take a city, one sees not only human beings slaughtered, but also dogs cut in half and the limbs of other animals hacked off (Polybius *Histories* 10.15, referring to the destruction of New Carthage in Spain in 209 B.C.).

The Macedonians were used to fighting Greeks and Illyrians, and so had only seen wounds inflicted by spears and arrows, and occasionally by lances. When they saw bodies dismembered by the Romans' Spanish swords, and arms sliced off at the shoulder, and heads separated from the trunk, neck and all, and entrails exposed, and other ghastly wounds, they trembled as they realized what weapons and what soldiers they would have to face (Livy *History of Rome* 31.34, referring to the Romans' use of the *gladius*, the short Spanish stabbing sword, against Philip V in the Second Macedonian War [200–196 B.C.]).

❁

In A.D. 272, Aurelian encountered stubborn resistance when he besieged Tyana [in south-central Turkey]. *In his frustration at the prolonged siege, he declared, "I shall not leave a dog in this town." By the time Tyana fell, Aurelian had decided to be merciful to the citizens and told his soldiers to kill only the dogs. Despite being deprived of their expected plunder, the troops took his decision in good spirit, as if it were a joke* (*Historia Augusta* Life of Aurelian 22).

❁

At the Battle of Chaeronea in 86 B.C., Sulla's army neutralized Mithridates' ninety scythed chariots by charging at them, thus depriving these fearsome weapons of the momentum they needed to break through the Roman lines. When the Romans repulsed the chariots, they jeered and clapped their hands, calling for more to be sent out, just as if they were at the races in the Circus. . . . By the same tactic of closing in fast, the Romans gave Mithridates' archers no room to draw their bows, forcing them to try to repulse their sword-wielding enemies with handfuls of arrows (Plutarch *Life of Sulla* 18, 21).

❁

Perhaps as many as a million people died in Julius Caesar's conquest of Gaul. In an unnamed battle in 57 B.C., *almost the whole tribe of the Nervii, along with their name, was wiped out. The survivors sent envoys offering submission. In describing the extent of the disaster, they said that only three of the six hundred members of their Senate and scarcely five hundred of their sixty thousand fighting men were still alive* (Caesar *Gallic War* 2.28).

❁

Pliny gives 1,192,000 as the number of those killed by Julius Caesar's forces in battle, not counting the civil wars. In an inscription commemorating the dedication of spoils in the Temple of Minerva in Rome, Pompey boasted of much greater achievements:

> *The commander Gnaeus Pompeius Magnus duly makes this dedication to Minerva, having completed a war of thirty years with the routing,*

scattering, slaughtering, or capture of 12,183,000 of our foes, and with the sinking or capture of 846 ships, and with the surrender of 1,538 towns and forts, and with the conquering of all the land from the Sea of Azov to the Red Sea (*Natural History* 7.97).

Records of battle casualties are rarely reliable. In the Battle of Sentinum (295 B.C.), for example, in which the Romans gained control of central Italy by defeating the Samnites and Gauls, the enemy lost twenty-five thousand men according to Livy (*History of Rome* 10.29), but a hundred thousand according to his near-contemporary Diodorus Siculus (*The Library* 21.4). To prevent generals from bolstering their claim to a triumph by exaggerating the number of enemy dead or by playing down Roman casualties, a law was passed (in the 60s B.C.) requiring them to swear that their reports were accurate (Valerius Maximus *Memorable Deeds and Sayings* 2.8.1).

Even making allowance for imprecision, the disproportionate figures for casualties on the opposing sides in a battle are often remarkable. For example:

- For various battles fought in the first half of the 2nd century B.C., Livy gives twelve thousand enemy dead as opposed to 73 Romans (*History of Rome* 35.1), fifty-three thousand to 349 (37.44), nine thousand to 109 (40.48), twenty thousand to 100 (44.42).
- According to Plutarch, in the Battle of Artaxata in 68 B.C., the Armenians lost a hundred thousand of their infantry and almost all their cavalry, whereas the Romans suffered a hundred wounded and five dead (*Life of Lucullus* 28).
- Strabo reports that, in a recent expedition to Arabia, ten thousand of the enemy were killed for the loss of two Romans (*Geography* 16.4.24).
- The satirist Lucian complains about a historian who records battle losses for the enemy of 70,236 killed, as opposed to two dead and nine wounded on the Roman side, adding that no one in his right mind would accept such statistics (*How to Write History* 20).

Augustus said that wars should be undertaken only if there was hope of considerable rewards, for seeking a victory involving small returns at a heavy price was like fishing with a golden hook: nothing one might catch could be balanced against the expense of its being lost (Suetonius *Life of Augustus* 25).

Caligula arranged his troops in battle order on the shore of the Ocean, with his catapults and other artillery deployed, as if he were actually about to go to war. No one knew or could guess what he was going to do. Suddenly he ordered the troops to gather shells and fill their helmets and the folds in their clothing, calling out that the shells were "spoils from the Ocean, owed to the Capitoline and Palatine" (Suetonius *Life of Caligula* 46; several years later, Claudius's troops did invade Britain).

When Spartacus's army was trapped by the Romans, he gave the impression of having a larger and better organized force than he actually did by tying dead bodies to stakes outside his camp and equipping them with weapons, so that from a distance they looked like sentries (Frontinus *Stratagems* 1.5.22).

During the Third Macedonian War (171–168 B.C.), to ensure that his horses would not be frightened by the Romans' elephants, King Perseus accustomed them to dummy elephants, which he smeared with a foul-smelling concoction and made to emit noises as loud as thunder (Cassius Dio *Roman History* 20 *fragment*).

In 141 B.C., *after subduing most of Spain, Quintus Metellus heard that he was to be replaced by his personal rival, Quintus Pompeius. He lost his right to a triumph because he sabotaged the transfer of command by:*

- *granting retirement to all who wanted it;*
- *giving leave without asking for reasons or fixing time limits;*
- *making the stores of grain vulnerable to looters by dismissing the guards;*

- *ordering the Cretan archers' bows and arrows to be broken and thrown into the river;*
- *denying fodder to the elephants.*

(Valerius Maximus *Memorable Deeds and Sayings* 9.3.7).

Sometimes a general should ride along the battle line and (if he happens to be on the right wing) shout to his men, "Our left wing is defeating the enemy right" (and vice versa if he is on the left). He should do this whether it is true or not, for deceit is needed in great crises. Similarly, if the enemy general is far away, on the opposite wing or holding the center of their battle line, he should shout out, "The enemy general (or king, or whoever it is) has been killed." And he should shout loudly enough to be heard by the enemy as well (Onasander *The General* 23.1).

The word for a military camp, *castra*, was popularly derived from the adjective *castus*, meaning "chaste," or from the verb *castrare*, "castrate," since sexual desire was castrated there. The emperor Septimius Severus (ruled A.D. 193–211) was the first to permit serving soldiers to marry.

Military camps were always laid out the same way, so that soldiers would know where to go if the alarm were sounded. Moreover, *when an enemy spy has infiltrated the camp, the soldiers should all be ordered back to their tents in the daytime; the spy will be detected immediately* (Vegetius *Military Affairs* 3.26). Mithridates the Great used this ploy against Romans in his camp (Cassius Dio *Roman History* 36.13).

When the Senate conferred on him a triumph due to Trajan, Hadrian declined it for himself, but had an effigy of Trajan borne along in the triumphal chariot, so that his predecessor should not lose the honor of a triumph even after death (*Historia Augusta* Life of Hadrian 6). Several ancient authorities attest that a public slave rode beside a triumphing general in his chariot, holding a golden crown set with jewels over his head and repeatedly saying to him, "Look behind you," meaning

"Watch out for what you cannot yet see in life to come, and do not be carried away into arrogance by your present good fortune" (Zonaras *Excerpts from History* 7.21). There would have been little need for a slave to accompany Trajan, reminding him of his mortality, since he was already dead and about to be deified.

It is customary for a general who is about to celebrate a triumph to invite the two consuls to a banquet, but that they should then be asked not to attend, so that on the day of his triumph there should be no one present with greater authority than the triumphator (Valerius Maximus *Memorable Deeds and Sayings* 2.8.6).

We tend to imagine just a few large-scale siege engines being deployed, but this was not always so:

- When Scipio took the Spanish city of New Carthage in 209 B.C., the armaments that he captured included 120 large catapults and 281 smaller ones intended for use in sieges.
- The eyewitness Josephus says that Vespasian and Titus employed 160 siege engines in their assault on Jerusalem in the late 60s A.D., requiring every tree within a radius of more than ten miles around the city to be cut down to supply the necessary timber (*The Jewish War* 3.166).
- In a vain attempt to conciliate the Romans and avoid the destruction of their city in the Third Punic War (149–146 B.C.), the Carthaginians handed over two thousand catapults and two hundred thousand other weapons (Polybius *Histories* 36.6).

In A.D. 60, when Nero's great general Corbulo was besieging Tigranocerta, the Armenian capital, he catapulted the head of a captured Armenian nobleman over the ramparts right into the midst of a council meeting, thereby persuading the inhabitants to surrender (Frontinus *Stratagems* 2.9).

You could appreciate the power of the catapult by the events of that night. A soldier standing on the wall near Josephus was struck by it. His head

Germans executing Germans under the supervision of the Roman cavalry, on the Column of M. Aurelius, which nowhere portrays even a single dead Roman.

was torn off by the stone missile, and the upper part of his skull was hurled six hundred yards (Josephus *The Jewish War* 3.246).

Spurius Carvilius constructed a colossal statue of Jupiter on the Capitol from the breastplates, greaves, and helmets taken from the Samnites defeated in the Battle of Sentinum (295 B.C.; Pliny *Natural History* 34.43). The statue was so big that it could be seen from the Alban Mount, some ten miles away, and the bronze filings left over from the construction were sufficient for Carvilius to have a statue of himself made from them, which stood at the feet of the statue of Jupiter.

Tunneling was an important part of siege warfare. According to legend, during the siege of the Etruscan city of Veii in 396 B.C., some

Roman soldiers who were digging a tunnel heard a soothsayer in the citadel directly above them declare that victory would be given to whoever should cut out the sacred parts of the victim which their king was sacrificing at that moment; the Romans burst out of their tunnel and seized the entrails, and the city was then captured (Livy *History of Rome* 5.21).

A comparable incident seems to have occurred during Livy's own lifetime. While Octavian was besieging Perugia (see p. 193), he received unfavorable sacrificial omens, but when a party of soldiers burst out from the city and carried off the sacrifice, they inadvertently brought the bad omens upon themselves (Suetonius *Life of Augustus* 96).

In the war with Mithridates the Great in the early 1st century B.C., Lucullus's army was impeded in its tunneling under the city of Themiscyra when the inhabitants drove bears, other wild animals, and swarms of bees into the tunnels.

Skeletons and weapons discovered in tunnels at Dura Europus in Syria are evidence of an underground battle when the Persians were besieging the Roman fort in the mid-3rd century A.D. The Persians seem to have asphyxiated a troop of twenty Roman soldiers with fumes from bitumen and sulfur; see www.independent.co.uk for January 18, 2009.

As a countermeasure to assault by a battering ram, a sack filled with straw is let down to the point of impact, for the blows of the battering ram are deadened by the soft billowing sack (St. Isidore *Etymologies* 18.11).

When a military unit was guilty of mutiny or dereliction of duty, it could be punished by *decimatio*. Although the term "decimate" nowadays refers to wholesale destruction, it was originally used to describe the beating or stoning to death of every tenth (*decimus*) man in an army unit, chosen by lot, by his nine lucky colleagues. *When a defeated army is punished with decimation, brave men are also chosen by lot.*

Setting an example on a large scale always involves a degree of injustice, when individuals suffer to ensure the public good (Tacitus *Annals* 14.44).

Macrinus, who ruled briefly in the early 3rd century A.D., *was arrogant and bloodthirsty and determined to rule in sound military style. He criticized the level of discipline demanded even in early times . . . going so far as to crucify soldiers and inflict punishments intended for slaves. Whenever his soldiers mutinied, he frequently decimated them, but sometimes he "centimated" them (a term he himself invented, referring to the execution of one man in a hundred* [centum]*), for he claimed to be merciful in "centimating" soldiers when one in ten or one in twenty deserved to die* (*Historia Augusta* Life of Macrinus 12).

The late-3rd-century emperor Maximian is said to have decimated a legion of Christian soldiers for refusing to suppress a revolt in Gaul by fellow Christians; the legion still refused, and he decimated it again; on a third refusal, he had them all killed. The legion's commander, Mauritius, is commemorated in the name of the Swiss ski resort of St. Moritz.

The Parthian cavalry were famous for their skill in archery. They massacred Crassus's army at Carrhae in 53 B.C. in perhaps the only great battle in antiquity to be decided by archery. They were particularly noted for their trick of shooting backwards when seeming to flee, a maneuver that would have been especially difficult without stirrups. This is the origin of the phrase "Parthian shot" (= "parting shot").

The tombstone of a Roman soldier in the Danube valley in the early 2nd century A.D. boasts that he was more skilled in archery than the Parthians, and could split an arrow in midair with a second one (a feat that will perhaps seem rather more credible if one bears in mind that an archer could shoot at an estimated rate of twenty arrows per minute) (*Corpus of Latin Inscriptions* 3.3676).

If a soldier requisitions your mule, just let it go without protesting. Otherwise you will suffer a beating and still lose your mule (Epictetus *Discourses* 4.1.79).

As well as their other equipment, Roman soldiers wear as a decoration on their helmets a circle of feathers with three purple or black plumes set straight up about one and a half feet. With this they appear twice their actual height and are a fearsome sight, intimidating to the enemy (Polybius *Histories* 6.23). Polybius's wording is a bit misleading:

A suit of Roman armor made of crocodile skin.

although they were proud of their ability to defeat enemies, such as the Gauls and Germans, who were physically much larger than themselves, the Romans were more than eighteen inches tall.

Slingers from a particular region of western Greece used a triple strap in their slings, rather than a single one, so that they could throw stones just as accurately as arrows are shot from a bow. They could shoot stones through quite small rings from a great distance, and hit the enemy not merely on the head but on any part of the face they aimed at (Livy *History of Rome* 38.29).

One of the Vindolanda Tablets (see p. 5) records the sending of creature comforts to a soldier serving on Hadrian's Wall: *I have sent you* [two?] *pairs of socks, two pairs of sandals, two pairs of underpants* (346).

The emperor Hadrian ruled that any soldier who attempted suicide because of boredom with life [taedium vitae] *should be dishonorably discharged* (Justinian's *Digest* 49.16.6.7).

nec bonum nec malum vagina gladium facit
A scabbard makes a sword neither good nor bad.
Seneca *Letters* 92.13

· VI ·

ROMANS AT SEA

Suave, mari magno turbantibus aequora ventis,
e terra magnum alterius spectare laborem
It is pleasant, when the winds are tossing the waters and the sea is high,
to watch from dry land someone else's great difficulty.
Lucretius *On the Nature of Things* 2.1–2

The Carthaginians used to keep their trading activities secret. When a Carthaginian captain saw that a Roman ship was following him, he deliberately ran his ship aground, thus wrecking the pursuing ship as well, and preventing the Romans from finding out his trading destination. He escaped on a piece of wreckage and was recompensed by the state for his losses when he returned to Carthage (Strabo *Geography* 3.5.11).

The First Punic War, fought against Carthage from 264 to 241 B.C., was the longest uninterrupted war in antiquity.

In 260 B.C., *the consul Gaius Duillius inflicted a surprise defeat on the Carthaginians in the Battle of Mylae off Sicily. He was awarded a triumph, and the right to be escorted by a torchbearer and a flute player on his way home from dinner* (Livy *History of Rome* Summary of Book 17). The modern Italian navy has named several warships in his honor.

When the Romans besieged the Sicilian Greek city of Syracuse in 214–211 B.C., they were kept at bay for a long time by Archimedes' inventions, which could pick up their ships with a metal claw (shaking the sailors out in midair), or sink them with huge missiles, or burn their sails with rays of sunlight reflected off metal panels. [This last feat is doubted by some scientists and historians in modern times, but it has been proved to work.] The Romans came to be so intimidated by Archimedes' machines that they would flee whenever they saw a coil of rope or a spar of wood on the battlements (Plutarch *Life of Marcellus* 17).

Although insurance was almost unknown, the state underwrote ships transporting materials to the army during the Second Punic War (218–201 B.C.). Two entrepreneurs were severely punished for making grossly inflated claims for worthless cargoes sent out in battered ships (Livy *History of Rome* 25.3).

When Hannibal was in exile from Carthage, he commanded the troops of King Prusias of Bithynia against King Eumenes of Pergamum. Outnumbered in a sea battle, he knew his only hope was to capture Eumenes himself. He identified Eumenes' ship by sending an emissary with a letter for him, ostensibly with peace terms (but actually making fun of him). He watched to see to which ship the emissary was directed and concentrated his attack on it, ordering his men to distract the crews of the other enemy ships by bombarding them with pottery jars full of poisonous snakes (Cornelius Nepos *Hannibal* 10).

In 188 B.C., *after Rome's victory over Antiochus the Great, the Seleucid king* [whose rule extended from the eastern Mediterranean to India], *Quintus Fabius Labeo was supposed to take away half of the king's ships in accordance with the terms of the peace treaty; it is said that he cut them all in half, so as to deprive Antiochus of his whole fleet* (Valerius Maximus *Memorable Deeds and Sayings* 7.3.4).

In the first half of the 1st century B.C., the Mediterranean was infested with pirates whose power was such that they not only preyed on shipping but also plundered coastal regions. Their ships were equipped with gilded sails, purple canopies, and silver-covered oars (Plutarch *Life of Pompey* 24).

As a young man, Caesar was captured by pirates who demanded a ransom of twenty talents for his release. He felt he was worth more, so he had the demand increased to fifty talents. In the thirty-eight days in which he was kept prisoner, pending the arrival of the ransom, he often told the pirates that he would come back and crucify them. They thought this was a great joke, but he did exactly that (Plutarch *Life of Julius Caesar* 2).

The Roman navy did not use galley slaves. The rowers, sailors, and marines were normally auxiliaries, who could expect to receive citizenship after serving for twenty-six years. As a desperate measure in the war against Sextus Pompeius [43–36 B.C.], Octavian did train twenty thousand slaves as oarsmen, but he gave them their freedom first (Suetonius *Life of Augustus* 16).

Two years before he engineered the naval victory over Antony and Cleopatra at Actium, Agrippa, in his capacity as magistrate responsible for the maintenance of Rome's water supply and sewers, sailed down the *Cloaca Maxima* into the Tiber.

Nero began a project to dig a canal across the Isthmus of Corinth, to provide an alternative to the long and dangerous route around the Peloponnese. He struck the first three blows at the earth with a golden pickaxe ceremoniously handed to him by the governor of Greece. He was not deterred by the misgivings of his Egyptian engineers that there would be disastrous flooding since the sea was at different levels on either side of the Isthmus, but he was forced to abandon the scheme because of the revolt in Gaul that led to his overthrow

(Philostratus *Nero* 3). The gods' opposition to the cutting of the canal was demonstrated by the violent deaths of all who tried to carry the project through: Demetrius I of Macedon, Julius Caesar, Caligula and Nero (Pliny *Natural History* 4.10). The Corinth Canal was eventually completed, without flooding or divine retribution, in 1893.

A provincial governor must be scrupulously vigilant in preventing fishermen from showing a light at night as if to guide sailors into port, but really intended to lure them on to the rocks, bringing ships and those aboard them into danger and gaining damnable plunder for themselves (Justinian's *Digest* 47.9.10).

More than twelve hundred shipwrecks from the period c. 300 B.C.–c. A.D. 200 have been located in the Mediterranean, far more than from the next millennium. This decrease does not suggest that maritime skills improved, but rather that prosperity declined, reducing the importance of overseas trade. The same decline is indicated by the fact that the skeletons of domesticated cattle from Roman times are larger than from later periods.

Most ancient wrecks are trading ships, often still laden with amphoras which preserve traces of their original content. Few can rival the Anticythera Wreck, named after the Greek island off which it was discovered by sponge divers in 1900. The ship may have been transporting plunder to Rome after Sulla's brutal sacking of Athens in 86 B.C. In addition to important pieces of sculpture, it also yielded the "Anticythera Mechanism," an astronomical calculator with a far more complex design than any other device known before the end of the Middle Ages. The apparatus may have been designed by Hipparchus of Nicaea (c. 190–c. 120 B.C.), the greatest of all ancient astronomers.

Pliny, who was commander of the important naval station at Misenum, has interesting opinions about seafaring. For example:

- *Pouring vinegar over ships gives them some slight protection against cyclones* (*Natural History* 2.132).

Cupids fishing.

- *I have it on the authority of some distinguished members of the equestrian order that they saw a merman exactly like a human being in the sea near Cadiz. He climbs on board ships in the night time, they say, and the part of the deck where he sits is immediately weighed down, and ships are actually sunk if he stays on board too long* (*Natural History* 9.10).
- *Oh, the vanity of mankind, when the remora, a little fish just six inches long, can immobilize ships with prows armed with bronze and iron, merely by attaching itself to them! They say that a remora held back Mark Antony's flagship during the Battle of Actium, when he was anxious to go around exhorting his troops* (*Natural History* 32.3).

⊕

Dreadful terrors suddenly stalked through all the world, such as neither myth nor factual history records for us. So begins Ammianus Marcellinus's graphic account (26.10) of the tsunami that devastated much of the eastern Mediterranean on July 21, A.D. 365.

❋

It was customary for those who survived shipwrecks to shave their heads in token of their gratitude (Juvenal *Satires* 11.81).

◎

aiunt ultra oceanum rursus alia litora, alium nasci orbem. facile ista finguntur, quia oceanus navigari non potest

They say that beyond the Ocean other shores and another world arise.
That sort of thing is easily invented, for the Ocean cannot be sailed.

Seneca *Suasoriae* 1.1

· VII ·

THE LAW

corruptissima re publica plurimae leges
Most laws are passed when the state is most corrupt.
Tacitus *Annals* 3.27

The laws are like spiders' webs: just as spiders' webs catch the weaker creatures but let the stronger ones through, so the humble and poor are restricted by the laws, but the rich and powerful are not bound by them (Valerius Maximus *Memorable Deeds and Sayings* 7.2 ext. 14).

Two four-horse chariots were brought up, and Mettius Fufetius, the king of Alba Longa, was tied to them [by order of Tullius Hostilius, the third king of Rome, as punishment for treachery]. *Then the horses were driven in different directions, with each chariot carrying off whatever parts of his mangled body were attached to it. Everyone turned their eyes away from such an awful sight. This was the first and last instance among the Romans of a punishment with so little regard for humanity: one of the things the Romans may boast about is that no other people has ever been satisfied with milder punishments* (Livy *History of Rome* 1.28).

In A.D. 61, the city prefect, an ex-consul named Pedanius Secundus, was murdered by one of his slaves, either because Pedanius would not free him after a price had been agreed or because of sexual rivalry. Ancient custom ordained that when a slave killed his owner, all slaves living under the same roof should be executed. Even though so many of them were women and children whose innocence was obvious, the Senate resolved to adhere to this practice, ignoring massive public protests and appeals for mercy: all four hundred of Pedanius's household slaves were executed (Tacitus *Annals* 14.42–45).

Originally, it was the responsibility of the victim's family to exact retribution for murder. There is no record of laws on murder in the surviving references to the *Twelve Tables*, Rome's earliest legal code, established in the mid-5th century B.C. The term *vendetta* is derived from the Latin word *vindicta* "retribution."

The traditional punishment for parricide is as follows: the condemned person is beaten with blood-colored sticks, then sewn up in a sack with a dog, a rooster, a viper and a monkey, and thrown into the deep sea, if the sea is nearby; otherwise, in accordance with the law passed by the deified Hadrian, he is thrown to wild beasts (Justinian's *Digest* 48.9.9).

No one may be both judge and defendant. It is not right that anyone should pass sentence on himself. . . . Anyone wishing to be an advocate can assume only one role in conducting cases. It is not possible for the same person to be both advocate and judge in the same case, for a distinction has to be made between these functions (*Theodosian Code* 2.2.1, 2.10.5).

Servilius Isauricus [probably the consul of 79 B.C.] *was once walking along a road when he met a horseman who was so disrespectful that not only did he not dismount for him, but he actually galloped right past. Isauricus subsequently saw the rider on trial in court* [he was presumably walking through the Forum, where court sessions were held in the open air]*; he mentioned the incident to the jurors, and they unanimously condemned the man with no further hearing* (Cassius Dio *Roman History* 45.16).

ORDER IN THE COURT

We tend to think of Roman courts as very formal, staid, and dignified. This was not always so:

- *When Lucius Piso, on trial* [in about 110 B.C.] *for offenses against Rome's allies, was groveling on the ground kissing the jurors' feet, a sudden rainstorm filled his mouth with mud, and the jurors decided he had suffered enough* (Valerius Maximus *Memorable Deeds and Sayings* 8.1.6).
- *We move tears by actions as well as by words, hence the custom of bringing in the defendants and their children and their parents dressed in squalid and unkempt clothing, and hence we see prosecutors displaying bloody swords, bones picked out of wounds, blood-covered clothing, exposed wounds, and scourged bodies* (Quintilian *Education of the Orator* 6.1.30).
- Quintilian goes on to acknowledge that such tactics are not always successful: When a boy was asked by the judge why he was crying, instead of replying that he was distressed at the thought of his father being severely punished, he said he was crying because his attendant had just pinched him.
- Quintilian decried the practice of eating and drinking while giving a speech in court (11.3.136), but such pauses will have given the advocate's hired supporters an opportunity to applaud his efforts. Such supporters were called *Sophocleses* [from the Greek term σοφῶς (*sophōs*, "bravo!") and the verb καλέω (*kaleō*, "call")] or *Laudiceni* ["people who get a dinner (*cena*) in return for their praise (*laudes*)"] (Pliny *Letters* 2.14.4).
- *Despite the normal uproar in the Julian Basilica when all four courts were in session concurrently, an exceptionally loud-voiced orator named Trachalus could make himself heard and understood so effectively that, much to the annoyance of the other lawyers in the court where he was speaking, even the audience at the other three trials applauded him* (Quintilian 12.5.6).

❁

A lawyer aims only for a semblance of the truth . . . for a litigant's reward is a favorable ruling, not a good conscience ("orator simile tantum veri petit . . . non enim bona conscientia sed victoria litigantis est praemium," a view of forensic law quoted, but not endorsed, by Quintilian at *Education of the Orator* 2.15.32).

The Julian Basilica, paid for from the spoils of Caesar's conquest of Gaul in the 50s B.C., dominated the southwest side of the Forum. Numerous boards for games scratched into the steps and aisles testify to the boredom of witnesses and spectators waiting for admission to court there.

When Gaius Visellius Varro was suffering from a serious illness, he allowed Otacilia, the wife of Laterensis, who had been his mistress, to record a loan to him of three hundred thousand sestertii. *The plan was that, if he died, she could claim this sum from his heirs. He intended the money to be a sort of legacy, and disguised his lustful generosity as a debt. Otacilia was annoyed when he did not realize her hopes of plunder by dying quickly, and changed from an obliging mistress into an insistent creditor, demanding the money which she had shamelessly wheedled from him with an empty contract. The judge dismissed her case, but would certainly have found both for and against Varro if the same legal formula had allowed it* (Valerius Maximus *Memorable Deeds and Sayings* 8.2.2).

Some lawyers preserve an austere silence to hide their ignorance of the law; others charge their clients every time they [i.e., the lawyers] *yawn; others, if the name of a famous writer is mentioned, think that it is a foreign word for a type of fish or some other sort of food* (Ammianus Marcellinus 30.4.8ff.).

Apuleius, the author of *The Golden Ass*, was tried for witchcraft, the charge being that he had used magic spells to persuade a rich widow to marry him. In his defense speech he said to his accuser: *You will protest that I am listing magic words used in Egyptian or Babylonian rites*—σελάχεια, μαλάκεια, μαλακόστρακα, χονδράκανθα, ὀστρακόδερμα, καρχαρόδοντα, ἀμφίβια, λεπιδωτά, φολιδωτά, δερμόπτερα, στεγανόποδα, μονήρη, συναγελαστικά (*Apology* 38).

They are actually technical terms that Apuleius used in a treatise on fish and other aquatic creatures.

Diocletian's edict on maximum prices (A.D. 301) ruled that an agricultural laborer or a sewer cleaner might earn up to twenty-five *denarii* per day, a trial lawyer up to one thousand, the top price for an unworked leopard skin.

The Romans had a great reverence for the law and legal proprieties:

- As one of the two censors in 204 B.C., *Livius Salinator did not hesitate to deprive thirty-four of the thirty-five tribes of their voting rights because, after condemning him, they had subsequently appointed him consul and censor. He considered that they must be guilty either of irresponsibility or of corruption. The only tribe he left uncensored was the Maecia, which had judged him deserving neither of condemnation nor of office* (Valerius Maximus *Memorable Deeds and Sayings* 2.9.6).
- Publius Sulpicius Rufus was killed in Sulla's proscriptions in the 80s B.C. The slave who betrayed him was given the reward promised for information and set free, but then he was thrown over a cliff for the crime of betraying his master (Livy *History of Rome* Summary of Book 77).
- A judge would not rule against an obvious impossibility if there was no law about it. A woman's claim to have given birth after a thirteen-month pregnancy was allowed because there was no statute determining the limit to a pregnancy (Pliny *Natural History* 7.40).
- *Since the period of mourning starts immediately after a person dies, a woman who finds out about her husband's death after the statutory period of mourning has expired puts on her mourning dress and also takes it off again on the same day* (Justinian's *Digest* 3.2.8). *Men are not under compulsion to mourn the death of their wives* (Justinian's *Digest* 3.2.9).
- In A.D. 362, Julian (the "Apostate"), the last pagan emperor, fined himself ten pounds of gold for exceeding his authority as a judge (Ammianus Marcellinus 22.7.2).

If some people were playing ball, and one of them struck the ball with unusual force so that it hit the hand of a barber, and the throat of a slave whom the barber was shaving was thereby cut, because the razor had been jolted, which party is at fault? Proculus [a 1st-century A.D. jurist] *says the barber is at fault, and he certainly does seem open to blame if he was shaving people where ball games were regularly played and there were a lot of people passing by. It is, however, reasonable to maintain that someone who entrusts himself to a barber whose chair is in a risky place has only himself to blame* (Justinian's *Digest* 9.2.11).

If a woman is a passenger on a ship and gives birth on board, the view to take is that nothing is owed for the child, since the fare is in any case slight and the child makes no use of the facilities provided for the passengers (Justinian's *Digest* 19.2.19.7).

The testimony of slaves was admissible only if obtained through torture. *We should resort to torturing slaves only when a defendant is already under strong suspicion and other arguments have brought a conviction so close that the confession of his slaves seems to be the only thing lacking* (Justinian's *Digest* 48.18.1.1).

While governing in Sicily [in 97 B.C.], *Lucius Domitius showed that he had a very determined character. When an extraordinarily large wild boar was brought to him, he ordered the shepherd who had killed it to be summoned and asked him how he had killed the beast; on learning that he had used a hunting spear, he had him crucified; to root out the highway robbery which was devastating the province, he himself had issued an edict forbidding the possession of weapons* (Valerius Maximus *Memorable Deeds and Sayings* 6.3.5).

The busiest roads are chosen for the crucifixion of criminals, so that as many people as possible may see them and take warning, for punishments are aimed less at the crime itself than at setting an example (Quintilian

Minor Declamations 274.13). *It is a widespread practice to hang notorious highway robbers in the places where they used to prowl, so that others may be deterred from committing the same crimes and the families of their victims can draw comfort from their being punished where they committed the murders* (Justinian's *Digest* 48.19.28.15).

When a guardian poisoned his ward in order to inherit his property, Galba had him crucified. The man invoked the law, saying that he was a Roman citizen and therefore not liable to such punishment. As if he were intending to mitigate the punishment as a consolation befitting the man's status, Galba ordered that his cross be set up much higher than the others and painted white (Suetonius *Life of Galba* 9).

According to Pliny (*Natural History* 8.47), the Greek historian Polybius reported that he and Scipio Aemilianus, who destroyed Carthage in 146 B.C., saw man-eating lions crucified there as a deterrent to other lions.

Magistrates often condemn criminals to be kept in prison or in chains. They ought not to do this, for such punishments are forbidden: prisons are for restraining people, not for punishing them (Justinian's *Digest* 48.19.8.9).

If an arbitrator in a dispute instructs the parties to come to a place of disrepute, such as an eating-house or a brothel, no penalty is incurred in disobeying the instruction (Justinian's *Digest* 4.8.21.11).

A man bequeathed "Taurus" *to someone in his will. He had had a rather valuable slave with that name, but his heir gave the beneficiary a bull* ("taurus") (Martianus Capella *On the Marriage of Philology and Mercury* 5.462; the will would not have distinguished between uppercase and lowercase letters).

A man who had a launderer called Flaccus and a baker called Philonicus had bequeathed his wife his baker, Flaccus. Which of them should be given to her, or should both? The most satisfactory decision was that that slave had been bequeathed whom the testator thought he was bequeathing. If this was not clear, the first thing to check was whether the owner had known the slaves' names. If so, the named slave was the one to be given over; but if he did not know his slaves' names, it is the baker who is deemed to have been bequeathed, just as if no name had been mentioned (Justinian's *Digest* 34.5.28).

❖

Lucius Verratius was an extremely evil and deranged fellow. He used to amuse himself by striking free men on the face with the palm of his hand. A slave would follow after him with a purse full of small coins. Whenever he had slapped anyone, he would tell the slave to count out twenty-five asses *on the spot, as the compensation ordained by the* Twelve Tables (Aulus Gellius *Attic Nights* 20.1.13). We are not told when Verratius lived, but with the passing of the centuries inflation had presumably rendered the compensation stipulated by the *Twelve Tables* wholly inadequate.

❖

lex videt iratum, iratus legem non videt
The law sees an angry person, but an angry person does not see the law.
Publilius Syrus *Sententiae* L 13

· VIII ·

FARMING

fertilior seges est alienis semper in agris
The crops are always more bountiful in other people's fields.

Ovid *The Art of Love* 1.349

More than 90 percent of the empire's population were rural poor, eking out a precarious existence. A centurion in the 2nd century B.C. is reported by Livy (*History of Rome* 42.34) as having inherited a cottage and one *iugerum* (about two-thirds of an acre) of land on which he and his wife raised eight children. Forensic examination of skeletons from all parts of the empire shows that diseases linked to undernourishment were endemic at all periods.

When Scipio Nasica was canvassing for office, he shook hands with a voter whose hands had been hardened by farm labor, and made the faux pas *of asking him jokingly if he was in the habit of walking on his hands. . . . This witticism cost him the election, for all the voting tribes from the countryside thought he was insulting them for their poverty and turned their anger against his abusive urban wit* (Valerius Maximus *Memorable Deeds and Sayings* 7.5.2).

Large-scale farming has ruined Italy, and now the provinces as well—six men owned half the province of Africa before Nero had them put to death (Pliny *Natural History* 18.35).

Vegetius explains that recruits for the army should be sought in the countryside because, with little technology, farming was unremittingly laborious. His logic: *A man who knows less about life's pleasures fears death less* (*Military Affairs* 1.3).

When the elder Cato was asked what he thought was the most profitable way of utilizing one's resources, he replied, "Grazing livestock successfully"; what second to that, "Grazing livestock fairly successfully"; what third, "Grazing livestock unsuccessfully"; what fourth, "Raising crops." When his questioner asked, "What about money-lending?" Cato replied, "What about murder?" (Cicero *On Duties* 2.89).

What is the best way to cultivate a field? Plow it well. What is the second best? Plow it. What is the third? Spread manure (Cato *On Farming* 61).

The *Twelve Tables* legislated against the removal of growing crops from a field by means of magic spells. The law was actually invoked in the 2nd century B.C. against a freedman who was obtaining better returns from his land than were his jealous neighbors. When he produced in court his well-maintained implements, his sturdy slaves, and his well-fed oxen, and argued that hard work was his only magic spell, he was unanimously acquitted (Pliny *Natural History* 18.41).

Something happened in our lifetime more ominous than anything ever heard of from earlier times: when the emperor Nero was overthrown, a whole olive grove belonging to Vettius Marcellus, a distinguished knight, crossed the public road and the crops that had been growing over there moved to where the olive grove had been (Pliny *Natural History* 17.245).

In a discussion of the propagation of plants, Pliny speculates whether trees enjoy the novelty of travel in the same way as people do (*Natural History* 17.66).

Cupids gathering grapes.

Vines should be freed for a few days from the trees to which they were attached, and allowed to wander and spread themselves, and lie on the ground they have gazed at for the whole year. Just as cattle released from the yoke and dogs after a hunt enjoy rolling about, so vines also like to stretch their lumbar regions (Pliny *Natural History* 17.209).

An estimated hundred thousand Germans were killed by Marius's army in 102 B.C. at the Battle of Aquae Sextiae in what is now southern France. *It was said that the people of Marseilles fenced their vineyards with their bones and that, after the bodies decomposed and the winter rains fell, the ground was so enriched by the putrefied matter sinking deep into it that it produced bumper crops for many years* (Plutarch *Life of Marius* 21).

I saw a tree at Tivoli laden with so many varieties of fruit. One branch had nuts, another berries, another grapes, or pears, or figs, or pomegranates, or types of apple. But it did not survive long (Pliny *Natural History* 17.120).

A cupid dragging off a goat.

On the large estates in the Gallic provinces, an enormous frame edged with teeth and mounted on two wheels is pushed by a team of draft animals through the crops,

September is the appropriate month for pressing grapes.

and the grain falls into the frame (Pliny *Natural History* 18.296). Several such reaping machines are portrayed on funerary monuments in France. It was probably the cheapness of slave labor, rather than any inherent flaw in the design of the machine, that prevented it from being adopted more widely. Palladius, probably writing in the mid-5th century A.D., gives a more detailed account, emphasizing how quickly it works (*On Farming* 7.2). It may be significant that Palladius almost never mentions farm work being carried out by slaves.

❁

If one of our animals is carried off by a wild beast and then escapes, it counts as part of the property shared out in an inheritance, for it is best to consider that any of our livestock carried off by a wolf or other wild beast does not cease to belong to us as long as it has not been eaten (Justinian's *Digest* 10.2.8.2).

❁

Quantity distinguishes a thief from a rustler: a person who steals a single pig will be punished as a thief, but a person who steals a herd of pigs will be punished as a rustler (Justinian's *Digest* 48.19.16.7). *The number of sheep driven off distinguishes a thief from a rustler: some have thought that ten sheep make a flock, but driving off four or five pigs or even a single horse or ox constitutes rustling* (Justinian's *Digest* 47.14.3).

❁

Sell surplus wine and grain, aging oxen, runt calves, runt sheep, wool, hides, old carts, old iron tools, old slaves, sickly slaves, and anything else you do not need (Cato *On Farming* 2).

❁

Some divide agricultural equipment into two categories: human resources and the aids without which people cannot cultivate the land. Others divide it into three categories: the articulate type of implement, the semiarticulate, and the mute; the articulate includes slaves, the semiarticulate oxen, the mute carts (Varro *On Farming* 1.17). Varro goes on to recommend using free labor in unhealthy places, since the death of a slave is a financial loss.

❁

necessitas feriis caret
Necessity never has a holiday.
Palladius *On Farming* 1.6.7

· IX ·

MEDICINE

medicus nihil aliud est quam animi consolatio
A doctor is merely a consolation for the mind.
Petronius ***Satyricon*** **42**

In 219 B.C., the Greek Archagathus was the first doctor to come to Rome. At first, he was wonderfully popular, but then his cruel cutting and cautery won him the nickname "the Executioner," and people began to detest the medical arts and all doctors (Pliny *Natural History* 29.12).

The elder Cato recommended that, to ensure that infants grow up strong and healthy, they should be washed in the urine of someone who has been living on a diet of cabbage (*On Farming* 157.10). Although Cato generally believed in old-fashioned remedies rather than in the new Greek medicines, he may here be influenced by a contemporary Greek treatise on the medicinal qualities of cabbage by Mnesitheus of Cyzicus.

Cato suggests putting a sprig of wormwood in one's rectum to prevent blisters on a journey (*On Farming* 159). He is probably thinking of horse riding rather than of sitting or reclining in a litter since, Cato being Cato, he would hardly have countenanced using a litter, in his time a relatively new mode of travel.

The Greeks are a quite worthless and unteachable race. When they bestow their literature on us, they will destroy our whole existence. They will do this all the sooner if they send us their doctors. They have conspired to murder all non-Greeks with their medicine. They make us pay for treatment, so we will have the more confidence in them and they can ruin us the more easily (the elder Cato, quoted by Pliny at *Natural History* 29.14).

If there were no doctors, there would be nothing more stupid than teachers (Athenaeus *Wise Men at Dinner* 666a; the great physician Galen was one of the guests attending the dinner, but he was so breathtakingly arrogant that he would hardly have regarded this as a personal attack).

King Pyrrhus of Epirus could cure ailments of the spleen by contact with the big toe of his right foot; when he was cremated, it did not burn and was kept in a casket in a temple (Pliny *Natural History* 7.20).

Mithridates VI of Pontus was an amateur physician. Some of his courtiers volunteered for surgery and cautery at his hands. This was flattery in action, not just in words, for he regarded their confidence in him as testimony to his skill (Plutarch *How to Distinguish a Flatterer from a Friend* 14). Commodus (ruled A.D. 180–192) also played at surgery, killing people with his deadly scalpels (*Historia Augusta* Life of Commodus 10).

During the rule of Nero, Thessalus rose to fame in the medical profession: he swept aside all received medical wisdom and denounced all doctors from every epoch with a sort of frenzy. You can get a clear idea of his sense of judgment and his attitude just by looking at his tomb on the Appian Way, where the inscription refers to him by the Greek term ἰατρονίκης (*iatronikes* "the Conqueror of Doctors"). *No actor or charioteer went out in public accompanied by a larger throng* (Pliny *Natural History* 29.9).

Scribonius Largus dedicated his *Compositiones*, a collection of 271 remedies, to Callistus, one of Claudius's most powerful freedmen. In the preface he complains that, whereas no one would trust an artist to paint his portrait until he had proof of his ability, scarcely anyone troubles to find out about a doctor before giving himself and his family into his care.

The word "abracadabra" is perhaps Semitic, but its original meaning is lost. It occurs first in the *liber medicinalis*, a versified medical textbook in Latin of uncertain date and authorship, associated with either Serenus Sammonicus, a scholar at the court of Septimius Severus (ruled A.D. 193–211), or his like-named son, a friend of Gordian I (who ruled briefly in A.D. 238). As a cure for fever, the poet recommends that the word be written on a piece of paper to be rolled up and worn round the neck in an amulet, thus:

A B R A C A D A B R A

A B R A C A D A B R

A B R A C A D A B

A B R A C A D A

A B R A C A D

A B R A C A

A B R A C

A B R A

A B R

A B

A

There is no doubt that all those doctors strive for publicity through some novel treatment, buying their fame at the expense of our lives. This is the cause of those awful diagnosis competitions at the patient's bedside, with no doctor agreeing with any other, for fear of seeming subordinate; it is also the cause of that miserable epitaph "I died of a surfeit of doctors" (Pliny *Natural History* 29.11).

Medical writings in any language other than Greek lack prestige even among the uneducated who do not know Greek. When it comes to health matters, people have less confidence if they know what is going on. That is why, by Hercules, anyone who claims to be a doctor is trusted straightaway. Medicine is the only profession in which this happens, even though there is no other profession in which falsehood is more dangerous. But we pay no heed to that danger, for everyone finds the sweetness of wishful thinking so seductive. Moreover, there is no law to punish ignorance that costs lives, and no precedent for redress. Doctors learn through endangering our lives, conducting experiments that lead to people's death. Only doctors have total immunity if they kill people. In fact, the criticism is transferred to the patient, who is faulted for self-indulgence: those who die are actually held to have brought their death upon themselves (Pliny *Natural History* 29.17).

Not everyone was quite so vehement in their opinions of doctors as Pliny, who caustically describes medical bills as a "down payment on death" (*mortis arra*) (*Natural History* 29.21), but medicine was a stock target for epigrammatic wit:

- *Diaulus used to be a doctor, now he's a mortician. He does as a mortician what he did as a doctor* (Martial *Epigrams* 1.47).
- *I was feeling poorly. You came to see me straightaway, Symmachus, accompanied by a hundred student doctors. A hundred fingers chilled by the North Wind took my pulse; I didn't have a fever, Symmachus, but now I do* (Martial *Epigrams* 5.9).
- *Baccara, from the Swiss Alps, has entrusted his penis for treatment to a doctor who's his rival in love. Baccara is going to be a Gaul* (Martial *Epigrams* 11.74). [The joke, such as it is, depends on a pun, *Gallus* meaning both "Gaul" and "eunuch."]
- *Yesterday, the doctor Marcus took the pulse of a stone statue of Zeus; even though he is made of stone, today Zeus is being carried out for burial* (Lucillius *Greek Anthology* 11.113).

- *Pheidon did not give me a purge or take my pulse—I just remembered his name, got feverish, and died* (Callicter *Greek Anthology* 11.118).

❁

A surgeon should be fairly young, with strong and steady hands, ambidextrous, with good eyesight, eager to cure his patient, but detached enough not to want to hurry or to cut less than is necessary. He has to perform his task as if the patient's screams had no effect on him (Celsus *On Medicine* 7 introduction).

❁

Gaius Marius [157–86 B.C., seven times consul and one of Rome's toughest military leaders] *was the first person to endure surgery without being tied down* (Cicero *Tusculan Disputations* 2.22). Having had the varicose veins removed from one leg, however, he declined to allow his other leg to be treated, the cure not being worth the pain (Plutarch *Life of Marius* 6).

❁

Lucius Apronius Caesianus, consul with Caligula in A.D. 39, had a son who was so fat that he could not move; he was cured by a primitive liposuction procedure (Pliny *Natural History* 11.213).

❁

Celsus gives a detailed account, unique in surviving ancient medical writings, of the procedures to be followed in the extraction of missiles, whether arrows (poisoned or not), spears, lead balls, or stones (*On Medicine* 7.5). Later in the same book (7.25) he gives a rather optimistic account of the process of "decircumcision."

❁

Dentistry, considered part of general medicine, was not very sophisticated. Augustus himself had spaces between his small and scabrous teeth (Suetonius *Life of Augustus* 79). False teeth were worn, but mostly for aesthetic reasons. They were removed before meals. Bad teeth and false teeth were common targets for epigrams:

- *If I recall, you used to have four teeth, Aelia, but one cough expelled two of them, and a second cough expelled the other two. Now you can cough carefree all day long: a third cough can't harm you.*

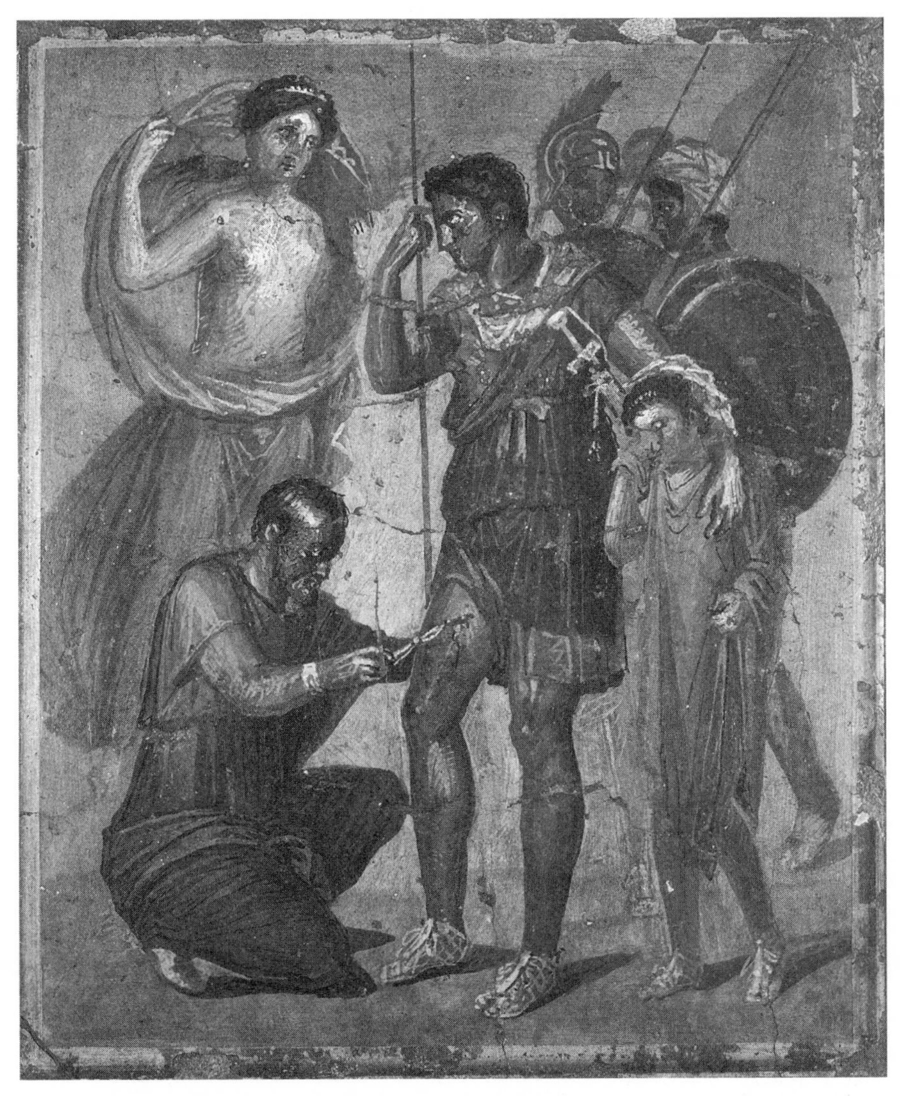

Aeneas receiving medical attention on a Pompeian fresco.

- *Thais has black teeth, but Laecania's are snowy-white. Why? Laecania has teeth she bought, but Thais has her own.*
- *You're not ashamed to wear teeth and hair that you've bought, but what will you do for eyes, Laelia? You can't buy them.*
  (Martial *Epigrams* 1.19, 5.43, 12.23)

Catullus mocks a rival's dazzling smile, attributing it to the Spanish habit of washing one's teeth with urine (poem 39). The ammonia in urine obtained from the *latrinae publicae* was considered essential for the laundering of clothes (see p. 188).

Calpurnianus, greetings. I've dashed off these verses for you. As you requested, I've sent you tooth-cleaner, an excellent whitening powder, made from Arabian plants to brighten your mouth and to smooth your swollen gums and remove food particles, so that no unsightly stain should be seen if you happen to draw back your lips and laugh (Apuleius *Apologia* 6).

Ointment made with a raven's eggs dyes the hair black. Anyone dying his hair this way has to keep his mouth full of olive oil and his lips shut. Otherwise, his teeth turn black along with his hair and it is very difficult to wash them white again (Aelian *On Animals* 1.48).

The deities most frequently honored in bath complexes are Asculapius, the god of medicine, and his daughter, Hygieia (*sc.*, Health). Hadrian allowed only the sick to go to the baths before the eighth hour (2 P.M.) (*Historia Augusta* Life of Hadrian 22.7). In the absence of chemical cleaning agents, the public baths were probably not very healthy:

- *Going to the baths is one of the worst things to do if one has a wound that is not yet free of morbid matter, for bathing makes it moist and dirty, and that often leads to infection* (Celsus *On Medicine* 5.28).
- Marcus Aurelius considered bathing to mean *olive oil, sweat, filth, greasy water, everything that is disgusting* (*Meditations* 8.24).

- Scribonius Largus commends a particular type of plaster as being very serviceable for wounds and bites, for inhibiting tumors and pus, and for not falling off if worn at the baths (*Compositiones* 214).

Cobwebs were used to stop bleeding from fractured skulls and shaving cuts [whereas brain hemorrhaging was treated with the blood and fat of geese and ducks] (Pliny *Natural History* 29.114).

The reason why there is so little research into the medicinal properties of various herbs is that only illiterate country folk who live surrounded by them make use of them; faced with hordes of doctors, the rest of us do not trouble to look for herbal remedies (Pliny *Natural History* 25.16).

Mandrake juice is drunk as an antidote to snakebites and as an anesthetic before surgery or injections, but care must be taken with the dosage: one whiff of it is enough to send some people to sleep (Pliny *Natural History* 25.150).

Especially because of its narcotic properties and the vaguely human shape of its root, mandrake was commonly associated with magic. Josephus describes how mandrake gatherers avoid its deadly root:

> *They dig a furrow round it, leaving just a very short part of the root in the earth. Then they tie a dog to the root. When the dog rushes to follow the person who tied it there, the root is pulled easily out of the ground, but the dog dies at once, as a substitute for the person trying to harvest the plant. (There is no danger in picking it up after the dog dies.) Despite all these risks, it has one property which makes it extremely prized: so-called demons, that is to say the spirits of evil people, enter the bodies of the living and kill them if they receive no help; a simple application of mandrake quickly drives them out* (*The Jewish War* 7.183-185).

Epileptics even drink the blood of gladiators. It is an appalling sight to see wild animals drink the blood of gladiators in the arena, and yet those who

Mandrake being harvested.

suffer from epilepsy think it the most effective cure for their disease, to absorb a person's warm blood while he is still breathing and to draw out his actual living soul (Pliny *Natural History* 28.4).

It is said that if someone takes a stone or some other missile that has slain three living creatures—a human being, a wild boar, and a bear—at three blows, and throws it over the roof of a house in which there is a pregnant woman, she will immediately give birth, however difficult her labor may be (Pliny *Natural History* 28.33).

Touching the nostrils of a she-mule with one's lips is said to stop sneezing and hiccups (Pliny *Natural History* 28.57).

Sexual intercourse is good for lower back pain, for weakness of the eyes, for derangement, and for depression (Pliny *Natural History* 28.58).

If a person whispers in a donkey's ear that he has been stung by a scorpion, the affliction is immediately transferred to the donkey (Pliny *Natural History* 28.155).

Strains and bruises are treated with wild boar's dung gathered in spring and dried. This treatment is used for those who have been dragged by a chariot or mangled by its wheels or bruised in any way. Fresh dung also may be smeared on (Pliny *Natural History* 28.237).

In treating fever, clinical medicine is almost entirely useless. I shall therefore note numerous remedies suggested by magicians, starting with amulets:

- *the dust in which a sparrowhawk has bathed, tied up with red thread in a linen bag;*
- *the longest tooth of a black dog;*
- *the wasp called the "false wasp," which always flies alone and should be caught in the left hand and attached under the patient's chin; other people use the first wasp they see that year;*

- *a viper's severed head, wrapped in a linen cloth, or its heart cut out while it is still alive;*
- *the muzzle and the ear-tips of a mouse in a red cloth (the mouse itself being set free again);*
- *the right eye plucked from a lizard while still alive, and then wrapped in goat skin with its severed head.*

(Pliny *Natural History* 30.98)

❁

If one wishes a child to be born with black eyes, the mother should eat a shrew during her pregnancy (Pliny *Natural History* 30.134).

❁

A man's urine in which a lizard has been drowned is an antaphrodisiac potion; so also are snails and pigeons' droppings drunk with olive oil and wine. The right section of a vulture's lung worn as an amulet in a crane's

Girls exercising on a 3rd/4th century A.D. mosaic.

skin is a powerful aphrodisiac, as is consuming the yolks of five dove eggs mixed with a denarius of pig fat and honey, or sparrows or sparrows' eggs, or wearing as an amulet a rooster's right testicle wrapped in ram's skin (Pliny *Natural History* 30.141).

❁

When Marcus Aurelius's army returned from campaigning in the East in A.D. 165, it brought back a disease, probably smallpox, which raged pandemically for twenty-five years, and may have carried off as many as six million people, which was perhaps a tenth of the population of the empire. Marcus Aurelius himself probably died of it.

❁

Whenever plague devastated the population, there was no dignity in the burial accorded to the poor. A pit one hundred and sixty feet long, one hundred feet wide, and thirty feet deep, containing an estimated twenty-four thousand corpses from the early imperial period, was discovered outside Rome in 1876; when it was opened, the stench was still intolerable.

❁

Galen devoted a short treatise to playing ball games as an inexpensive and safe way to keep fit. In *On Exercise with a Small Ball* (*Minor Writings* 1.93), he expressed his conviction that *most gymnastic exercises, by contrast, are counterproductive, leading to fatty deposits such as can even inhibit breathing. People who exercise that way are not likely to be good military or political leaders; it would be better to give such responsibilities to a pig.*

❁

Especially in modern Rome, there are doctors dealing with many specialist fields: dentists, otologists, proctologists. . . . Medicine being such a vast subject, and Rome and Alexandria being such huge cities, they can all make a living (Galen *On the Divisions of the Medical Art* 2).

❁

Dissection of human corpses was permissible at certain periods in Alexandria, but not elsewhere in the Greco-Roman world. Galen urged medical students unable to travel to Egypt to grasp any lucky chance to examine bone structure—a corpse washed out of its grave by a river in flood, or the skeleton of a highwayman killed by a traveler whom he had attempted to rob (*On Anatomical Procedures* 1.2).

I have never tried to dissect ants, gnats, fleas, or other such tiny creatures, but I have often dissected animals that creep, such as cats and mice, and animals that crawl, such as snakes, and many species of birds and fish (Galen *On Anatomical Procedures* 6.1).

I hear that in Rome nowadays even doctors advertise their services (Epictetus *Discourses* 3.23.27).

An epitaph for a woman doctor, from Rome: *To my holy goddess, to Primilla, a physician, daughter of Lucius Vibius Melito. She lived forty-four years, of which she spent thirty with Lucius Cocceius Apthorus without a quarrel. Apthorus built this tomb for his excellent, devoted wife and for himself* (*Corpus of Latin Inscriptions* 6.7581).

Much of the Romans' water supply was channeled through lead pipes. (The English word "plumbing" is derived from the Latin term *plumbum*, meaning "lead.") It has been suggested that infertility caused by lead poisoning contributed to the eventual fall of the empire. The Romans, however, were fully aware that water conducted through terra-cotta pipes was healthier and better tasting (Vitruvius *On Architecture* 8.6.10–11). A more dangerous source of lead poisoning would have been cauldrons and cooking pots made at least partially of lead.

A lead water pipe displaying the name of the ruling emperor, Marcus Aurelius.

Life expectancy for the population as a whole was not much more than twenty-five years. War killed many men, but childbirth killed more women, and there was regularly a shortage of women of marriageable age. Nevertheless, longevity was not uncommon. In the census records for A.D. 74, Pliny had no difficulty in finding many people supposedly well over a hundred years old, with some who even claimed to be one hundred and forty (*Natural History* 7.164).

A justification for vivisection: *It is not cruel, as most people maintain, that remedies for innocent people's ailments in all future ages should be sought through the sufferings of just a few criminals* (Celsus *On Medicine* Proem 26).

Alexander of Abonoteichus, an obscure town in what is now northern Turkey, who styled himself as a priest of Asculapius, the god of healing, gave responses to questions submitted to him in a sealed letter and accompanied by an appropriate payment. To expose him as a fraud, the satirist Lucian sent a sealed question that his slave led Alexander to believe was a request for a cure for a pain in the side. The response, given in oracular fashion as a line of hexameter poetry, was "I bid you smear yourself with bear grease and the foam from a horse's mouth." When the question was unsealed, it read "Where does Homer come from?" (*Alexander or The False Prophet* 53; for more on Alexander, see p. 89).

non quaerit aeger medicum eloquentem, sed sanantem
A sick person does not look for a
smooth-talking doctor, he wants
one who will cure him.
Seneca *Letters* 75.1

· X ·

RELIGION AND SUPERSTITION

expedit esse deos et, ut expedit, esse putemus
It is convenient that the gods should exist,
and, since it is convenient, let's suppose that
they do exist.
Ovid *The Art of Love* 1.637

Rome's agricultural origins can be seen in the gods Vervactor, Reparator, Imporcitor, and Obarator, who oversaw various stages of plowing; in Occator, Runcina, Saritor, Spiniensis, and Subruncinator, all deities of weeding; in Robigo and Robigus, who protected crops from mildew; and in Stercutus, who taught humans the technique of manure spreading.

Everyone sets a single doorkeeper in front of his house to guard it, and, because he is human, he is quite adequate for the task. But Romans in the old days used to post three deities there, namely Forculus to watch the doors [fores], *Cardea to watch the hinges* [cardines], *and Limentinus to watch the threshold* [limen]*: Forculus was incapable of watching the hinges and the threshold as well as the doors* (St. Augustine *City of God* 4.8).

We Christians laugh when we see so many gods assigned to specialized tasks, like workers in the silversmiths' quarter where, in the production of one little pot, it passes through the hands of so many craftsmen, even

A multi-phallused wind chime that once hung in Pompeii as a charm to avert bad luck.

though it could have been made by a single expert (St. Augustine *City of God* 7.4).

The *ancile* was the shield of Mars, given by Jupiter to Numa Pompilius, Rome's second king. Rome would prosper so long as the *ancile* was safe. On the advice of the nymph Egeria, Numa had eleven identical shields made to protect it from theft. Special priests, the Salii, were responsible for its safety.

There is a savage and barbaric aspect to the rituals conducted in the grove of Diana at Aricia, south of Rome along the Appian Way. The priest is always a runaway slave who has won the position by killing his predecessor. He always carries a sword and is always looking out for assailants, ready to defend himself (Strabo *Geography* 5.3). *The Golden Bough*, Sir James Frazer's monumental anthropological work, grew out of an

The phallus with legs is on a street corner in Leptis Magna, in Libya. As the evil eye (see also p. 90) makes clear, the purpose of such charms was to avert harmful spirits.

attempt to explain this strange institution of the *rex nemorensis*, the "King of the Wood."

Gaius Sallustius Crispus Passienus [the great-grand-nephew, by adoption, of Sallust the historian] *was twice consul* [A.D. 27 and 44], *subsequently becoming even more distinguished when he married the younger Agrippina, thus gaining Nero as a stepson. He loved a very ancient tree in the grove of Diana at Tusculum. He habitually kissed it and hugged it, and would sleep under it and pour wine out round it* (Pliny *Natural History* 16.242).

The distinguished Servilian family feed gold and silver to a small copper coin, and it eats both. I have not been able to discover the origin or nature of this phenomenon, but shall quote the words of the elder Messalla [consul in 53 B.C.]*: "The family of the Servilii have a sacred coin, to which they scrupulously make a magnificent sacrifice every year. They say it seems sometimes to grow larger, sometime to grow smaller, and that this means distinction or obscurity for the family"* (Pliny *Natural History* 34.137).

The Sibylline Books were a collection of prophecies and warnings sent by the gods to help the Roman state. A foreign priestess came to Tarquinius Superbus, the last king of Rome, offering to sell him nine books of oracles. He refused to pay the exorbitant price that she demanded. She burned three of the books and offered the remaining six for the same price. Again Tarquinius refused. She burned three more and offered the remaining three for the same price. Tarquinius bought them (Dionysius of Halicarnassus *Roman Antiquities* 4.62).

Although the *flamen dialis*, the chief priest of Jupiter, enjoyed many privileges, he was also subject to many restrictions, and the significance of some was unknown even to the Romans. He could not, for example, be absent from Rome for a night; ride a horse; touch or mention dogs, she-goats, beans, or ivy; or be naked outdoors.

The chief priest was the *pontifex maximus*, a title also bestowed on the pope from the 6th century until recently. It is not known what the term *pontifex* actually means.

A festival was celebrated every July 25 in honor of the goddess Furrina, even though her sphere of influence was unknown. Cicero speculated that she might have something to do with the Furies, the goddesses of vengeance (*On the Nature of the Gods* 3.46).

Even the Salian priests themselves have no clear understanding of the hymns they sing, but religious scruples forbid the making of any changes (Quintilian *Education of the Orator* 1.6.41).

The *fetiales* were a college of priests whose duties were confined solely to the declaring of wars and the making of treaties. In declaring war, they performed an elaborate sequence of rituals culminating in throwing a spear into enemy territory. As Rome's empire expanded and its enemies came to be inconveniently far away, a strip of land near the temple of Bellona, the goddess of war, in the Field of Mars was declared to be non-Roman, and the spear was thrown into it.

This expedient was first employed for the war with King Pyrrhus of Epirus (280–275 B.C.), when one of the enemy soldiers was captured and forced to buy that strip of land (see the expanded Servius commentary on Vergil *Aeneid* 9.52). Octavian made a point of resorting to this ancient custom in his capacity as *fetialis* when he declared war on Cleopatra, thereby drawing attention away from the fact that the war was actually a civil war against Antony (Cassius Dio *Roman History* 50.4).

Roman religious ceremonies had to be carried out exactly as ritual ordained. The same sacrifice might be performed thirty times if some detail was omitted or any other procedural offense was committed (Plutarch *Life of Coriolanus* 25).

Probably in 221 B.C., *when Quintus Fabius Maximus and Gaius Flaminius were being appointed as dictator and Master of the Horsemen, respectively, a shrew was heard to squeak, and this omen forced both of them to withdraw from their appointments* (Valerius Maximus *Memorable Deeds and Sayings* 1.1.5).

In the temple of Jupiter all the pictures and other ornaments are on subjects to do with women. They were intended for the temple of Juno, but the porters got the cult images mixed up when they were installing them. This arrangement was kept for religious reasons, as if the deities had decided on their own dwellings, with the ornaments that should have been in the temple of Jupiter likewise being in that of Juno (Pliny *Natural History* 36.43).

Augustus's spirit was thought to haunt the small room in which he had been born in his grandfather's country house. A new owner of the house, either in ignorance or to test this belief, went to spend the night in the room. Several hours later, he was found lying almost half-dead up against the bedroom door, still wrapped in the blankets, having been hurled out of the bed by a sudden mysterious force (Suetonius *Life of Augustus* 6).

To quash the rumor that he himself was responsible for the Great Fire [see p. 177], *Nero provided scapegoats whom he executed with the most refined tortures. The masses hated these people for their depraved behavior and called them Christians, after Christus, who was put to death by Pontius Pilate, who governed Judaea during the rule of Tiberius. Although his death had temporarily checked the destructive superstition, it burst out again, not just in Judaea, the center of that evil, but even in Rome itself, for everything that is horrible and shameful comes flooding to Rome from every direction and thrives there. The first to be arrested were those who confessed to being Christians. These people then informed on a huge multitude who were convicted not so much of arson as of hatred of the human race. They were mocked as they died; some were covered in animal skins and torn to pieces by dogs, others were crucified, and others were burned as torches to provide illumination after the daylight failed* (Tacitus *Annals* 15.44).

Soon after becoming emperor, Vespasian was asked by a blind man in Alexandria to smear his eyes with spit, and by another to step on his shriveled hand. He did so, and both were cured immediately (Tacitus *Histories* 4.81).

Perhaps because the state religion and most privately adopted cults offered only vague expectations of an afterlife, Romans set great store on elaborate funeral monuments. Since, with few exceptions, burial within the city was prohibited, many massive tombs of the rich and powerful were built along the great arterial roads leading out from Rome.

It's a big mistake to have nice homes while we're alive, and not bother about the one we'll have to inhabit for a lot longer time (Petronius *Satyricon* 71).

Poor people were sometimes buried in large amphoras cut in half, or their ashes were stored in smaller wine jars.

There is no people so sophisticated and educated or so brutish and barbaric that it does not believe that the future can be foreseen and understood and predicted by certain individuals (Cicero *On Divination* 1.2).

Marcus Marcellus [who captured Syracuse in 211 B.C.] *was consul five times, and outstanding both as a military commander and as an augur* [a priest who predicted the future by observing birds]. *He used to say that he traveled in a closed litter whenever he had something particularly important to do and did not want to be obstructed by any ominous signs he might otherwise see* (Cicero *On Divination* 2.77).

Something that looked like ships gleamed down from the sky. . . . Something that looked like a big fleet was said to have been seen in the sky at Lanuvium, near Rome (quoted by Livy *History of Rome* 21.62 and 42.2 from official lists of *prodigia*, unusual occurrences).

For various reasons the left side was regarded as unlucky, or even ill-omened. The Latin term for "on the left" is *sinister*. The Greeks, being more given to euphemism intended to ward off evil, called the left, and still call it, "better than best" (ἀρίστερος [*aristeros*]). A militaristic state such as Rome, dependent on the firm discipline of its infantry battle line, would have taken a dim view of a soldier who preferred to carry his shield on his right arm, thus leaving his comrade on the left vulnerable. Some gladiators, however, were left-handed and might for that reason be regarded by their opponents as particularly daunting adversaries (Seneca *Controversies* 3 *Preface* 10). The emperor Commodus took pride in fighting in the arena with his sword in his left hand (Cassius Dio *Roman History* 73.19).

It was regarded as ill-omened if both oxen in a team defecated simultaneously while yoked (Cicero *On Divination* 2.77).

The swan has an advantage over humans in what really matters, for it knows when the end of its life is imminent. Moreover, in bearing death's approach with contentment, it has received the finest gift that nature can bestow. For it is sure that there is nothing painful or distressing in death. By contrast, humans are afraid of death, about which they know nothing, and they think it a very great evil. The swan is so contented at the ending of its life that it sings a funeral song, as it were, in memory of itself (Aelian *On Animals* 5.34).

Elsewhere, Aelian says that he has not personally heard a swan singing and that he doubts anyone else has (*Miscellaneous History* 1.14). The notion that dying swans sing can be traced back to lines 1444f. of Aeschylus's *Agamemnon*, first performed in 458 B.C. Oddly enough, however, the only swan commonly found in Greece is the mute swan (*cygnus olor*), which neither remains mute in its lifetime (it grunts, snorts, and hisses) nor sings as it dies. No type of swan, in fact, can be said to sing at any time.

Death is rest and night is suitable for rest. I therefore deem it proper that funerals be conducted at night. There are many reasons to forbid them in the daytime. Everyone is then going about his business, and the whole city is packed with people on their way to the courts, or to or from the market, or sitting down to work at their craft, or going to the temples to make sure that the good hopes they have from the gods are fulfilled. It is quite intolerable for people to put a corpse on a bier and shove their way through crowds of people engaged in such activities. Those who happen to meet a funeral are filled with disgust, either because they regard it as ill-omened or because those who are on their way to the temples are forbidden to go on till they have purified themselves (Julian "the Apostate" [ruled 361–363] *Letters* 56).

About one hundred and thirty curses written on lead tablets have been found in the waters at Bath (Aquae Sulis "The Waters of Sul [= Minerva]") in southern England. They tend to be rather banal:

- *The person who has stolen my bronze bowl is accursed. I hand that person over to the temple of Sul, whether a woman or a man, whether slave or free, whether a boy or a girl, and may the person who did this pour his own blood into the bowl itself. I give that thief to the deity to find, whether a woman or a man, whether slave or free, whether a boy or a girl.*
- The still legible part of another says *Solinus to the goddess Sul Minerva. I give my bathing robe and cloak to your divinity and majesty. Do not allow sleep or health to the person who robbed me, whether a man or a woman, whether slave or free, unless he reveals himself and brings those articles to your temple.*

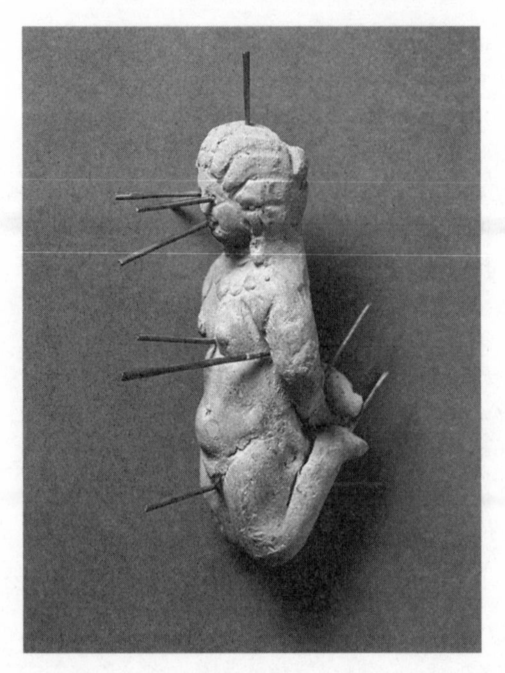

A voodoo doll from Roman Egypt.

From *The Interpretation of Dreams* by Artemidorus of Daldis, in southwest Turkey, compiled in five books in the 2nd century A.D.:

- *Dreaming that one is blind is favorable for runners, since a runner who takes the lead in a race is like a blind man in that he does not see his fellow runners. . . . Such dreams are auspicious for poets also, since they need total calm when they are going to compose, and loss of sight would ensure that they are not distracted by shapes or colors* (1.26).
- *Dreaming about turnips, rutabagas, and pumpkins presages disappointed hopes, since they are massive but lack nutritional value. They signify surgery and woundings with iron implements for sick people and travelers, respectively, since these vegetables are cut into slices* (1.67).
- *Dreaming that one is eating books foretells advantage to teachers, lecturers, and anyone who earns his livelihood from books, but for everyone else it means sudden death* (2.45).

- *Dreaming that one is dead or is being crucified foretells marriage for a bachelor* (2.49, 53).
- *Dreaming that one is eating many onions is favorable for a sick man, for it means that he will recover and mourn for someone else, whereas dreaming that one is eating just a few onions signifies death, since the dying shed just a few tears, whereas those who mourn shed many* (4.55).

❋

Artemidorus's fifth book is a collection of "case histories" amassed at festivals in Italy, Greece, and Asia Minor (now Turkey). Some examples:

- *A man dreamed that he had slipped from his body in the way a snake sloughs its old skin. He died the next day. His soul, in preparation for leaving his body, gave him these images* (40).
- *A man dreamed that Asclepius, the god of medicine, wounded him in the stomach with a sword and that he died. A tumor subsequently developed in his stomach, but he was cured by surgery* (61).
- *A man dreamed that he had a mouth with big, beautiful teeth in his rectum, and that through it he spoke, ate, and performed all the normal functions of a mouth. He was subsequently exiled from his homeland for making incautious statements. I have not included the reasons, for the outcome was easily predictable* (68).
- *A man dreamed that he had three penises. At that time he was a slave, but subsequently he was freed. He then had three names instead of one, for he acquired the extra two from his former owner* (91). [It was customary for a male slave, when freed, to adopt the personal name (praenomen) and family name (nomen) of his former owner; see p. 17.]

❋

Hannibal was said to be an exspert in interpreting the entrails of sacrificed animals, but when he was serving as a military advisor to Prusias of Bithynia and the king hesitated to join battle "because the entrails prevented it," he replied, "Do you mean to say that you rely more on a little bit of calf's flesh than on an experienced general?" (Cicero *On Divination* 2.52). The specific context is unknown, but Prusias lost the war.

❋

An Etruscan life-size model of a sheep's liver, used in divination.

When Caesar landed in Greece [in 48 B.C., in pursuit of Pompey's army], *the omens were unfavorable: some of his soldiers were killed by lightning while still on board the ships, the standards were infested with spiders, and snakes followed him when he disembarked, obliterating his footprints* (Cassius Dio *Roman History* 41.14).

April 21, 753 B.C., is the traditional date for the founding of Rome, as determined by the scholar and antiquarian Marcus Terentius Varro (116–27 B.C.). Varro was advised by the astrologer Lucius Tarutius Firmanus, who calculated June 24, 772 B.C., between 7 and 8.15 A.M., as the date and time of Romulus's conception (i.e., just after the moment when the vestal virgin Rhea Silvia was raped by the god Mars) (Plutarch *Life of Romulus* 12). Tarutius seems to have made his calculations by a kind of horoscope in reverse, determining the time of Romulus's conception from the events in his life, rather than making predictions about his life from the time of his conception.

Every day there is proof that astrology is useless. How many predictions do I remember Pompey, Crassus, and Caesar himself receiving from the astrologers that none of them would die other than in old age, at home, and covered in glory? I am amazed that anyone could continue to put their trust in such people, when the falseness of their predictions is every day made clear by what actually happens (Cicero *On Divination* 2.99).

Intending to have Thrasyllus the astrologer thrown off a cliff if he showed himself to be a charlatan, *Tiberius asked him to read his own horoscope. Thrasyllus hesitated at first, then he began to tremble and to shake with shock and terror the more he looked at the horoscope, and finally he shouted out that a dreadful danger was looming over him. Tiberius embraced him and congratulated him on foreseeing the peril and assured him that he would be safe. Whatever Thrasyllus said thereafter he regarded as oracular, and he kept him in his intimate circle of friends* (Tacitus *Annals* 6.21). Apart from being Tiberius's court astrologer, Thrasyllus is also credited with being the scholar whose arrangement of the works of Plato in tetralogies is still used today.

Tiberius himself became so proficient in divination that, after having a dream in which he was instructed to give money to a certain person, he realized that he was the victim of enchantment and had the man put to death (Cassius Dio *Roman History* 57.15). Domitian was also skilled enough in the art to cast the horoscopes of potential rivals, executing those who seemed dangerous to his rule, and Hadrian was said to have predicted what he would be doing right up to the very hour of his death (*Historia Augusta* Life of Hadrian 16.7).

Astrologers are treacherous to the powerful and unreliable to the merely hopeful; they will always be banned from our state, and yet always retained (Tacitus *Histories* 1.22).

When Marcus Aurelius was fighting the German tribes, the charlatan prophet Alexander of Abonoteichus produced an oracle predicting that victory would be ensured if two lions were thrown into the Danube.

The evil eye being attacked by a bird, a trident, a sword, a scorpion, a snake, a dog, a centipede (?), a cat (?), as well as a naked retro-ithyphallic musician. The Greek words KAI ΣY (*kai su*, "you also") seem to suggest that harm done by the evil eye will be reciprocated.

Two lions were duly thrown into the river. They swam to the other side, only to be slaughtered by the enemy forces, who thought that they were some strange sort of dogs or wolves, and twenty thousand Romans were massacred (Lucian *Alexander or The False Prophet* 48). Alexander apparently tried to justify his prophecy by pointing out that he had not actually specified for which side the victory would be assured. Two large but not precisely identifiable animals are depicted swimming across a river in one of the panels on the Column of Marcus Aurelius; some scholars believe they are these lions. (Since the animals on the Column would originally have been painted, they would have been easier to identify.)

In A.D. 172, Marcus Aurelius's army was trapped by superior numbers of the Quadi, a German tribe, and was suffering from heat and thirst, but the Rain God came miraculously to their aid, and the Romans won an unexpected victory (Cassius Dio *History of Rome* 71.8), as commemorated here on the Aurelian Column.

The Rain God.

Astrologers have various arguments they use to escape responsibility for their predictions. For example, they claim that spirits do not obey, and cannot be seen by, people with freckles (Pliny *Natural History* 30.16).

We came to the tombs, and my friend went to do his business among the gravestones, while I moved off singing and counting the stars. Then, when I looked back at my companion, he had taken off all his clothes and laid them at the roadside. My heart was in my mouth; I stood there practically dead. He pissed in a circle around his clothes, and suddenly turned into a wolf. Don't think I'm joking: nothing could induce me to tell lies about this. As I started to tell you, after he had turned into a wolf, he began to howl and ran off into the woods. At first, I didn't know where I was; then I went to pick up his clothes, but they had all turned to stone (Petronius *Satyricon* 62).

When I was in Italy, I heard about women in a certain region, innkeepers initiated in the dark arts, who were said to give travelers cheese tainted with a certain substance that turned them straightaway into pack animals. When they had transported the witches' equipment, they were turned back again. They kept their rational human mind, just as Apuleius claims to have happened to him in his work titled "The Golden Ass" St. Augustine *City of God* 18.18).

If one regrets having inflicted a blow, whether struck at close quarters or with a missile, and then immediately spits into the palm of one's hand, the person who has been struck immediately feels less aggrieved. This may seem incredible, but it is easy to confirm it by putting it to the test (Pliny *Natural History* 28.36).

num quis, quod bonus vir esset, gratias
dis egit umquam?
Isn't it true that no one has ever given thanks
to the gods for making him a good man?
Cicero *On the Nature of the Gods* 3.87

· XI ·

THE LIFE OF THE MIND

si hortum in bibliotheca habes, deerit nihil
If you have a garden in your library, you'll have all you need.
Cicero *Letters to his Friends* 9.4

Nasica [Publius Cornelius Scipio Nasica, consul in 191 B.C.] *went to visit the poet Ennius but, when he asked for him at the door, a slave girl said that he was not at home. Nasica realized that she had been told by her master to say this, and that he was in fact in the house. A few days later, Ennius went to visit Nasica but, when he asked for him at the door, Nasica shouted out that he was not at home. Ennius exclaimed, "What! Don't I recognize your voice?" Nasica retorted "You're a cheeky fellow; I believed your slave girl when she told me you weren't at home, but you won't believe me myself!"* (Cicero *On the Orator* 2.276).

When Terence's comedy *Hecyra* ("The Mother-in-Law") was first performed, it failed because the audience preferred to go off and see a display of tightrope walking.

Lucius Mummius, the Roman commander responsible for the sack of Corinth in 146 B.C., *was so unsophisticated that, when he was giving out permits for the removal to Italy of paintings and statues by the greatest artists, he warned the contractors that any works that were lost would have to be compensated for with others just as good* (Velleius Paterculus

Histories 1.13). Mummius's soldiers played board games while sitting on paintings that had been thrown to the ground (Strabo *Geography* 8.6.23).

Two hundred and fifty years later, the Greek Dio Chrysostom was still criticizing Mummius's philistinism, but he added sardonically that it was not important that he labeled statues wrongly, since the ignorant Roman masses did not know the difference (*Oration* 37.42).

Vergil was extremely shy. He very rarely came to Rome and, if he was spotted in a public place, he would take refuge in the nearest building to escape from those who were following him and pointing him out (Suetonius *Life of Vergil* 11). Vergil is the only Roman poet known to be mobbed by the masses in this way. Such adulation seems to run counter to the report that he removed a reference to the Campanian city of Nola from the *Georgics* when the inhabitants refused to allow him to channel water to his farm (Aulus Gellius *Attic Nights* 6.20).

Augustus's advisor Maecenas, the leading literary patron of the period, closely associated with such great poets as Vergil and Horace, invented a system of speed-writing (Cassius Dio *Roman History* 55.7) and built Rome's first warm-water swimming pool.

About eighteen hundred papyri, preserved in a carbonized form, have been found at Herculaneum in the Villa dei Papiri, which may once have belonged to the father of Julius Caesar's third wife, Calpurnia, and is the model for the J. Paul Getty Museum in Malibu, California. Many of them contain important and otherwise unknown works by the 1st century B.C. Greek philosopher and poet Philodemus, and there are excellent prospects for the recovery of other lost Greek literary texts. For more about the Herculaneum papyri, visit www.herculaneum.ox.ac.uk.

Ovid was not unaware of the flaws in his poetry, rather he cherished them, as the following story will show. When his friends once asked him to remove three lines from his poetry, he agreed, on condition that he should be allowed to make an exemption of three lines over which they were to have no control. The stipulation seemed fair; they secretly wrote down the three which they wanted removed, and he wrote down the ones he wanted to be kept safe. The same verses were on both tablets (Seneca *Controversies* 2.2.12).

⊕

In his poetic autobiography, *Tristia* ("Sad Poems") 4.10, Ovid records that his father (a conservative country gentleman who lived to be ninety) tried to force him to give up writing poetry because there was no money in it, but that whatever he said turned out to be poetry. This passage may have inspired a wonderful, but apocryphal, anecdote: once, when his father was beating him for persisting with his poetry, Ovid cried out, *parce mihi; numquam versificabo, pater!* ("Spare me, father, and I'll never write verses again"), which scans as a pentameter.

THE PERILS OF RECITATION

- *Caligula held Greek and Latin oratory competitions at Lugdunum* [Lyon, in southern France]. *The losers had to give prizes to the winners and compose speeches in their honor. The competitors who pleased him least had to erase their speeches with a sponge or with their tongue, unless they preferred a whipping or to be thrown into the nearby river* [the Rhone] (Suetonius *Life of Caligula* 20).
- *When he was young, the future emperor Claudius was encouraged by Livy to write history. He had difficulty getting through the first reading of his work, which he himself rather spoiled. There was a comical incident at the beginning of the performance, when a fat man broke several benches. More than once, even after calm was restored, Claudius could not help giggling when he recalled the incident* (Suetonius *Life of Claudius* 41).
- *When Nero was singing, no one was allowed to leave the theater, even in an emergency. Some women therefore gave birth during his performances, and many people, weary with listening and applauding, secretly jumped over the wall or pretended to be dead and were carried out to be buried* (Suetonius *Life of Nero* 23). Even the future emperor Vespasian

incurred Nero's displeasure by going away or falling asleep during his recitals (Suetonius *Life of Vespasian* 4).

- *There are many things which we want to seem to want, but do not actually want. A speaker produces some vast work, in very tiny writing and very tightly folded: when he has read a large part of it, he says, "I'll stop now, if you wish," but those who would really like him to be quiet shout out, "Read on! Read on!"* (Seneca *Letters* 95.2).
- Horace similarly complained in the final lines of his *Art of Poetry* that, when an author has once grabbed on to someone, *he holds him fast and kills him by reading to him, like a leech that won't let go till it is full of blood.*
- Juvenal specifies fires, falling buildings, and poets reciting in August as hazards to life in Rome (*Satires* 3.7ff.).
- One of Martial's better epigrams is a complaint against an offensively persistent poet: *et stanti legis et legis sedenti, / currenti legis et legis cacanti* ("You read to me when I'm standing; / You read to me when I'm sitting; / You read to me when I'm running; / You read to me when I'm shitting") (3.44.10–11).

Have you never read about the man from Cadiz [in southern Spain] *who was so impressed by the name and fame of the historian Livy that he came from the farthest region of the world just to look at him, and went straight back home as soon as he had done so?* (Pliny *Letters* 2.3.8).

This story would appeal strongly to the younger Pliny himself and to his friend Tacitus the historian. In a different letter (9.23), Pliny tells another friend that *during a casual conversation on learned topics at the Circus games, a knight asked Tacitus if he was an Italian or a provincial; when Tacitus told him that he surely knew him from his acquaintance with literature, the knight asked, "Are you Tacitus or Pliny?"*

The emperor Tacitus rather implausibly claimed to be a descendant of the historian by the same name, and he decreed that ten copies of the historian's works should be made each year and deposited in the libraries (*Historia Augusta* Life of Tacitus 10). We might have had the missing books of the *Histories* and *Annals* if the emperor had not been killed by his own troops in July 276 after a rule of only eight months.

During the German retreat through Italy in 1944, a detachment of SS troops attempted to steal the most authoritative manuscript of Tacitus's *Germania*, a text that portrays the German tribes as living a simple and noble life untainted by the decadence of Rome. The manuscript evaded capture by being hidden under the floor in the kitchen of its Italian owner's castle. Even so, its adventures were not over: it was damaged in the flood that devastated Florence in 1966. It is now safely housed in the Museo Nazionale in Rome.

Tacitus's other works have also attracted thieves. The sole manuscript of *Annals* 1–6 was stolen from the monastery of Corvey in France in the early 16th century and taken to Rome. The primary manuscript of the *Histories* and *Annals* 11–16 was written at Monte Cassino in the mid-11th century but was in Florence by the early 15th century. Boccaccio, the author of the *Decameron*, is strongly suspected of complicity in its theft.

Alexander the Great kept Homer's *Iliad* and a dagger under his pillow (Plutarch *Life of Alexander* 8; his father, Philip, had slept with a golden drinking goblet there [Pliny *Natural History* 33.50]). Aelius Verus, Hadrian's adopted son and designated successor, preferred Apicius's cookbook and Ovid's *Amores* as his bedtime reading, and he called the epigrammatist Martial his Vergil (*Historia Augusta* Life of Aelius Verus 5).

Although he had such a poor memory that he could not even remember the names of the Homeric heroes, Calvisius Sabinus wanted to be thought learned, so he had a slave learn the works of Homer by heart, another those of Hesiod, and nine more those of one of the nine Greek lyric poets. These slaves stood ready during banquets to supply him with quotations to parade (Seneca *Letters* 27).

Although he lived in Rome for many years, the great physician Galen felt no need to learn Latin or any other language but Greek. *Everyone can learn Greek, which is a mellifluous language. Should you wish, however, to learn any of the languages spoken by barbarians, you should be aware that some of them sound like the noises made by pigs or frogs or crows, for they are without charm, and some of them speak as if they were snoring or hissing or squeaking* (*On Variation in the Pulse* 2).

Aristodemus of Nysa (in western Turkey) points to certain customs found among the Romans as proof that Homer was a Roman, namely the playing of checkers and the fact that people get up from their seats as a token of respect for their superiors (*Fragments of Greek Historians* 3.307).

Having decided to write an epic account of Roman history, Nero wondered how long the poem should be. Some people urged him to write it in four hundred books. (Vergil's *Aeneid*, by contrast, has twelve books; Ovid's *Metamorphoses* has fifteen; and Silius Italicus's *Punica*, the longest surviving Latin poem, has seventeen.) When the Stoic philosopher Annaeus Cornutus told Nero that four hundred books were too many and that no one would read them, he was banished (Cassius Dio *Roman History* 62.29).

The younger Seneca was likewise a Stoic philosopher, but also inordinately wealthy. He was said to have precipitated Queen Boudicca's uprising when he called in a loan of forty million *sestertii* that he had made to various people in the new province of Britain (Cassius Dio *Roman History* 62.52).

Seneca's nephew, Lucan, was the author of the daringly republican *Civil War*, an epic poem vehemently critical of Julius Caesar and, by implication, of the imperial system of government. According to Tacitus (*Annals* 15.49, 56), he joined a conspiracy against Nero not through political idealism, but because the emperor had forbidden him to publish his poetry. When detected and arrested, Lucan sought leniency by betraying his own mother for her part in the conspiracy.

Many of the serious works of Antiphilus, a Greek artist of the later 4th century B.C., were taken to Rome. He once drew a grasshopper dressed up in a bizarre costume, and hence "grasshopper" (*gryllos*) became the term for comic drawings in general (Pliny *Natural History* 35.114). The word "cartoon" merely denotes that the figure is drawn on paper (Latin *carta*).

The earth has a circumference of slightly more than 24,900 miles. In the 3rd century B.C., Eratosthenes calculated it as 24,700 miles. For more than fifteen hundred years, however, cartography was dominated by Claudius Ptolemy of Alexandria (c. A.D. 90–168), whose wayward miscalculation of the earth's circumference as 17,800 miles was partly responsible for Columbus's assumption that the Caribbean was actually India.

He's not just telling lies now, he's philosophizing (Plautus *The Captives* 284).

Despite the best efforts of such writers as Lucretius, Cicero, and the younger Seneca, the Romans were not a philosophically minded people:

- Pliny records that some writings of Pythagoras, discovered in King Numa's coffin in the early 2nd century B.C., were burned because they were philosophical (*Natural History* 13.86).
- In 93 B.C., the proconsul Lucius Gellius made a fool of himself by calling a meeting of the various philosophical sects in Athens and offering to act as a mediator to put an end to their arguments (Cicero *On the Laws* 1.53).
- When an Epicurean philosopher had finished a lecture, he asked if anyone had any questions. Papirius Paetus, a friend of Cicero's, did not ask him, as he expected, whether there are countless universes or just one; he said that the only question that had been on his mind all

day was where he could get invited to dinner (Cicero *Letters to his Friends* 9.26).

- Despite the protests and pleas of the Epicurean community in Athens, Gaius Memmius wished to demolish Epicurus's house, which stood in the way of his building plans (Cicero *Letters to his Friends* 13.1). Cicero's letter was written in the summer of 51 B.C., probably very soon after the publication of Lucretius's *On the Nature of Things*. The Memmius to whom Lucretius dedicated his Epicurean masterpiece is almost certainly the same man. Memmius's attitude contrasts sharply with that of Alexander the Great, who spared the house of the poet Pindar when he sacked Thebes, and of Demetrius I, also king of Macedon, who is said to have given up the opportunity of burning the city of Rhodes when he found that the painter Protogenes' masterpiece might be destroyed in the fire (Pliny *Natural History* 7.109, 35.104).
- Galen remarked scornfully that the Romans regarded Greek philosophy as being about as useful as drilling holes in millet seeds.
- *A philosopher in a rich Roman's household is a mere status symbol. He will not be required to expound philosophy, only to look after the sick and pregnant lapdog of his patron's wife* (*On Salaried Positions* 34).

nemo aegrotus quidquam somniat tam
infandum, quod non aliquis dicat philosophus
No sick person ever dreams anything so
outrageous that some philosopher or other
doesn't maintain precisely that very thing.
Varro *Menippean Satires* 122

· XII ·

FOREIGNERS

barbara barbaribus barbarant barbara barbis
(*Select Latin Inscriptions* 351; untranslatable gibberish playing with the word *barbarus* [barbarian], in the form of a hexameter verse, found inscribed on a wall in Pompeii.)

Roman scholars were aware that *barbarus* was not a purely Latin word, since it was also found in Greek. Nevertheless, it was suggested that a barbarian was someone with a beard (*barba*) who lived an unsophisticated life in the countryside (*rus*) (Cassiodorus on *Psalm* 113.11). It is sometimes supposed that "barbarian" signifies bleating like a sheep, but there is no authority for this.

The elder Cato observed that *the Athenians were amazed how swiftly and pointedly he* [Cato] *spoke, for whatever he said in a few words the interpreter relayed at great length and in many words. He thought that it was generally true that what the Greeks said came from their lips, but what the Romans said came from their hearts* (Plutarch *Life of the Elder Cato* 12).

The Greeks are a nation of actors. If you laugh, your Greek friend shakes with a louder fit of giggling; he weeps if he sees his patron's tears (not that he feels any sorrow); if you ask for a brazier in the winter, he puts on his cloak; if you say "I'm hot," he sweats (Juvenal *Satires* 3.100–103).

❁

Such subservience ran rampant in Roman society, which was very status-conscious, and it was not confined to Greeks. The late Republican orator *Caelius Rufus was very irascible. A client reclining beside him at dinner decided the best way to avoid a quarrel with him was to agree with everything he said. Caelius could not bear his acquiescent attitude and shouted out "Contradict me, so that there can be two of us!"* (Seneca *On Anger* 3.8.6).

HANNIBAL

- Hannibal (247–183/2 B.C.) came close to destroying Rome in the Second Punic War. His name means "grace of Baal [the patron deity of Carthage]." Archaeology confirms that the practice of sacrificing children to Baal was not mere Roman propaganda.
- When Hannibal wished to go to Casinum (eighty miles southeast of Rome, now the site of the Abbey of Monte Cassino), his guide, misled by his pronunciation of the town's name, brought him instead to Casilinum (much farther south, twenty-five miles from Naples). Hannibal was now in danger of being trapped by the Romans, so, after flaying and crucifying the guide, he tied torches to the horns of two thousand cows and drove them off into the night. Having tricked the Romans into thinking that this was his army on the move, he led his men to safety in the opposite direction (Livy *History of Rome* 22.13).
- When Hannibal was camped near Rome, confident that the inhabitants were in a panic, two incidents discouraged him and prompted him to withdraw. One was that a fully equipped force marched out from the city, not to fight him, but to strengthen the Roman army in Spain; the other was that the very spot on which he was camped fetched a high price at an auction in Rome (Livy *History of Rome* 26.11).

MITHRIDATES VI OF PONTUS (134–63 B.C.)

- Mithridates was Rome's most dangerous foreign enemy in the 1st century B.C. He arranged for the massacre of perhaps more than a hundred thousand Roman officials and merchants, along with their families, in Asia Minor (now Turkey) in a single day.

Mithridates.

- *When Mithridates was a baby, lightning burned his clothing but left him unscathed, except for a scar on his forehead hidden under his hair* (Plutarch *Table-Talk* 1.6).
- *It is well known that Mithridates is the only person who has ever spoken twenty-two languages. Throughout his reign of fifty-six years, he never spoke through an interpreter to any of his subjects* (Pliny *Natural History* 25.6). Frederick II (*stupor mundi*, "The Wonder of the World"), who ruled the Holy Roman Empire from 1220 to 1250, could speak a mere nine languages.
- *When he defeated Mithridates, Pompey discovered in his personal notebook a recipe for an antidote to poisons: two dried walnuts and two figs ground up with twenty leaves of rue and a pinch of salt. Taking this on an empty stomach safeguards a person against poison for a whole day* (Pliny *Natural History* 23.149). Pliny elsewhere credits Mithridates with a much more elaborate universal antidote to poison, concocted with fifty-four ingredients (29.24). Celsus records a detailed and complex version of the recipe (*On Medicine* 5.23).

- *When his long reign finally came to its close, Mithridates lamented that he had found no antidote to the deadliest of all poisons, one which infects every royal house, the treachery of soldiers, children, and friends. He attempted suicide by poison but failed, because of the immunity which he had developed through taking small doses regularly* (Appian *The Wars against Mithridates* 16.111). In Italian and Romanian, the verbs *mitridatizare* and *a mitridatiza* are still used to refer to administering an antidote to poison.
- Mithridates also took measures against other forms of assassination. *He had little confidence in armed guards to protect him while he slept, so he had a bull, a horse, and a stag trained to watch over him. If anyone approached him while he was asleep, these animals would immediately detect the intruder by sensing his breathing and wake Mithridates, the bull by bellowing, the horse by neighing, the stag by bleating* (Aelian *On Animals* 7.46).

The nationality of slaves for sale must be declared, since it often attracts or deters a buyer. It matters to know the nationality, since there is an assumption that some slaves are good because they belong to a nation with a good reputation, whereas others are bad because they belong to a nation with a bad reputation (Justinian's *Digest* 21.1.31.21).

After capturing Rome c. 387 B.C., the Gauls agreed to leave on payment of one thousand pounds of gold. While the gold was being weighed, the Romans complained that the scales were incorrect. The Gallic leader, Brennus, threw his sword on the other side of the scales, to weigh it down even more, crying *vae victis!* ("Woe to the conquered!").

Brennus may not have been the Gallic leader's actual name, but rather a Celtic word for "king," just as the name of the Illyrian queen Teuta, who opposed the Romans in the next century, may be simply a version of an Illyrian word for "queen." Attila the Hun was the *flagellum dei* ("Scourge of God") in the fifth century; the origin of his name is uncertain, but it may be a Gothic word *atta* meaning "father" in a diminutive form (i.e., "daddy").

Gallic warriors fight naked, and the whiteness of their body makes their wounds seem the more horrible. They are not much troubled by gaping wounds. But when an arrowhead or a lead bolt from a slingshot buries itself in their body and they cannot remove it, they throw themselves on the ground in rage and shame at such a seemingly insignificant wound (Livy *History of Rome* 38.21).

The Celts love danger more than any other people, and they make noble death in war the subject of their poetry. They fight wearing garlands, and set up trophies, and glory in their deeds and leave memorials of their bravery, just as the Greeks do. They regard running away as so shameful that they do not even try to escape from a house that is falling down, actually allowing themselves to be caught in buildings that are on fire. Many even hold their ground when the sea is dashing against them. Some of them seize their weapons and attack the waves, accepting their onslaught while brandishing their naked swords and spears, as if they could frighten or wound them (Aelian *Miscellaneous History* 12.23).

The Gauls are almost all very tall and fair-skinned, with reddish hair. Their eyes are intimidatingly fierce, they love quarreling and are overbearingly arrogant. Indeed, a whole band of foreigners could not match any one of them in a brawl if he should call on his gray-eyed wife to help him, for she is far stronger than he is. She is especially hard to face when she swells her neck, grinds her teeth, swings her massive snow-white forearms, and begins to kick and throw punches like bolts shot from the taut strings of a catapult (Ammianus Marcellinus 15.12.1).

Soap was invented by the Gauls for reddening the hair. It is made from animal fat and ashes. The best type is made from beechwood ash and goat fat. It can be either solid or liquid. The Germans also use it, the men more than the women (Pliny *Natural History* 28.191). The Romans did not use soap for washing, preferring, like the Greeks, to anoint themselves with olive oil, which they then scraped off with a *strigil.*

Diodorus Siculus notes that a Gallic noble would typically shave his cheeks but grow a mustache right over his mouth, so that food got tangled up with it, and whatever he drank passed through a sort of sieve (*The Library* 5.28).

When a Gaul heard Caligula proclaiming oracles from a high platform while dressed as Jupiter, he started to laugh. Caligula had him summoned, and asked him, "Who do you think I am?" The Gaul replied, "A big buffoon." But he came to no harm for he was merely a shoemaker: it seems easier for the powerful to bear the candor of the masses than that of those of high rank (Cassius Dio *Roman History* 59.26).

Before Caesar's conquest, the Gauls had been Rome's great northern enemies. Their capture of the city in the early 4th century B.C. was one of the most devastating catastrophes in Roman history. Another Gallic disaster, though reported by Livy (*History of Rome* 23.24), has tended to pass almost unnoticed. In 216 B.C., an army of twenty-five thousand men led by Lucius Postumius, the consul-elect, was annihilated by the Gauls in the Silva Litana in northern Italy. The trees that stood on either side of the road along which the Romans would pass were cut through in such a way that they did not actually fall over. Only when the Romans were in the ambush did the Gauls topple the trees, thus ensuring that the Romans were either killed by the falling trees or unable to escape. Hardly ten got away, and very few were taken prisoner. Postumius's skull was covered in gold and used as a drinking cup. Roman losses—two legions and many thousands of allies—were greater than in the massacre of Varus's three legions by the German tribes in the Teutoburg Forest in A.D. 9, but the event is scarcely remembered, largely because it is eclipsed by the disaster at Cannae, which occurred in the same year.

London is mentioned in classical Latin literary texts only once, at Tacitus *Annals* 14.33, recording the destruction of the town by Queen Boudicca in A.D. 60/61.

The Romans knew little about Ireland. Writing in the early 1st century A.D., the Greek geographer Strabo reports that *there are several small islands around Britain and a large one, Ierne* [*sc.*, Ireland], *running along its north side, and broader than it is long. I can say nothing definite about Ierne, except that its inhabitants are wilder than the Britons, for they eat human flesh as well as plants, considering it proper to eat their fathers when they die* (*Geography* 4.5.4).

After Zenodorus had been commissioned by the Arverni, a Gallic tribe, to sculpt a colossal statue of Mercury, Nero summoned him to Rome to sculpt an enormous statue of himself (Pliny *Natural History* 34.45). Pliny claims that the Arverni paid Zenodorus forty million *sestertii*, the same amount as had been imposed by Julius Caesar as annual tribute on the whole of Gaul (Suetonius *Life of Julius Caesar* 25).

When some Vettonians [a Spanish tribe] *first visited a Roman camp and saw some officers strolling up and down for pleasure, they thought they must be mad and tried to escort them back to their tents, for they assumed that soldiers should be either resting or fighting* (Strabo *Geography* 3.4.16).

It is an appalling indication of the inhuman savagery of the Cantabrians [a Spanish tribe] *that they sing songs of triumph when fixed to a cross* (Strabo *Geography* 3.4.18).

In the Baltic Sea, there are islands inhabited by people whose ears are so enormous that they cover their bodies with them and do not need clothes (Pliny *Natural History* 4.95). *By contrast, the Shade-Foot people of India keep themselves cool by lying on their backs and shading themselves from the sun with their single enormous foot* (7.23). *Also in India are found the Mouthless people, who live on air and the odors of roots, flowers, and apples; it is said that they may die if subjected to a particularly strong smell* (7.25).

Some of the survivors of the massacre of Crassus's legions by the Parthians at Carrhae in 53 B.C. may have come in contact with the

Chinese, who were unknown to the Romans except as silk producers. A Chinese document of 36 B.C. refers to a group of more than a hundred soldiers in the Hunnish army behaving in a disciplined manner not typical of the Huns, arranging themselves in a fish-scale formation [perhaps the *testudo* (tortoise); see p. 137] and practicing drills.

The earliest reliable evidence for direct contact between the Romans and the Chinese appears in Chinese records of A.D. 166, which report a meeting between the emperor of China and a Roman embassy sent by "Antun," presumably a reference either to Antoninus Pius, who died in 161, or to his successor, Marcus Aurelius Antoninus.

By the Augustan age, silk dresses (described by Petronius as *ventus textilis* "woven wind" [*Satyricon* 55]) were fashionable. Silk was extremely expensive, for it had to be imported along the trade route from China, which guarded its monopoly on silk production very closely. Silkworms were first brought to the West in A.D. 552.

THE TOGA

The toga was the formal garb of Roman citizens, distinguishing them from foreigners and slaves. It was not a very practical garment, being hot, cumbersome, and hard to keep clean.

- Romulus was normally thought to have been borne up to heaven as a god, but an alternative story had him cut to pieces by the senators, who disguised the murder by each carrying off a body part hidden in his toga (Plutarch *Life of Romulus* 27).
- "Candidates" are so called because it was customary for those seeking election to wear a *toga candida*, a "white toga," as they canvassed for votes. Livy records that, in 432 B.C., there was apparently great controversy over a law forbidding candidates to attempt to gain unfair advantage by wearing an artificially whitened toga; he goes on to observe that *nowadays this seems a trivial matter, scarcely worth serious consideration, but it then sparked a huge conflict between the patricians and the plebeians* (*History of Rome* 4.25).

- The toga was originally worn by both sexes. When the *stola* was adopted as the formal garb of respectable women, prostitutes and women divorced for adultery were forbidden to wear it, and they continued to wear a version of the toga.
- As part of his attempt to impose a return to the traditional Roman way of life, the *mos maiorum* (literally "the custom of the ancestors"), Augustus sought to reintroduce the dress code of former times. *He once saw a crowd wearing dark cloaks in front of the Assembly and he shouted out indignantly, "Just look at them, the Romans, the masters of the world, the toga-wearing race"* [Romanos, rerum dominos, gentemque togatam (Vergil *Aeneid* 1.282, from Jupiter's great speech promising Venus dominion for her descendants)]. *He ordered the city magistrates not to permit anyone thereafter to appear in or near the Forum except in their toga and without a cloak* (Suetonius *Life of Augustus* 40).
- As an example of Claudius's legal pedantry, Suetonius cites his ruling that a man accused of wrongfully claiming to be a citizen should wear a Roman toga or a Greek cloak, depending on whether the lawyers for the defense or for the prosecution were speaking (*Life of Claudius* 15).
- Despite the general dislike of the encumbering and clumsy toga, the artist who painted many of the frescoes in Nero's new palace, the *domus aurea* ("The Golden House"), was so conscious of his own dignity that he wore his toga even when he was up on the scaffolding (Pliny *Natural History* 35.120).
- Juvenal points out that one of the many advantages of living in the countryside is that *no one puts on his toga unless he is dead*, that is, to be buried in it (*Satires* 3.171–172).
- The Britons were quicker than the Gauls in adopting Roman ways. *Those who had till recently rejected the Romans' language became eager to learn Latin rhetoric. Our style of dress became popular, and many people wore the toga. This led gradually to decadence and corruption, porticoes, baths, and sophisticated banquets. In their innocence, they called this process "civilization," whereas in reality it contributed to their enslavement* (Tacitus *Agricola* 21).
- The Romans thought the wearing of trousers a barbaric custom: Gaul beyond the Alps was once known as *Gallia bracata* "Trousered Gaul," whereas Gaul on the Italian side was known as *Gallia togata*

"Gaul in a Toga." The emperor Honorius forbade the wearing of trousers in Rome as late as A.D. 397.

- In the later empire, the toga fell into neglect; it is mentioned scarcely half a dozen times in all of Justinian's *Digest*. At the end of the 6th or in the early 7th century, St. Isidore suggests that looking at old paintings or statues is a good way of discovering what the toga looked like (*Etymologies* 19.24).

❁

Marcus Cornelius Fronto, tutor to the emperors Antoninus Pius, Marcus Aurelius, and Lucius Verus, was from the province of Numidia in North Africa. His ancestors were probably Italian settlers, but he liked to call himself a "Libyan born of Libyan nomads." He laments that it is impossible to establish a warm friendship with anyone in Rome and that there is not even a specific Latin term for the affection felt between friends (*Letters* p. 111 van den Hout).

This ivory statuette of Lakshmi, the Hindu goddess of fertility, is a surprising survivor from the ruins of Pompeii.

The ancient Egyptian practice of mummification of the dead continued throughout the Ptolemaic period (323–30 B.C.) and the centuries of Roman occupation. When Octavian visited Alexandria in 30 B.C., he viewed the mummy of Alexander the Great, but, when he touched it, part of the nose fell off. The Alexandrians were very eager to show him the mummies of the Ptolemaic rulers also, but he said, "I wanted to see a king, not corpses" (Cassius Dio *Roman History* 51.16).

Pliny says of Sri Lanka, a land practically unknown to the Romans: *No one has a slave, or sleeps till daybreak, or takes a siesta; their houses are of a modest height; the price of wheat never increases; they have no law courts or legal disputes* (*Natural History* 6.89).

The people of Byzantium are said to be so amazingly addicted to wine that they live in taverns and rent their homes to people visiting the city. . . . When the enemy were attacking the walls during a determined siege, the Byzantines drifted away and spent the day in their usual haunts. So Leonides, their commander, had taverns set up for them on the walls. By this trick, he finally managed to persuade them not to desert their posts (Aelian *Miscellaneous History* 3.14).

In the 2nd century A.D., Appian records that he had himself seen embassies from impoverished barbarian tribes turned away by the emperor when they came begging to be made subject to Rome (*Roman History* Preface 7).

Helvetii, Gallica gens olim armis virisque,
mox memoria nominis clara
The Swiss, a Gallic people once famous
for their manly courage in war, now a distant
memory.
Tacitus *Histories* 1.67

· XIII ·

SLAVES

servitutem mortalitati fere comparamus
We regard slavery as more or less the same as death.
Justinian's *Digest* 50.17.209

In the early 4th century B.C., *Rome's neighbors in Latium asked the Romans to send them women to marry. The Romans suspected that this was a mere trick to obtain hostages, but did not have the military strength to refuse. A slave girl persuaded the magistrates to send her with a group of other slave girls, disguised as freeborn women. During the night, when the girls had removed the Latin soldiers' swords, the Romans attacked the camp, and a massacre ensued* (Plutarch *Life of Camillus* 33).

As a desperate measure in the aftermath of the Battle of Cannae in 216 B.C., slaves were recruited into the Roman army. On the eve of a battle, the Roman commander promised freedom to any slave who brought back the head of an enemy. *Nothing impeded the Romans so much as the granting of freedom in return for enemy heads. Each of the bravest fighters, as soon as he had killed one of the enemy, wasted time cutting off his head, and then, holding the head rather than his sword in his right hand, he quit the battle line, leaving the fighting to the sluggish and fainthearted* (Livy *History of Rome* 24.15).

A barefoot slave serving at a banquet.

Cato believed that most unrest among slaves was caused by sexual frustration, so he allowed his male slaves to have intercourse with his female slaves—for a fixed price (payable to him) (Plutarch *Life of the Elder Cato* 21).

It is easy to see how household slaves, who lived closely with their owners and enjoyed a fairly comfortable environment, might hope to earn small amounts of money. Slaves in brutal occupations, on large agricultural estates or in mines, would have had few such opportunities. The Latin term for household slaves is *vernae*. Such slaves could expect relatively humane treatment, but one of the etymologies proposed for the term in antiquity, *vere nati*, "born in the spring," suggests that they were bred like animals.

Elagabalus [ruled A.D. 218–222] *used to play jokes on his slaves, as when he ordered them to bring him a thousand pounds of cobwebs, with a prize for the contest. He is said to have amassed ten thousand pounds of cobwebs, and to have declared that one could understand from this how large Rome was* (*Historia Augusta* Life of Elagabalus 26.6).

Gold mining is more arduous than the labors of the Giants. Mountains are hollowed out by the digging of long tunnels by the light of torches. The miners work in shifts as long as the torches last, and do not see daylight for months at a time. . . . Sudden cracks appear and crush the miners, so that it now seems less perilous to dive for pearls and purple mollusks in the depths of the sea. We have made dry land so much more dangerous! (Pliny *Natural History* 33.70).

Not all such labor was quite so brutal. Slaves in the Sicilian quarries had lives settled enough that they could raise families. Some of those children, never having seen a city before, ran off screaming when they went to Syracuse and saw horses in harness and oxen being driven along (Aelian *Miscellaneous History* 12.44).

Spartacus and about seventy other slaves escaped from a training camp for gladiators in Capua in 73 B.C. They quickly attracted thousands of slaves and destitute country folk, and they battled Roman armies for two years, devastating much of the Italian countryside in the process. When the revolt was finally crushed, more than six thousand slaves were crucified along the Via Appia, the road between Rome and Capua.

Spartacus's revolt had been preceded by slave uprisings in Sicily in 135–132 and 104–103 B.C. The earlier of these revolts was led by a Syrian named Eunus, who impressed his followers by emitting sparks and flames from his mouth when he spoke, a trick he managed with a fire in a nutshell (Diodorus Siculus *The Library* 35.2). St. Jerome later attributed much the same trick to Simon bar Kokba, the leader of the Second Jewish Revolt (A.D. 132–135).

Not wishing to be distracted by their presence, the ex-consul and triumphant general Pupius Piso told his slaves to speak only when spoken to and answer his questions as briefly as possible. He once laid an elaborate dinner in honor of Clodius Pulcher [see p. 23]. *When Clodius failed to show up, Piso repeatedly sent his slave to see if he was on his way. Eventually he asked the slave, "Did you deliver the invitation?" The slave said he had. "Then why isn't he here?" "Because he declined to come." "Why didn't you tell me straightaway?" "Because you didn't ask me that"* (Plutarch *On Talkativeness* 511).

Plutarch illustrates Pompey's sudden debasement after his defeat by Caesar in the Battle of Pharsalus in 48 B.C. by noting that, while taking shelter in a fisherman's hut, he had to take off his own shoes (*Life of Pompey* 73). The younger Cato was regarded as a model of frugality because he had taken only twelve slaves with him on that same campaign (Valerius Maximus *Memorable Deeds and Sayings* 4.3.12).

When Quintus Fufius Calenus, Julius Caesar's lieutenant, captured Megara, one of the few Greek cities to resist him, he sold the survivors into slavery to show that he had treated them as they deserved. Since, however, he did not actually want Megara to be utterly destroyed, he sold them very cheaply to their own relatives (Cassius Dio *Roman History* 42.14).

Hostius Quadra was a rich miser whose sexual habits disgusted Seneca, but not sufficiently to prevent him from denouncing them in detail. When Quadra was killed by his slaves, Augustus came very close to ruling that the murder was justified (Seneca *Natural Questions* 1.16).

It is estimated that, by the end of the 1st century B.C., perhaps as much as 90 percent of the free population of Italy had ancestors who had been slaves. Two factors contributed strongly to this remarkable integration: slavery was not racially based, and slaves, on gaining their freedom, were normally also granted citizenship.

Caenis, Vespasian's concubine, had once been the slave of Antonia, the daughter of Mark Antony (Suetonius *Life of Vespasian* 3).

An inscription on a dog collar reads *Hold me, lest I escape, and bring me back to my owner, Viventius, in Callistus's forecourt* (*Corpus of Latin Inscriptions* 15.07193).

An inscription on a slave collar reads *I am Asellus* [Little Donkey], *slave of Praeiectus, who is an official in the Department of the Grain Supply. I have escaped from my post. Detain me, for I have run away. Take me back to the barbers' shops near the temple of Flora* (*Select Latin Inscriptions* 8727).

It was once proposed in the Senate that slaves should be distinguished from free people by their dress, but then it was realized how great a danger this would be, if our slaves began to count us (and discovered how far they outnumbered the free population) (Seneca *On Mercy* 1.24).

A slave is not diseased if he has a tooth missing. Most people are without some tooth or other, and are not therefore diseased. We are born without teeth, and this does not mean that we are not really healthy until we cut our teeth. On any other reckoning, no old person would be healthy (Justinian's *Digest* 21.1.11).

Being left-handed is not a disease or a defect, unless a slave favors his left hand because of a weakness in his right; such a slave is crippled, not left-handed (Justinian's *Digest* 21.1.12.3).

A slave is not diseased if he wets his bed while drunk and asleep or because he is too lazy to get up. If, however, he cannot retain his urine because of a defective bladder, his sale may be canceled because of that defect. It cannot be canceled simply because he wets his bed (Justinian's *Digest* 21.1.14.4).

Some flaws in slaves are psychological rather than physical, as for example when a slave is always wanting to watch the games, or gazes intently at pictures, or tells lies, or is afflicted with other such defects (Justinian's *Digest* 21.1.65).

If their owner is suffering a deadly assault, slaves should help him with weapons, with their hands, by shouting, by interposing their bodies; if they do not do so when they might have, it is right that they should be punished (Justinian's *Digest* 29.5.19).

Even after they had been freed, former slaves still had an obligation to provide services for their former owners. *If a freedman practices the art of dancing, it is proper that he should provide this service free of charge not only for his patron, but also at entertainments put on by his patron's friends. Similarly, a freedman who practices medicine should treat his patron's friends without payment whenever the patron wishes him to do so. For it is not right that, in order to benefit from his freedman's services, a patron should have either to give entertainments constantly or to be ill all the time* (Justinian's *Digest* 38.1.27).

Just as a [pregnant] *slave girl who runs away is regarded as stealing herself, so she makes her child a runaway also* (Justinian's *Digest* 47.2.61).

The rise of Christianity did very little to curb slavery. Even St. Augustine, in the 5th century, thought it acceptable for slaves to be obtained by kidnapping, provided the kidnapping took place outside the boundaries of the empire (*Letters* CSEL 88.8, 10).

minus est quam servus dominus qui servos timet
An owner who fears his slaves is less than a slave.
Publilius Syrus *Sententiae* M 14

· XIV ·

ANIMALS

mus syllaba est; mus caseum rodit; syllaba ergo caseum rodit
"Mouse" is a syllable; a mouse nibbles cheese; therefore a syllable nibbles cheese.
Seneca *Letters* 48.6

In the northern forests, there are animals called elk. Their shape and their dappled hides are like those of roe deer, but they are slightly bigger and have no horns. They have legs without tendons or joints, and do not lie down to sleep, nor, if they have accidentally fallen down, are they able to get up again. Trees serve them as beds: they lean against them and sleep at a slight incline. When hunters have found their usual haunts by observing their tracks, they either undermine the roots of all the trees in that spot or they cut them so that the upper trunks of the trees still seem to be standing firmly. When the elk lean against the trees in their normal way, they knock the weak trees over with their weight, and they themselves collapse along with them (Caesar *Gallic War* 6.27).

Aelian (*On Animals* 13.6) records the strange case of the mysterious plundering of the stocks of pickled fish stored by some Spanish fish merchants in a warehouse in Pozzuoli. The doors, walls, and roof remained intact, yet a large quantity of fish was missing every morning: the culprit turned out to be an octopus that came up through the sewer every night.

Birds imitate the human voice, and parrots can actually conduct a conversation. . . . They are particularly risqué if they drink wine (Pliny *Natural History* 10.117).

According to Pliny, the most amazing belief about hyaenas is that they imitate human speech among the shepherds' huts and learn the name of one of them, so as to call him outside and tear him to pieces (*Natural History* 8.106). He also reports the belief that those who have a hyaena's tongue between the sole of their foot and their shoe are not barked at by dogs (28.100).

In A.D. 28, at the height of the treason trials that marred Tiberius's rule, a certain Titius Sabinus was arrested. *His dog could not be driven away from the prison door. When Sabinus was thrown down the Steps of Sorrow outside the prison, it sat howling beside his corpse. Crowds gathered, and it took such scraps of food as people threw to it and laid them by the dead man's mouth. When his corpse was thrown into the Tiber, it jumped in and tried to keep it from sinking* (Pliny *Natural History* 8.145).

Tuna fish take such delight in swimming and feeding together that they move in a solid cube with six equal sides, with all of them facing outward as they move along. Hence, if a tuna-spotter ascertains the exact number of fish on the surface, he can tell immediately how big the whole school is, since its depth, breadth, and length are all the same size (Plutarch *On the Cleverness of Animals* 29).

In winter, fishermen take picks and break through the ice wherever they fancy, making a circular hole down into the water; you would say it was like the mouth of a well or of a jar with a very big belly. And so the fish, trying to escape from the covering ice and longing for daylight, eagerly and in vast numbers approach the aperture that has been opened up; they push against each other and are as easy to catch as if they were in a narrow ditch (Aelian *On Animals* 14.26). Aelian begins the next book with an account of fly-fishing for trout.

EXOTIC PETS

- Quintus Sertorius, a generally sympathetic but largely forgotten figure, set up a "counter-Senate" in Spain in the 70s B.C. as an alternative to the government in Rome. He owed much of his success to the belief which he fostered among the native Spanish tribes that he received divine inspiration communicated to him via a magical white doe.
- *A runaway slave named Androcles took a thorn from the foot of a lion in the African desert. He was later captured and sent to Rome, where he was condemned to be eaten by a lion in the arena. The lion spared him, for it was the very one he had treated in Africa. The emperor Caligula freed them both. Androcles would then take the lion around Rome on a leash, and people would give him money and scatter flowers over the lion* (Aulus Gellius *Attic Nights* 5.14).
- Hanno, a Carthaginian general in the 3rd century B.C., was said to have had a lion trained to carry his baggage when he was on campaign (Plutarch *Political Precepts* 3).
- One of the several queens of Egypt named Beronice had a lion that used to dine with her, just like a person. It also licked her face and smoothed away her wrinkles (Aelian *On Animals* 5.39). There may be a pun here, since Aelian's word for "it smoothed," ἐλέαινε (*eleaine*), is very similar to λέαινα (*leaina*), which means "lioness." Irrelevant coincidence is also possible: *leaina* is an anagram for *Aelian*.
- Valentinian I (ruled A.D. 364–375) kept two man-eating bears, Mica Aurea ("Gold Speck") and Innocentia, outside his bedroom (Ammianus Marcellinus 29.3.9).

In India, if a monkey sees someone putting on his shoes, it imitates the action of putting on shoes. . . . Therefore hunters lay out shoes made of lead, with nooses attached beneath them, so that when monkeys put their feet into them they are caught in a trap from which they cannot escape (Aelian *On Animals* 17.25).

We go about like inflated animal skins and are worth less than flies; flies have at least something to commend them, but we are worth no more than bubbles (Petronius *Satyricon* 42).

Hedgehog skins are used to give a polished finish to clothing. Vast profits have been made through fraudulently cornering the trade in them. Nothing has been the subject of more legislation by the Senate than this monopoly, and every emperor has been approached by people in the provinces with complaints about it (Pliny *Natural History* 8.135).

Even after it has been removed from the creature's body, a seal's skin retains its feeling for the sea, for it always bristles when the tide is going out (Pliny *Natural History* 9.42).

Cats were regarded as sacred in Egypt. In the mid-1st century B.C., the historian Diodorus Siculus was an eyewitness when an Egyptian mob lynched a member of a Roman embassy who had accidentally killed a cat (*The Library* 1.83).

In the province of Africa, offshore from the town of Hippo, a dolphin befriended a boy, playing with him and allowing him to ride on its back. The deputy governor of the province poured ointment over its back as a misguided religious offering. The unfamiliar smell of the ointment caused the dolphin to flee out to the deep sea for many days. When it returned, it seemed listless and depressed at first, but gradually recovered its strength and played with the boy again. Accommodating the VIPs who came flocking to see it put a strain on the town's resources, so the local council had the dolphin secretly killed (Pliny *Letters* 9.33).

Among all the species of insect, the first rank and the greatest admiration is rightly given to bees, for they are the only insect created for the benefit of mankind (Pliny *Natural History* 11.4). The Romans thought that queen bees were actually king bees, and that honey, the ancient world's predominant source of sugar, was gathered as a sort of dew.

There was a widespread and quite erroneous belief that bees could be generated from the corpse of an ox that had been beaten to death and left to rot. No ancient farmer would have wasted any of his livestock

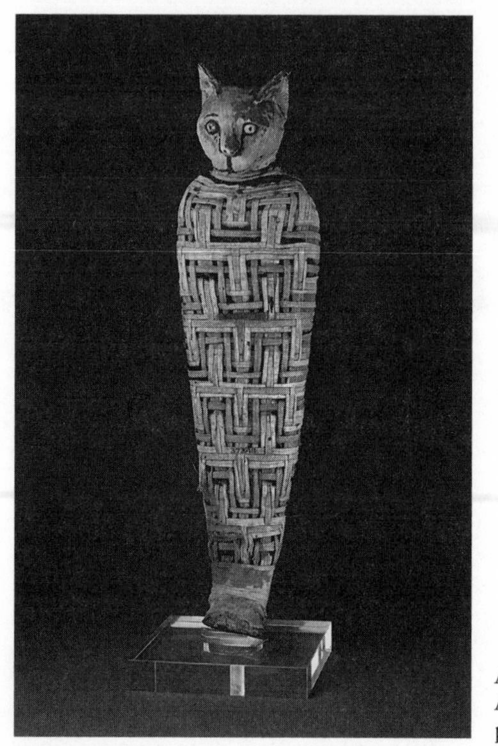

A cat mummy from Abydos in the Roman period.

to obtain a swarm of bees, but Vergil describes the process at length in the fourth book of the *Georgics*.

❁

The Romans accepted the Greek notion that goats breathe through their ears. Aristotle had attempted to refute this view, but Varro repeats it (*On Farming* 2.3), as does Pliny (*Natural History* 8.202). An early-3rd-century A.D. Greek poem, the *Cynegetica* ("On Hunting with Dogs"), attributed to Oppian, claims that wild goats breathe through a channel between their horns, and that one can suffocate them by pouring wax round their horns (2.338–342). It was not known in antiquity that several species of turtle breathe rectally.

After grazing all night on land, turtles go back to the sea at dawn, full but tired. They doze off on the surface of the water, and their snoring gives their location away to hunters (Pliny *Natural History* 9.36).

Latin does not have a very large vocabulary, and the Romans were not particularly observant about many aspects of the natural world (hence king bees, goats breathing through their ears). There seem to have been few terms used exclusively of groups of animals, comparable to such long-established English phrases as "cete of badgers," "nye of pheasants," "sounder of wild pigs," "unkindness of ravens." It is surprising, therefore, that the range of specialized terms for animal calls is so extensive. The emperor Geta (ruled A.D. 211) liked to quiz grammarians about such words (*Historia Augusta* Life of Geta). For example:

Camels and rams	*blatterant*
Panthers	*cauriunt*
Frogs	*coaxant*
Storks	*crotolant*
Owls	*cuccubiunt*
Swans	*drensant*
Weasels	*drindrant*
Leopards	*feliunt* and *rictant*
Geese	*gingriunt* and *glicciunt* and *sclingunt*
Incubating hens	*glocidant*
Mice	*mintriunt* (but shrews *desticant*)
Peacocks	*paupulant*
Sparrowhawks	*plipiant*
Wild boars	*quiritant*
Tigers	*rancant* (but bears *uncant* and lynxes *urcant*)
Ducks	*tetrissitant*
Blackbirds	*zinziant*

SNAKES

Snakes have a particular liking for wine, when they get the chance (Pliny *Natural History* 10.198). Aristotle had recorded specifically that vipers can be caught when drunk on wine laid out on shards of pottery by stone walls (*History of Animals* 594*a*).

In his account of events in 255 B.C., during the First Punic War, *Livy records that in Africa, beside the river Bagradas, there was a snake so huge that it kept Atilius Regulus's army away from the river. It seized many soldiers in its huge jaws and crushed others in the coils of its tail. Javelins could not pierce its skin, and it eventually succumbed to a hail of heavy flint rocks shot from catapults from all sides. All the soldiers regarded it as more formidable than Carthage itself. The river was so tainted with its gore and the surrounding region was so polluted with the pestilential odor of its corpse that the Romans had to move their camp* (Valerius Maximus *Memorable Deeds and Sayings* 1.8 ext. 19).

Just before the Battle of Actium [in 31 B.C.], *a two-headed snake eighty-five feet long appeared in Etruria; it caused great damage before it was killed by lightning* (Cassius Dio *Roman History* 50.8).

Suetonius reports that Augustus displayed a (presumably live) snake that was about seventy-five feet long (*Life of Augustus* 43).

Aelian, who may have spent his whole life in Italy, claims that snakes in Ethiopia grow to one hundred and eighty feet long (*On Animals* 2.21), while Strabo refers skeptically to a captive snake in India two hundred and ten feet long (*Geography* 15.1.28).

SOME STRANGE BEASTS

There is universal agreement among those who have discussed it that the phoenix is sacred to the Sun, and has a beak and plumage unlike those of other birds. There are various opinions about its life span. Five hundred years is the most common view, but some people maintain that it appears every 1,461 years, most recently in the reigns of Sesostris, Amasis, and Ptolemy III, and that it flew to the city of Heliopolis with a huge escort of other birds that were amazed at its unfamiliar features. . . . They say that, when the years alloted to it have passed and its death is approaching, the phoenix constructs a nest in its own country and pours a life-giving substance over it, from which an offspring arises. The new phoenix's first concern is to bury its father, which it does with great care: it makes a long test flight with a load of myrrh, and when it is capable of sustaining a heavy burden on a long journey, it picks up the body and carries it to the altar of the Sun, where it cremates its father. The details are uncertain and exaggerated with legends, but that the bird is seen from time to time in Egypt is not questioned (Tacitus *Annals* 6.28).

I personally have seen a hippocentaur [part horse, part human] *preserved in honey, brought from Egypt to the emperor Claudius* (Pliny *Natural History* 7.35).

According to Pliny (*Natural History* 8.75, drawing on Aristotle *History of Animals* 501*a*), *Ctesias* [a Greek physician at the Persian court in the early 4th century B.C.] *records that in India there is a beast called the manticore, which moves very rapidly, and has a particular liking for human flesh. It has the following characteristics:*

- *a triple row of teeth that come together like the teeth of a comb;*
- *the face and ears of a human being;*
- *gray eyes;*
- *a hide the color of blood;*
- *the body of a lion;*
- *a tail that inflicts stings just as a scorpion does;*
- *a voice comparable to the sound of a reed-pipe and a trumpet played in unison.*

The basilisk is found in the province of Cyrenaica [roughly, eastern Libya]. *It is not more than a foot long and is distinguished by a white spot*

PHOENIX FELIX ET TV: "Phoenix, you also, [be] prosperous."

on its head like a diadem. Its hissing puts all other snakes to flight, and it moves with its body upright, not with winding coils, as other snakes do. It destroys bushes without even touching them, but merely by breathing on them, and it burns up grass and splits rocks, such is its malign power. It is believed that a horseman once killed a basilisk with his spear, but that its destructive force ran up along the spear and killed both horse and rider (Pliny *Natural History* 8.78).

❁

The precious stone known as draconitis or dracontias is formed in the brains of dragons. It only turns into a gem if the dragon's head is cut off while it is still alive, for the creature spitefully prevents the process if it realizes that it is dying. . . . It is said that the hunters go out in two-horse chariots, scattering soporific drugs as soon as they spot a dragon, and then chop off its head when it falls asleep (Pliny *Natural History* 37.158).

Pliny is skeptical about the claim put forward by magicians that salamanders have the power to extinguish fire. He argues that if this were so they would surely have been exploited for this purpose in Rome, where fire was a constant danger (*Natural History* 29.76). That notion had, however, been entertained by Aristotle (*History of Animals* 552*b*).

India produces one-horned horses and donkeys. Drinking vessels are made out of their horns. If anyone drinks fatal poison from one of these, the attempt on his life does him no harm at all, for the horn of both the horse and the donkey seems to be an antidote to the poison (Aelian *On Animals* 3.41). This passage foreshadows the myth of the unicorn, as does Pliny's description of the rhinoceros as a one-horned Indian animal with the head of a deer, the body of a horse, the feet of an elephant, and the tail of a wild boar (*Natural History* 8.76).

They say that there is an animal in Macedonia called the bonasus, *which has a horse's mane, but is in other respects like a bull. Its horns curve backward and are useless for fighting, so it defends itself by running away. As it runs away, it emits manure over an area of up to two acres, and contact with this burns its pursuers like fire* (Pliny *Natural History* 8.40, expanding on Aristotle *Parts of Animals* 863*a*, who mentions the manure, but not its range and firepower).

According to Ulpian, Rome's greatest legal expert, the gorgon lives in Africa, and is like a sheep or a calf. It kills anyone it meets with the power of its breath or by a glance from its eyes. The Romans got to know of it in the war against Jugurtha, the king of Numidia, in 107–106 B.C. Some soldiers tried to kill one by rushing at it with their swords, but it killed them by glaring at them. This was repeated several times, until some Numidian horsemen killed it with their javelins and brought it back to Marius, the Roman commander (Athenaeus *Wise Men at Dinner* 221*b*).

No one now believes in the existence of the Hydra of Lerna [killed by Hercules as one of his Twelve Labors] *or of the three-headed Chimaera, but the amphisbaena is a snake with a head at both ends. When it is going forward, it uses one head as a tail, the other as a head, and when it is going backward, it uses its heads in the opposite manner* (Aelian *On Animals* 9.23).

ELEPHANTS

Pliny reports that, when they are surrounded by hunters, elephants position those with the smallest tusks at the front, to make the hunters think that their ivory is not worth fighting for. When they are exhausted with fighting, they break off their tusks by bashing them against a tree, and ransom themselves by leaving them as plunder (*Natural History* 8.8).

It is usually the oldest male which leads a herd of elephants on the march, but they send the smallest ones ahead when they are crossing a river, for fear that the bigger ones should wear away the riverbed and cause the depth to increase (Pliny *Natural History* 8.11).

The elephant drivers carried a chisel and a mallet. When an elephant began to run amok and to rush at their own men, its driver positioned the chisel between its ears where the head is joined to the neck and hammered it in as vigorously as possible. This is the quickest way to kill such a large animal when it is out of control. Hasdrubal [Hannibal's brother] *was the first to introduce the technique* (Livy *History of Rome* 27.49).

Panic among their elephants contributed significantly to the Carthaginians' defeat at the Battle of Zama in 202 B.C. The 1937 epic film *Scipione l'africano*, directed in part by Benito Mussolini's son Vittorio, inaccurately portrays the Roman legions winning the battle thanks to their heroic resistance to a massive charge by the Carthaginian

A war elephant.

elephants. (The role of Scipio, the Roman commander, is played by Annibale [*sic*] Ninchi.)

Elephants expend up to twenty-five times as much energy traversing hills as they require for flat terrain. Most of Hannibal's elephants perished crossing the Alps, and all thirty-seven of them were dead before the decisive Battle of Cannae.

The Romans experienced great problems transporting elephants in their advance across the mountains of central Greece before the Battle of Pydna in 168 B.C. According to Livy's account, *a series of thirty-foot platforms was constructed, and each platform was tipped over when an elephant reached the far end of it, so that the animal was forced on down to the next platform. Some of the elephants went forward standing on their feet, but others slid down on their rumps* (*History of Rome* 44.5).

Elephants on Display

- *When Pompey attempted to enter Rome in a triumph procession in a chariot drawn by four elephants, it got stuck in the city gate* (Plutarch *Life of Pompey* 14).
- In a show put on by Germanicus Caesar, twelve elephants, six male and six female, acted the roles of diners at a banquet (Aelian *On Animals* 2.11).
- The future emperor Galba displayed tightrope-walking elephants at the *Floralia* games (Suetonius *Life of Galba* 6).
- At a festival in honor of his mother, Nero had an elephant with its rider descend a tightrope from the top of a theater (Cassius Dio *Roman History* 62.17).
- *A troupe of elephants was being trained in Rome recently to perform complex and dangerous routines. One of them was very slow to learn and was repeatedly berated and punished. It was seen all alone in the moonlight practicing what it had been taught* (Plutarch *On the Cleverness of Animals* 12).

POULTRY SECTION

scire ex vobis volo, ovumne prius exstiterit an gallina
I want to know from you whether the egg came first or the chicken (Macrobius *Saturnalia* 7.16).

⊕

When the Gauls were about to take the Capitol in the early 4th century B.C., geese sacred to Juno gave the alarm, whereas the guard dogs failed do so. Nearly five hundred years later, in commemoration of this event, dogs were still being crucified annually on a cross of elder wood (Pliny *Natural History* 29.57), whereas a goose was carried along in a litter in a solemn procession (Aelian *On Animals* 12.33).

The customer seems to have brought her own shopping bag.

In 368 B.C., Appius Claudius Crassus spoke against the admission of plebeians to the consulship, arguing that only patricians could take the auspices by observing the behavior of the sacred chickens: *"People may mock our religious scruples: 'What does it matter if the sacred chickens will not eat, if they are slow in leaving their coop, if one of them squawks discordantly?' These are small matters, but it was by not despising such small matters that your ancestors made Rome supreme"* (Livy *History of Rome* 6.41).

In 249 B.C., Appius's great-grandson, Publius Claudius Pulcher, was in command of the Roman fleet, fighting the Carthaginians at the Battle of Drepana off Sicily. On being told before the battle that the sacred chickens would not eat, he said, "Then let them drink!" and had them thrown overboard (Suetonius *Life of Tiberius* 2). The Romans were defeated, losing ninety-three of the one hundred and twenty ships in their fleet.

When Livia was engaged to Octavian, an eagle dropped a white hen into her lap. It was unharmed and had a little olive twig in its mouth. The priests who divined the future from the behavior of birds commanded that the hen and its offspring be looked after and that the olive twig be planted and tended. Augustus and all his successors used to carry a branch of this olive tree and wear a garland made from it whenever they held a triumph (Pliny *Natural History* 15.136).

The place where Livia's grove grew was called "the Chicken-Run." In the last year of the reign of Nero [the last of the Julio-Claudian emperors], *the whole grove withered from the roots up, and all the chickens died* (Suetonius *Life of Galba* 1).

A unit of ten soldiers ate a chicken that one of them had stolen from a provincial. When Pescennius Niger [ruled A.D. 193–194] *ordered them all to be beheaded, the army came close to mutiny, so he made each of the ten pay the price of ten chickens as compensation and prohibited the use of cooking fires throughout the whole army* (*Historia Augusta* Life of Pescennius Niger 10).

No soldier is to steal anyone else's chickens or lay hands on his sheep. No soldier is to steal grapes, or grind corn belonging to anyone else, or extort olive oil, salt, or firewood. Soldiers are to be content with their own allowances and live off plunder taken from the enemy, not off the provincials' tears (*Historia Augusta* Life of Aurelian [ruled A.D. 270–275] 7).

Cornelius Fidus, who was married to the poet Ovid's stepdaughter, once burst into tears in the Senate when Domitius Corbulo, Nero's great general, called him a "plucked ostrich" (*struthocamelus depilatus*) (Seneca *On the Constancy of the Wise Man* 17.1).

An ostrich imagines that it escapes detection when it hides its head in a bush (Pliny *Natural History* 10.2).

The emperor Commodus demonstrated his skill at archery by shooting ostriches in the head in the arena. Cassius Dio records (*Roman History* 73.21) that Commodus came across the arena to where he and the other senators were sitting, holding the head of an ostrich in his left hand, his bloody sword in his right. He waggled his head at them, grinning but saying nothing. Dio adds that many of the senators would have been killed on the spot if they had not followed his example in chewing laurel leaves plucked from their garlands so as to prevent themselves from laughing.

A salesman duped Salonina, the wife of Gallienus [who ruled with his father, Valerian, A.D. 253–260, and alone 260–268], *into buying glass jewelry as if it were genuine, and she demanded that he be punished. The emperor had him hauled off as if to be thrown to a lion, but he had a chicken released from the cage. Everyone wondered what the point of this bizarre incident might be, and he announced through a herald, "He practiced deceit, and had it practiced on him." Then he let the salesman go* (*Historia Augusta* The Two Gallieni 12).

MOSTLY ABOUT PIGS

The inhabitants of the Greek city of Megara, when besieged by Antigonus Gonatas, king of Macedonia, routed his elephants by hurling at them pigs that had been doused with oil and set on fire (Aelian *On Animals* 16.36). The military use of elephants became common in the 3rd and 2nd centuries B.C.; their fear of pigs seems to have been exploited as a standard countermeasure.

When some pirates beached their ship on the coast of Tuscany and went inland, they came across a pen full of pigs. They took the pigs back to their ship, cast off, and sailed on. The pig keepers kept quiet while the pirates were actually on shore, but as soon as they were as far out to sea as a shout could carry, they called the pigs back with their familiar call. When the pigs heard the call, they all crowded on to the one side of the ship and capsized it. The pirates perished straightaway, but the pigs swam back to their keepers (Aelian *On Animals* 8.19).

Many Roman *cognomina* ("nicknames") are uncomplimentary. In Varro's *On Farming*, a speaker named Tremelius Scrofa (*scrofa* means "sow") gives advice on breeding pigs, but is at pains to insist, "My family does not have a piggy cognomen, and I am not a descendant of Eumaeus, Odysseus's [pig keeper]" (2.4.1). He explains his cognomen as having been awarded to his grandfather when, on campaign in Macedonia, he made good a boast that he would scatter the enemy as a *scrofa* scatters her piglets. There is, however, another version: the slaves of an early Tremelius had stolen a neighbor's pig. Tremelius hid it under the blankets of the bed in which his wife was sleeping, and, when the neighbor came to search for it, he swore that the only *scrofa* in the house was the one lying in the bed (Macrobius *Saturnalia* 1.6.30). In his speeches against Verres, the rapacious governor of Sicily, Cicero makes endearingly frequent puns on *verres* ("boar"), but refers respectfully to Scrofa as Gnaeus Tremelius.

After assassinating his son-in-law, the emperor Numerian, Aper was stabbed to death by an officer named Diocles, who had been told by a Gallic druidess that he would become emperor if he killed the wild boar (sc., *aper*). After hearing that prophecy, Diocles had always made a point of killing wild boar with his own hand when hunting, but when a succession of emperors took power (Aurelian, Probus, Tacitus, Florianus, Carus, Carinus, and Numerian) he exclaimed, "I'm the one who kills the wild boar, but the other man gets to enjoy the meat!" This time the prophecy was fulfilled, thanks to his victim's name. Diocles was acclaimed emperor by the army and ruled from 284 to 305 under the name Diocletian (*Historia Augusta* Lives of Carus, Carinus and Numerian 13–15).

Marcus Aemilius Lepidus, consul in 137 B.C., *was useless in conducting a war, since his excess weight and bulging rolls of flesh made him so bulky that he could move only with difficulty* (Diodorus Siculus *The Library* 33.27); it is perhaps not surprising that he had the cognomen *Porcina* ("Piggy"). Publius Cornelius Scipio Nasica, consul the year before, had the cognomen *Serapio*, because he looked like a pig dealer by that name (Pliny *Natural History* 21.10).

Milan was founded in the early 4th century B.C. A pig with a fleece of wool (*lana*), sent as an omen by the gods, was discovered in the middle (*medius*) of the site where the city was to be founded, and hence it was named *Mediolanum* (Sidonius Apollinaris *Letters* 7.17.20, Claudian *The Marriage of Honorius and Maria* 182).

The time when normal people are returning from work and need food is the time when athletes are just getting up. They live the way pigs do, except that pigs do not exert themselves excessively or cram themselves with so much food (Galen *An Exhortation to Study the Arts* 28).

Testudo volat, "A tortoise is flying" (Claudian *Against Eutropius* 352), is an example of the impossible, equivalent to "pigs might fly." A winged sow appears on some coins of Clazomenae and is reported by Aelian as ravaging that Greek island (*On Animals* 12.38).

In the Massacre of the Innocents (St. Matthew 2.16), Herod attempted to counter a prophesied threat to his rule by murdering all boys under two years old. When Augustus heard that Herod's own son had been killed in the massacre, he remarked that he would rather be Herod's pig than his son (Macrobius *Saturnalia* 2.4). He was presumably speaking Greek, punning on the similarity between ὗς (*hus*, "pig") and υἱός (*huios*, "son"). The pun is the more ingenious if one recalls that Diogenes, the 4th-century B.C. Cynic philosopher, had criticized the inhabitants of the Greek city of Megara in similar terms, saying that they were ignorant and vulgar, and treated their animals so much better than their children that he would rather be a Megarian's κριός (*krios*, "ram") than his υἱός (Aelian *Miscellaneous History* 12.56).

PLINY ON TOADS

- *To ward off diseases that attack millet, carry a toad around the field at night, before hoeing, and bury it in a clay jar in the middle of the field. This prevents sparrows and worms from harming it. But it must be dug up before sowing; otherwise the ground turns sour* (*Natural History* 18.158).
- *Some people advise hanging a toad by one of its back legs over the threshold of a granary before bringing the crops in* (18.303).
- *Marine centipedes, likewise toads and frogs, burst if you spit on them* (28.38).
- *The liver of a chameleon smeared with a toad's lung acts as a depilatory* (28.117).
- *The ashes of a toad mixed with stale grease are useful in treating gout and arthritis* (32.110).
- *Sick pigs are cured if they drink water in which a toad has been thoroughly boiled* (32.141).

ANIMALS IN THE MILITARY

Soldiers have adopted the names of many animals for their equipment (Servius's commentary on Vergil *Aeneid* 9.503):

- *aquilae*, "eagles," the standards of the legions. Originally, there had been other standards as well: the wolf, the Minotaur, the horse, and the wild boar. In Marius's sweeping reforms of military organization at the end of the 2nd century B.C., all the other standards were abolished (Pliny *Natural History* 10.16).
- *aries*, "(battering) ram."
- *caput porci*, "pig's head," a type of wedge formation.
- *cervus*, "stag," a *cheval de frise*, an obstacle made of pointed stakes.
- *corvus*, "raven," the name of several siege weapons, but also, and most famously, of a type of grapnel used to form a bridge to an enemy ship by piercing the deck with an iron point reminiscent

of a bird's beak. This device was used in the Romans' first successful naval engagement against the Carthaginians, off Mylae in northeast Sicily in 260 B.C., as a way both to immobilize the enemy's smaller and more maneuverable ships and to simulate conditions in a land battle, a style of fighting with which the Romans were more familiar.

- *cuniculus*, "tunnel." The original meaning is "rabbit" (Ital. *coniglio*, Sp. *conejo*, Port. *coelho*), then "rabbit burrow."
- *ericius*, "hedgehog," a spiked defensive barrier.
- *lupus*, "wolf," a type of defensive grappling iron designed to pluck soldiers from ladders and suspend them in midair (Livy *History of Rome* 28.3).
- *muli Mariani*, "Marius's mules," a term for the legionaries. As part of his reforms, Marius increased the amount of equipment that soldiers had to carry in an effort to reduce dependence on slow and unwieldy supply columns.
- *musculus*, literally "little mouse," but also a type of small fish that helps whales, hence a movable shelter used to prepare the terrain before larger siege engines are brought up (Vegetius *Military Affairs* 4.16).
- *onager*, "wild ass," a type of large catapult *so named because wild asses kick stones back at hunters from long distances, capable of piercing their pursuers' chests or crushing the bones in their skulls* (Ammianus Marcellinus 23.4.7).
- *papilio*, "butterfly," a large [military] tent, from which the English word "pavilion" is derived.
- *scorpio*, "scorpion," a type of catapult so named because its firing arm stands straight upright, like a scorpion's tail.
- *terebra*, "woodworm," a siege engine for boring through walls (Vitruvius *On Architecture* 10.13.7).
- *testudo*, "tortoise"; *the* testudo *is formed by positioning the light-armed troops, the cavalry, and the baggage animals in the center, with some of the infantry in a rectangle on the outside with their shields facing outwards, while the others hold their shields over the rest. This formation is so strong that even horses and vehicles can be driven over it. It is used to attack city walls or as a tactic against archers: the whole formation crouches (and even the horses are trained to kneel or lie down), making the*

enemy think they are exhausted; then, when the enemy comes close, they suddenly stand up and throw them into a panic (Cassius Dio *Roman History* 49.30).

❁

mus syllaba est; syllaba caseum non rodit; mus ergo caseum non rodit
"Mouse" is a syllable; a syllable does not nibble cheese; therefore a mouse does not nibble cheese.

Seneca *Letters* 48.6

· XV ·

SPECTACLES

(populus Romanus . . .) qui dabat olim
imperium, fasces, legiones, omnia, nunc se
continet atque duas tantum res anxius optat,
panem et circenses

The Roman people, who once dispensed
military commands, symbols of office,
legions, everything, now holds itself in check
and prays anxiously for only two things,
bread and circus games.

Juvenal *Satires* 10.78–81

Chariot racing was the most popular spectator sport. The Circus Maximus, as its name implies, was the largest but not the only venue in Rome for the races: it may have had a capacity of a hundred fifty thousand in the Augustan age, rising in later centuries to more than a quarter of a million people. (On July 9, 2006, six hundred thousand people watched Italy beat France in the soccer World Cup Final on three enormous television screens in the Circus Maximus.) The Colosseum, where gladiatorial shows were held, could accommodate perhaps no more than fifty thousand, whereas the world's largest soccer venue, the Maracana Stadium in Rio de Janeiro, has a capacity of approximately two hundred thousand, and the largest sporting venue of any kind, the Indianapolis Motor Speedway, has a permanent seating capacity of two hundred fifty thousand and an infield spectator capacity of more than one hundred fifty thousand.

A cupid in a dolphin chariot.

Augustus sent a messenger to a Roman knight who was drinking at the games to say, "When I want to have lunch, I go home." The knight replied, "You aren't afraid of losing your seat" (Quintilian *Education of the Orator* 6.3.63).

During the games in the Circus Maximus, crystals of selenite are strewn over the sand, giving it a bright sheen that is much admired (Pliny *Natural History* 36.162). Because it is easily split into very thin plates, selenite was also sometimes used instead of glass in windows.

Several curses on charioteers survive, perhaps paid for by people who had bet on a chariot team from another stable. For example:

> *I adjure you, sacred beings and sacred names, help this spell: bind, bewitch, foil, strike, overturn, plot against, destroy, kill, break the charioteer Eucherius and all his horses tomorrow in the Circus at Rome.*

> *Let him leave the starting gate slowly, let him not pass anyone, let him not take the turns well, let him not win any prizes, let him crash, let him be tangled, let him be broken, let him be dragged along in the races in the morning and in the afternoon. Now! Now! Quickly! Quickly!* (*Greek Inscriptions on Roman Topics* 1.117).

When the rabble supported a charioteer in a team other than the one he favored, Caligula shouted out, "I wish the Roman people had just a single neck!" (Suetonius *Life of Caligula* 30).

When he was a boy, Nero's main theme of conversation was chariot racing in the Circus, even though he was told not to talk about it. Once, when he was complaining to his fellow students about a charioteer from the Green team being dragged along, his paedagogus *scolded him; Nero lied and told him that he was discussing the episode in Homer in which Achilles ties Hector's corpse to his chariot and drags it round Troy* (Suetonius *Life of Nero* 22).

Nero often took part in chariot races. At the Olympic games, he even drove a ten-horse chariot, despite having criticized King Mithridates in one of his poems for doing precisely that. He fell from his chariot and had to be helped back in; even though he could not stay the course and stopped before reaching the finishing line, he was crowned as victor (Suetonius *Life of Nero* 24).

Marcus Aurelius Mollicius Tatianus, born here in Rome, who lived twenty years, eight months, and seven days, and who won 125 crowns of victory, eighty-nine for the Reds, twenty-four for the Greens, five for the Blues, seven for the Whites. Twice he won a prize of forty thousand sestertii (*Corpus of Latin Inscriptions* 6.10049*b*, an epitaph for a charioteer). From such inscriptions it has been calculated that the mean age at death for charioteers was twenty-two and a half years. This driver's brother, Polynices, won many more victories, 739, and lived rather longer, twenty-nine years, nine months, and five days (6.10049*a*).

The first gladiatorial show in Rome was put on in the cattle market during the consulship of Appius Claudius and Quintus Fulvius [264 B.C.], *when three pairs fought at the funeral games arranged in honor of Brutus Pera by his sons Marcus and Decimus* (Valerius Maximus *Memorable Deeds and Sayings* 2.4.7). It is often said that the Romans adopted gladiatorial games from the Etruscans, but there is little reliable evidence for this.

Writing in the Augustan period, Nicolaus of Damascus records that *when drunken diners have finished eating they call in the gladiators and applaud with pleasure when one of them has his throat cut* (quoted at Athenaeus *Wise Men at Dinner* 153f.).

I put on gladiatorial games three times in my own name, and five times in the name of my sons or grandsons. About ten thousand gladiators fought in these games (*The Deeds of the Divine Augustus* 22). In A.D. 107, Trajan displayed that same number of gladiators in the games that accompanied his triumph over the Dacians (Cassius Dio *Roman History* 68.15).

The *Tabula Larinas*, a senatorial decree of A.D. 19, partially preserved on a bronze tablet first published in 1978, prohibited the recruitment of the sons, daughters, grandsons, granddaughters, great-grandsons, and great-granddaughters of senators and knights to fight in gladiatorial contests if they were under the age of twenty.

In the emperor Gaius's training camp, there were twenty thousand [!] *gladiators, but only two who did not blink when under pressure; for that reason they were unbeatable* (Pliny *Natural History* 11.144).

Awnings the color of the sky and adorned with stars were recently drawn on ropes over the emperor Nero's amphitheaters (Pliny *Natural History* 19.24). Sailors were employed in this task. *vela erunt*, literally "there will be sails [*sc.*, to provide shade]," appears in several announcements of shows to be put on in Pompeii.

A fresco depicting the Pompeii riot in A.D. 59. A graffito, rather riskily scratched on a wall in Pompeii, reads *Happiness to the people of Puteoli and Nuceria, but for the Pompeians and Pithecusans a hook* [sc., to drag away their corpses].

Enthusiasm for the games was instilled early: a terra-cotta baby's bottle found at Pompeii is decorated with the figure of a gladiator.

In A.D. 59, *violence broke out between the settlers at Nuceria and Pompeii, from a trivial beginning at a gladiatorial show put on by Livineius Regulus, whose removal from the Senate I have reported elsewhere. People from the two towns started bantering with each other, then they turned to insults, then they threw stones, and finally they took up weapons. . . . The Senate prohibited the people of Pompeii from putting on such public shows*

A gladiator's helmet.

for ten years and disbanded their illegal clubs. Livineius and the others who had incited the riot were punished with exile (Tacitus *Annals* 14.17).

Commodus (ruled A.D. 180–192) frequently fought as a gladiator, armed with iron weapons, whereas his opponents had lead ones (Aurelius Victor *The Caesars* 17.4), and he charged the state a million *sestertii* for each performance. At least seven other emperors are said to have had gladiatorial training: Caligula, Titus, Hadrian, Verus, Didius Julianus, Caracalla, and Geta.

St. Augustine relates the poignant story of Alypius, a young Christian whose companions dragged him against his will to a gladiator fight: *for a time, he refused to open his eyes, but eventually he did and was immediately addicted to the thrill of bloodlust* (*Confessions* 6.9; Alypius went on to become a bishop).

Rare evidence for the presence of musicians in the arena during gladiatorial contests.

Although gladiatorial games were officially prohibited by Constantine the Great in A.D. 325, they continued until 404, when Honorius abolished them after a monk who tried to stop a fight was stoned to death by indignant spectators. Christian writers also spoke out against the Circus, but chariot racing continued until at least A.D. 549.

It is widely supposed that, before the games began, gladiators hailed the emperor with the words "We who are about to die salute you" [*nos morituri te salutamus*]. The evidence is very tenuous:

> *Just before a sea fight put on in the Fucine lake, the participants* [who were not gladiators] *addressed Claudius with the words, "Hail, commander. Those who are about to die salute you." The emperor muttered, "Or not"* [a feeble witticism implying that some might survive the battle], *and the men therefore refused to fight, as if they had been pardoned. Claudius jumped from his seat and limped ludicrously around the shore of the lake, urging them to fight with threats and promises* (Suetonius *Life of Claudius* 21).

It is also widely supposed that spectators signaled for a defeated gladiator to be put to death by turning their thumbs down. Textual and pictorial evidence, however, suggests that turning the thumbs up was the signal for death. There is, moreover, little evidence for the common belief that the public was admitted when gladiators were having a banquet the evening before they fought in the arena.

An attendant dressed as Mercury, the god who escorted the souls of the dead to the Underworld, poked the corpses of gladiators and criminals killed in the arena with a red-hot iron to determine whether they really were dead. Another attendant, dressed as Dis, the god of the Underworld, dispatched with a sledgehammer those who were still alive (Tertullian *Apology* 15).

If we are obliged to take evidence from an arena fighter or some other such person, his testimony is not to be believed unless given under torture (Justinian's *Digest* 22.5.21).

The traffic in wild animals for the amphitheater reduced or exterminated many species within and beyond the empire. Already in 50 B.C., Cicero, as governor of Cilicia (in southeastern Turkey), wrote to Marcus Caelius Rufus, who was preparing to put on games to gain political popularity:

> *As regards the leopards, the matter is being handled diligently by the usual hunters in accordance with my instructions. But there is a*

Killing leopards.

surprising shortage, and they say that the leopards which are still here are complaining bitterly that they are the only animals in my province being hunted, and apparently they have decided to leave for Caria (*Letters to his Friends* 2.11.2).

Scaurus had 150 leopards sent to Rome, Pompey the Great 410, the Divine Augustus 420 (Pliny *Natural History* 8.64).

In the 1st century B.C., an artist from the south of Italy named Pasitiles went to make an engraving of a lion in the dockyards where African beasts for the shows were being held. He had a narrow escape when a panther got out of one of the other cages (Pliny *Natural History* 36.40).

When the cost of buying meat to feed wild beasts that he had bought for a show was too high, Caligula decided to give them criminals to tear apart. Glancing at a line of prisoners, but paying no attention to the charge sheets, he stood in the middle of the colonnade and ordered everyone "from this bald man to that bald man" to be led away (Suetonius *Life of Caligula* 27).

Nero imitated the deeds of Hercules. They say that a lion was trained so that he could kill it either with a club or by strangulation, while the people watched him fighting naked on the sand of the amphitheater (Suetonius *Life of Nero* 53).

It has recently been discovered that if you sprinkle a concoction based on copper in the mouths of bears and lions in the arena they are unable to bite (Pliny *Natural History* 34.127).

When Augustus criticized a dancer named Pylades for his scandalous behavior, Pylades replied, *It is to your advantage, Caesar, if the people are distracted by performers like me* (Cassius Dio *Roman History* 54.17). *When Pylades played the mad Hercules, he actually shot arrows into the audience, and he did the same when he performed the same role for Augustus at a banquet, but the emperor did not mind facing him just as*

A flutist and a dancer with castanets.

the Roman people had done (Macrobius *Saturnalia* 2.7). Augustus later banished Pylades from Italy for gesturing obscenely at a member of the audience who tried to hiss him off the stage (Suetonius *Life of Augustus* 45).

❁

The way Caligula supported his favorite performers was nothing short of madness. He used to shower kisses on the pantomime actor Mnester even during performances. If anyone made even the slightest noise while Mnester was on stage, Caligula would have him dragged from his seat and flog him with his own hand. He sent a centurion to order a Roman knight who had caused a disturbance to sail off at once from the harbor at Ostia with a sealed message for King Ptolemy in Mauretania. What the message said was "Do nothing good or bad to the man I have sent" (Suetonius *Life of Caligula* 55, the point being that the poor fellow spent the whole journey imagining what terror lay in store for him in Mauretania).

❁

Rome was not the only city with a fanatical interest in spectacles; by making a sudden attack on Carthage on October 19, A.D. 439, when the population was attending the consular games in the circus, the largest edifice in Roman Africa, Gaiseric's Vandals took the city virtually unopposed.

❂

The Colosseum is the most prominent symbol of ancient Rome, but the remnants of more than two hundred amphitheaters survive in various parts of the Roman world. The vast majority are in Italy and the western provinces, an indication of the greater influence of Greek theater in the East. The oldest datable amphitheater is at Pompeii (70s B.C.).

❂

The combination of sweat, dirt, and olive oil scraped with a *strigil* from the bodies of top athletes was sometimes sold to the public at huge prices by officials in charge of gymnasia and was used as an ingredient in unguents to counter various ailments (Pliny *Natural History* 15.19, 28.50).

❂

Flowers native to North Africa still grow in and around the Colosseum. Their seeds were perhaps brought to Italy in the manes and fur of lions and other exotic beasts displayed in the arena. In the 19th century, with fewer tourists and less weed killer than nowadays, as many as 420 different types of plant were catalogued there, and the abundant and unusual spring flowering in the Colosseum was often noted.

❂

spectatum veniunt, veniunt spectentur ut ipsae
Women come to look and to be looked at themselves.
Ovid *The Art of Love* 1.99

· XVI ·

FOOD AND DRINK

glans aluit veteres et passim semper amarunt
In the old days people lived on acorns, but
love affairs were all around.
Tibullus 2.3.69

Banquets were becoming more elaborate and expensive. Cooks, regarded in the old days as the least valuable slaves and treated accordingly, started to command high prices, and cooking, once a menial task, acquired the status of an art form. What was conspicuously luxurious then, however, was hardly even the first hint of the decadence that was to come (Livy *History of Rome* 39.6, referring to the 180s B.C.).

People used to denounce luxury by complaining that more was being paid for a cook than for a horse. Now a cook costs more than three horses, and a fish costs more than three cooks (Pliny *Natural History* 9.67).

You should eat to live, not live to eat ([esse oportet ut vivas, non vivere ut edas] *Rhetorical Instructions for Herennius* 4.39, attributed to Cicero).

The diet of the vast majority of the population was extremely bland and dull. The ancient world was without such staples as coffee, tea, chocolate, potatoes, and tomatoes. Of the two grain crops most widely produced nowadays, rice and corn, the former was known but little grown, the latter completely unknown.

The poor rarely ate meat. A family entitled to a meat dole might receive five pounds of pork each month for five months of the year, a rather measly allowance (*Theodosian Code* 14.4).

In his treatise *On Farming*, Varro gives instructions on how to fatten dormice (3.15), and Apicius's cookbook has a recipe for stuffed dormice (8.9), but there had once been a decree by a censor (probably in 169 B.C.) forbidding the serving of dormice at dinner (Pliny *Natural History* 36.4).

Julius Caesar punished his baker for serving better bread to him than to his guests (Suetonius *Life of Julius Caesar* 48), and Hadrian was said to have food intended for those at other tables served to him instead, to ensure that the cooks were not cheating him (*Historia Augusta* Life of Hadrian 17). Juvenal contrasts the splendor of the food served to a philistine host with that served to his hapless guests. For example, for him, a huge Sicilian lamprey; for them, an eel like a water snake, fattened in the Tiber sewers (*Satires* 5.99–106).

People who drink wine in which eels have been drowned lose their appetite for drinking wine (St. Isidore *Etymologies* 12.6.41).

In his *Wise Men at Dinner*, Athenaeus catalogues and describes, among much else, more than fifty varieties of bread (109*f*–113*d*).

Augustus's advisor Maecenas made donkey meat a fashionable delicacy (Pliny *Natural History* 8.170; Pliny also records that the hard skin of an elephant's trunk was sought after by gourmets, not because it was actually thought to taste good, but because eating the trunk was as close as they could come to chewing on the vastly expensive but quite inedible ivory of the tusks [8.31]).

Galen observes that anyone who eats the flesh of horses or donkeys would have to be an ass himself (*On the Thinning Diet* 443). Although

A loaf of bread baked in Pompeii on August 24, A.D. 79.

horse meat is much appreciated in many parts of modern Europe, neither the Romans nor the Greeks ate it except in dire circumstances.

When he was trying a case in the Forum of Augustus, Claudius caught the scent of a meal being prepared for the Salian priests in the temple of Mars nearby, and so he abandoned the court and climbed the temple steps to join the priests (Suetonius *Life of Claudius* 33).

Eating mushrooms fell out of fashion after Agrippina, Claudius's second wife, murdered him with one that was poisoned, but she replaced them with another poison for the whole world and especially for herself—her own dear Nero (Pliny *Natural History* 22.92). *Nero made the memorable remark that mushrooms are the food of the gods, for it was by means of a mushroom that Claudius became a god* (Cassius Dio *Roman History* 61.35).

Leeks became a fashionable food when Nero started eating them to strengthen his voice for singing (Pliny *Natural History* 19.108).

Domitian once invited a group of important senators and knights to dinner in a room painted entirely black, with black furnishings. The plates were shaped like gravestones, and the waiters were boys painted black. The food was black, the sort used in offerings to the dead. Domitian spoke only of death and murder. They all expected to die but, when they arrived home, he sent them expensive gifts (Cassius Dio *Roman History* 67.9).

The game of *cottabus*, which involved flicking wine from one's cup at a target, was inordinately popular in Greece but seems not to have caught on in Rome. Even so, banquets could be messy affairs: Vitruvius (*On Architecture* 7.4.5) advises constructing dining rooms with drains and charcoal paving to soak up wine poured or spat out. Such a pavement also prevented barefoot slaves from catching cold.

When we recline at a banquet, one slave wipes away the disgorged food while another crouches beneath the table to gather up the drunken guests' leftovers (Seneca *Letters* 47).

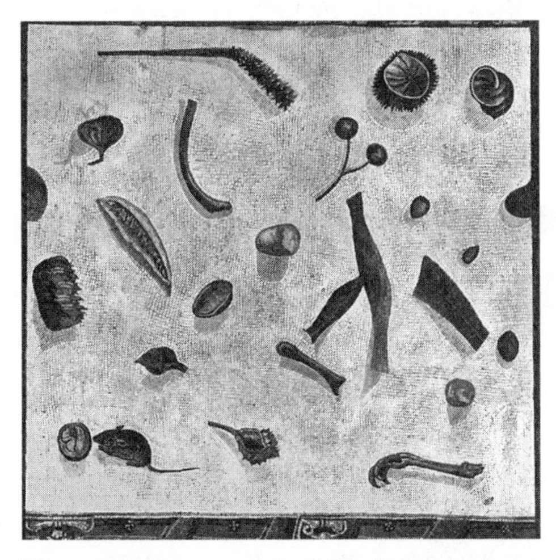

The unswept house mosaic. (Note the scavenging mouse.)

There is a common misconception that rich Romans had a special room, a *vomitorium*, to which they withdrew to throw up so that they could continue eating. There is no evidence for such a room. The term does not appear until the end of the 4th century A.D., when Macrobius notes that *the entranceways through which people enter the theater and amphitheater in droves, pouring themselves on to the seats, we call these passages* vomitoria *even nowadays* (*Saturnalia* 6.4.3).

Vitellius, who ruled for eight months in A.D. 69, often dined four times in one day, a feat made possible by the use of emetics. On a serving dish so big that he called it "the shield of city-guarding Minerva," he dedicated to Minerva a concoction of parrot wrasse livers, pheasant and peacock brains, flamingo tongues and lamprey roe, brought by naval vessels from regions as far apart as Parthia and the Straits of Gibraltar (Suetonius *Life of Vitellius* 13). *The dish itself cost 1 million* sestertii *to make, in a kiln specially constructed in open countryside* (Pliny *Natural History* 35.163).

Clodius Albinus (ruled A.D. 196–197) was said to be able to consume inordinate quantities of fruit at a sitting: five hundred dried figs, one hundred peaches, ten melons, and twenty pounds of grapes, as well as one hundred small birds and four hundred oysters (*Historia Augusta* Life of Clodius Albinus 11).

Fearing that Cleopatra might try to poison him before Actium, Mark Antony employed a *praegustator* (food taster). The practice became fashionable, and the *praegustator* was a fairly important figure in imperial households. The names of several are known, mostly from their tombstones, which never record the cause of death.

Cleopatra poisoned the tips of the flowers Antony was to wear in a garland at a banquet. When the party was in full swing, she suggested that they should drink their garlands by strewing the flowers in their wine. When Antony was about to drink his, Cleopatra put her hand over his cup and called for a condemned prisoner, who drank the wine and died on the spot (Pliny *Natural History* 21.12).

The empress Livia smeared poison on figs growing on the trees from which Augustus usually plucked the fruit with his own hands; she then ate those that had not been tampered with, and offered him the poisoned ones. He duly fell ill and died (Cassius Dio *Roman History* 56.30).

Marcus Aurelius was rumored to have cut a sow's udder (a great delicacy) in half with a knife poisoned on one side, and to have offered the poisoned side to Lucius Verus, his co-emperor (*Historia Augusta* Life of Marcus Aurelius 15, Life of Verus 11).

Roman taste for the silphium plant, an expensive ingredient in many recipes, led to its extinction. It was once the symbol of Cyrene in Libya, which prospered through exporting it. The plant could not be domesticated, and eventually became so rare that a single stalk of it was presented to Nero (Pliny *Natural History* 19.39).

Truffles may have been more abundant in Roman times than they are now: few people nowadays have ever eaten, or would wish to eat, a

One of four pepper pots discovered in England in 1992, as part of a hoard buried early in the 5th century. All four have perforations for sprinkling ground pepper. It has been conjectured that the woman represented is Helena, the mother of Constantine the Great (ruled A.D. 303–336).

whole truffle, but Pliny mentions that a magistrate damaged his front teeth on a coin round which a truffle had grown (*Natural History* 19.35).

The rich loved spices so much that recipes sometimes specifically stated when pepper, a highly expensive import, was *not* to be used. It is an ingredient in 349 of the 468 recipes in the *De Re Coquinaria* (*On Cooking*), attributed to Apicius, the only surviving ancient cookbook. In A.D. 92, special *horrea piperataria*, "pepper warehouses," were constructed near the Via Sacra, as a bazaar for Eastern goods. They burnt down twice, in A.D. 191 and 283.

Alaric the Visigoth was paid off with gold, silver, silk, and three thousand pounds of pepper as his price for not plundering Rome in the early 5th century. (Since the Visigoths were said to cook their meat by riding around with it between their saddlecloth and their horse's back, the pepper would have been especially welcome.)

I hope that such dishonest tricks get you in trouble, innkeeper: you sell water but drink unmixed wine yourself (*Corpus of Latin Inscriptions* 4.3948, an elegiac couplet scrawled on the wall of a bar in Pompeii).

House rules inscribed on the wall of a dining room in Pompeii, in the form of three elegiac couplets:

- *Let the water wash your feet, and let the slave wipe them dry; let a cloth drape the couch, but be careful with my linen.*
- *Turn your lustful looks and your wheedling eyes away from other men's wives, and put on a decorous expression.*

A *thermopolium* (a shop selling hot food) in Pompeii.

- *Postpone disputes and tedious wrangling if you can—otherwise, turn your steps back to your own house.*
  (*Corpus of Latin Inscriptions* 4.7698)

IRON RATIONS

- *When the Gauls took Rome* [in the early 4th century B.C.] *and were besieging the Capitol, they knew their only hope of taking it was to starve the Roman garrison out. The Romans used a very clever plan to deprive the victorious Gauls of their only incentive to persevere with the siege—they began throwing down loaves of bread from various parts of the Capitol. The Gauls were amazed when they saw this and thought the Romans had an abundant supply of grain, so they were driven to come to an agreement for ending the siege* (Valerius Maximus *Memorable Deeds and Sayings* 7.4.3).
- When Casilinum was under siege by Hannibal, who had plowed the ground between his camp and the city walls to deprive the starving inhabitants of even grass to eat, the defenders threw seeds into the furrows to give the impression that they had enough food to last until harvest time (Livy *History of Rome* 23.19). A mouse (or perhaps a rat; Latin makes no distinction) changed hands for an exorbitant sum during the siege; the buyer survived, but the seller starved to death (Frontinus *Stratagems* 4.5.20).
- *When the Spanish city of Numantia was being besieged by Scipio and the inhabitants had used up all their food, they finally turned to cannibalism. After the city was captured, some of them were found carrying body parts in their garments. In this case, necessity is no excuse: a person who was free to die did not have to live like that* (Valerius Maximus *Memorable Deeds and Sayings* 7.6 ext. 2).
- *Pompey found some loaves made of grass in the siege works at Dyrrachium* [in western Greece, where he was besieging Caesar in 48 B.C.]; *he said he was fighting with wild animals and ordered the loaves to be hidden from his troops, lest their morale be broken by this evidence of the stubborn determination of Caesar's men* (Suetonius *Life of Julius Caesar* 68).

FISH SAUCE

- *Garum*, which could command prices far above those of the finest wines, was a fermented sauce made from fish entrails. Although it is thought of nowadays as quintessentially Roman, it is first mentioned in the 5th century B.C. by the Athenian dramatists Aeschylus and Sophocles, and was named after the γάρος (*garos*), a not precisely identified fish that was originally its primary ingredient. Later on, a wide variety of fish (especially mackerel) and other sea creatures were used.
- The ruins of several *garum* factories survive in the western Mediterranean. Because of the strong odor caused by the fermentation process, all are located on the outskirts of cities (just as workshops such as tanneries were concentrated on the far bank of the Tiber) (Juvenal *Satires* 14.201ff.).
- *Garum* was an easy target for those who castigated rich living. Seneca rants: *What about garum, the high-priced gore of rotten fish? Don't you think it burns a person's insides with its salty putrefaction? Do you suppose that such festerings ingested practically straight from the cooking fire itself can be extinguished in our very entrails without causing damage? What disgusting and pestilent belches it causes!* (*Letters* 95). Even so, *garum* is the most prevalent condiment in the recipes transmitted in Apicius's *On Cooking:* it is used in more than ten times as many dishes as salt.
- *Garum* was also widely used in medicine, whether taken internally for various ailments or applied externally for burns (though Pliny cautions that the patient should not be told that it is being applied [*Natural History* 31.97]), bites (especially crocodile bites, according to Pliny), earache, hemorrhoids, and many other complaints. Pliny further notes that eating an odd number of African snails marinated in wine or *garum* had recently been found to cure stomach disorders (30.44).
- *There used to be perfume in the little onyx jar; it turned to* garum *after Papylus sniffed it* (Martial *Epigrams* 7.94).

IN THE KITCHEN

I don't season my dinners the way other cooks do, bringing in whole prairies on their platters, turning guests into cows by heaping up herbs that they season with yet more herbs. They put in coriander, fennel, garlic, rock parsley, and add sorrel, cabbage, beet, spinach, and a whole pound of asafoetida, and nasty mustard, which makes the eyes of anyone who grinds it water even before he grinds it. When these fellows season dinners, they don't season them with seasonings, but with screech owls, which eat out the insides of the guests while they are still alive. This is why people live such short lives, heaping into their stomachs herbs like this, ghastly even to name, not just to eat. People eat herbs that cattle don't eat (Plautus *Pseudolus* 810–824).

For the treatment of urine retention: Take a cabbage and parboil it. Pour off most of the water. Add a generous amount of olive oil, salt, and a pinch of cumin. Boil for a short time. Drink the broth cold, and eat the cabbage itself, to facilitate digestion. Repeat daily (Cato *On Agriculture* 156).

His hand goes round in a circle; gradually the individual ingredients lose their particular qualities, and there is one color instead of many [color est e pluribus unus], *not entirely green, since the milky morsels resist this, and not shining milk-white, since it is varied with so many herbs* (*Moretum* 101–104). Some scholars believe that *e pluribus unum* ("One from Several"), one of the earliest mottoes of the United States, is derived from this passage in the *Moretum*, a poem falsely attributed to Vergil, which describes how an old peasant blends the various ingredients in a dish prepared from cheese and garlic mixed with vegetables.

Remove the flamingo's entrails, wash and dress it, put it in a pot, add water, salt, dill, and a little vinegar. Parboil, then add a bunch of leeks and coriander. When it is nearly cooked, add some wine-lees to give it color. Crush pepper, cumin, coriander, asafoetida root, mint, and rue, add a little vinegar, dates, and the gravy from the bird. Strain it into the same pot, bind the gravy with starch, pour it over the bird, and serve. The same method is used for cooking parrots (Apicius *On Cookery* 6.6).

Milk-fed Snails: Take the snails and sponge them. Remove the membrane so that they can come out of their shells. Put milk and salt in the container with them for one day, then only milk on the following days. Remove waste matter every hour. When they are so fattened that they cannot withdraw into their shells, cook them in olive oil (Apicius 7.16).

A flamingo ready for the oven.

Stuffed Cuttlefish: First cook the cuttlefish with pepper, lovage, celery, and caraway seeds, honey, broth, wine, and the usual condiments. Split the cuttlefish and pour the juice over it. Boil their brains, after removing the veins, then grind them up with pepper and sufficient raw egg. Add whole peppercorns. Sew the paste in the cuttlefish and boil till the stuffing is cooked (Apicius 9.4).

OYSTERS

The Romans were extremely fond of oysters. Gourmets could distinguish *primo morsu*, "at first bite," the region from which a particular oyster came (Horace *Satires* 2.4.31ff., Juvenal *Satires* 4.140ff.).

Sergius Orata laid down the first oyster beds, at Baiae on the Bay of Naples, just before the War against the Allies [91–87 B.C.]. *His motive was not gluttony, but greed for money, for he made a great profit from his idea. He also benefited from his invention of shower baths, and from his business of repairing country homes and then selling them* (Pliny *Natural History* 9.168).

Oysters must be fresh to be edible. Writing in the late 5th century A.D., Anthimus notes that if one has oysters that smell, one does not need any other type of poison (*On Dietetics* 49).

The difficulty in transporting oysters enhanced their appeal. They were sent to Rome from as far away as England, and Apicius is said to have devised a method of packing oysters so that he could send them to Trajan while he was campaigning in the Parthian desert (Athenaeus *Wise Men at Dinner 7d*).

It is difficult to argue with one's stomach, since it has no ears (as Cato the Elder used to say), so we must do our best to make the quantity of what we eat easier to deal with by closely monitoring the quality of what we eat (Plutarch *Advice on Health* 18).

A skeleton might be passed around at banquets as a *memento mori* (literally, "remember to die") to remind guests that life was short and should be enjoyed (Petronius *Satyricon* 34).

Little old women often tolerate not eating for two or three days, but deprive an athlete of his food for just one day and he'll appeal to Jupiter, Olympian Jupiter, for whose games he's in training, and he'll howl that he cannot endure it (Cicero *Tusculan Disputations* 2.40).

Athletes had a special diet, eating food so high in protein that an ordinary person would quickly be made unwell by it (Galen *On the Power of Foods* 2).

When people unwittingly eat human flesh, served by unscrupulous restaurant owners and other such people, the similarity to pork is often noted (Galen *On the Power of Foods* 3).

A rather surrealistic Pompeian mosaic, representing the tenuous frailty of human fate. The wheel of fortune, a butterfly (symbolizing the soul), and a skull with improbably splendid teeth and ears are all balanced on a builder's leveling instrument, from which are suspended royal robes and a beggar's rags.

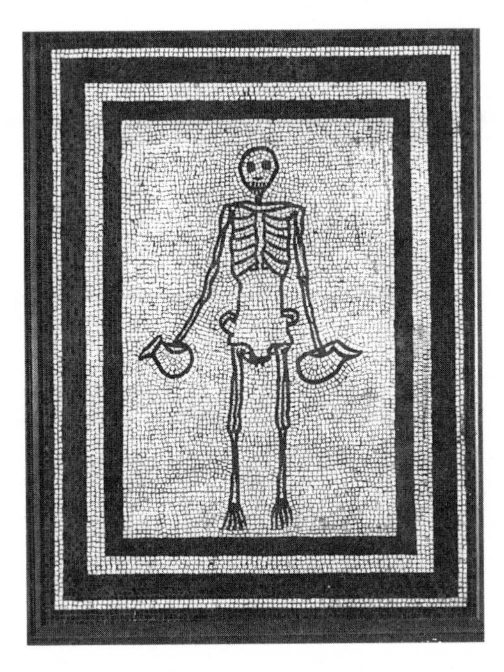

Memento mori.

The term for "swimming pool" in most Romance languages (e.g., Italian and Spanish *piscina*, French *piscine*) is derived from *piscina*, the Latin word for a pond in which fish (*pisces*) were bred for the dining tables of gourmets.

The best sea bass were those caught in Rome itself, near the Tiber island, which is slightly upstream from the mouth of the *Cloaca Maxima* (Pliny *Natural History* 9.169). In *On the Power of Foods* 3, Galen several times emphasizes that fish caught near sewers do not taste good.

uxor erat saepe horridior glandem ructante marito
[In the old days] a wife was often shaggier than her acorn-belching husband.
Juvenal *Satires* 6.10

· XVII ·

DECADENCE

Non est, Tucca, satis, quod es gulosus:
Et dici cupis et cupis videri
Tucca, you're not content with being a glutton;
You want to be notorious and conspicuous for it.
Martial *Epigrams* 12.41

Crassus had a pet eel that he adorned with earrings and a jeweled necklace. When it died, he mourned for it as if it had been his daughter. Domitius criticized him for this excessive behavior, but Crassus retorted that his conduct was better than that of Domitius, who had buried three wives without shedding a tear. Although this anecdote is reported by several authors, the precise identity of the two men is unclear. They were probably Lucius Licinius Crassus and Gnaeus Domitius Ahenobarbus, who, as censors together in 92 B.C., were responsible for the overseeing of moral standards.

Authoritative sources agree that in the consulship of Marcus Lepidus and Quintus Catulus [78 B.C.], *there was no house in Rome more beautiful than that of Lepidus himself, but less than thirty-five years later it was not even in the top hundred* (Pliny *Natural History* 36.109).

In the middle of the first century B.C., *Publius Servilius Rullus was the first to serve a whole wild boar at a banquet, whereas two or three may be eaten nowadays just as a first course* (Pliny *Natural History* 8.210).

IMPEDIMENTA

- The Parthians are said to have been shocked to find pornography in the baggage of a Roman officer at Carrhae (Plutarch *Life of Crassus* 32).
- Severe Roman moralists were appalled that soldiers carried "womanish" items such as mirrors (Seneca *Natural Questions* 1.17.10).
- The younger Scipio was disgusted to discover wine coolers set with precious stones in the baggage of one of his officers (Plutarch *Sayings of the Romans* Scipio 17 [201]).
- *Caesar used to carry mosaics and stone floorings about with him while on military campaigns* (Suetonius *Life of Julius Caesar* 46).

Horace parodies the pretentious sophistication of gourmets by having a dinner host commend a wild boar as having been captured when a gentle south wind was blowing (*Satires* 2.8.6f.).

In Nero's *domus aurea* ("The Golden House"), the main dining rooms were circular and revolved day and night in accordance with the movements of the heavens (Suetonius *Life of Nero* 31). In September 2009, archaeologists announced the chance discovery of what they believe to be the mechanism that drove the rooms around.

Papirius Fabianus, an outstanding natural scientist [his works are almost entirely lost], *attests that marble regenerates itself in quarries, and quarrymen also declare that the wounds that they inflict on mountainsides close over of their own accord. If this is true, we can be optimistic that the resources for sumptuous living will never be exhausted* (Pliny *Natural History* 36.125). Despite this prospect of renewal, Pliny also reports that an ancient decree of the Senate prohibited mining in Italy (3.138).

Quintus Hortensius (Cicero's rival as a forensic speaker) *used to irrigate his plane trees with wine. During a case in which they were on opposite sides, he asked Cicero as a favor to swap the times at which they were to speak, since he had to go off to see personally to the pouring of wine round a plane tree that he had planted at his estate near Tusculum* (Macrobius *Saturnalia* 3.13). This anecdote seems to imply that advocates were not required to be present in court to hear the arguments put forward by the other side.

Cleopatra's cooks had to have several complete banquets at different stages of preparation, for they never knew when Antony might call for dinner to be served immediately (Plutarch *Life of Antony* 28; his authority for this gossip is a friend of his grandfather, who was given a tour of the kitchens in the palace at Alexandria by one of the royal chefs).

When Cleopatra bet Antony that she could spend ten million *sestertii* on a single meal, she was out to impress—and won the wager by drinking a pearl dissolved in vinegar. (Scientists doubt whether the

Cupids drinking wine.

pearl could actually have been dissolved so quickly.) The twin to Cleopatra's pearl was later cut in two and set in the earrings of the statue of Venus in the Pantheon.

The tasteless dedication to pretentious excess shown by Lollia Paulina, Caligula's third wife, was hard to parallel. She would bedeck herself with emeralds and pearls whenever she attended even the most modest gathering, taking the receipts with her to show to anyone who doubted that her jewelry had cost forty million *sestertii* (Pliny *Natural History* 9.117, reporting his personal observation).

When their husbands criticize them for their love of pearls, women respond by pointing to their husbands' mensarum insania, *their mad passion for collecting tables made of fine African citrus wood. There still survives such a table for which Cicero once paid half a million* sestertii, *which is the more amazing given his modest means and the greater value of money then* (Pliny *Natural History* 13.91).

FIRST-CLASS TRAVEL

- *When his slaves had lifted him from the bath into his litter, a rich and idle fellow asked, "Am I sitting down now?"* (Seneca *On the Shortness of Life* 12.8).
- Augustus liked to travel so slowly by litter that he would take two days to reach Praeneste (Palestrina) or Tibur (Tivoli), neither of which is much more than twenty miles from Rome (Suetonius *Life of Augustus* 82).
- The emperor Septimius Severus, who suffered from gout, was carried most of the way from Rome to northern England in a litter.
- The medical writer Celsus compares traveling in a litter to tossing in a ship on stormy seas (*On Medicine* 2.15).
- *I am as exhausted when I return from a ride in my litter as I would be if I had been walking rather than just sitting. For it is hard work being carried along for a long time, perhaps since it is not natural: nature gave us feet with which to do our own walking. . . . Our decadent lifestyle has condemned us to weakness—what we have for a long time been reluctant to do, we have ceased to be able to do* (Seneca *Letters* 55).

- Lucian compares lolling in a litter to being carried out for burial. He goes on to pillory those who, when they do actually go on foot, send slaves ahead to warn them of uneven ground and to remind them that, strange as it may seem, they are in fact walking (*The Wisdom of Nigrinus* 34).
- *Nero never traveled with a train of fewer than a thousand carriages drawn by mules shod with silver* (Suetonius *Life of Nero* 30). This is all the more extravagant since most horses and mules were not shod at all.

When his slave dropped a crystal cup, Vedius Pollio ordered him to be thrown alive to his lampreys, which had been trained to eat human flesh. The slave appealed to Augustus, who happened to be dining with Pollio. After trying in vain to persuade Pollio to be merciful, Augustus had all his other crystal cups broken and the lamprey pond filled in (Cassius Dio *Roman History* 54.23).

The ex-consul Petronius (who is generally presumed to be the author of the *Satyricon*) had a goblet made of fluorspar for which he had paid three hundred thousand *sestertii*. Just before committing suicide, he broke it to ensure that it did not come into Nero's possession (Pliny *Natural History* 37.20).

An ex-consul recently bought a fluorspar goblet for seventy thousand sestertii, *even though it held only three pints. He loved it so much that he used to gnaw the rim, but this damage served only to enhance its value* (Pliny *Natural History* 37.18).

At a very conservative estimate, India, China, and the Arabian peninsula drain the empire of one hundred million sestertii *every year. That's the cost of luxury goods for our women* (Pliny *Natural History* 12.84).

Perfume is the most meaningless of all luxuries. Pearls and precious stones are at least heirlooms, and clothes last for a certain time, but perfume fades immediately and is used up as soon as it is applied. The most one can say for it is that, when people are otherwise occupied, it attracts them to take notice of a woman passing by. Perfume costs more than four hundred denarii *per pound: that is what we pay out to give pleasure to other people, for the person who is wearing the perfume does not appreciate it* (Pliny *Natural History* 13.20).

At the funeral of Felix, a charioteer for the Reds, one of his fans threw himself on to the pyre—a trivial tale, though the supporters of the other factions tried to prevent the incident from reflecting glory on Felix by claiming that the fan had merely passed out, overcome by the incense used in the ceremony (Pliny *Natural History* 7.186).

Nero burned more than a whole year's output of Arabian incense at the funeral of his second wife, Poppaea [whom he had killed by kicking her in the stomach when she was pregnant] (Pliny *Natural History* 12.83).

Poppaea was not cremated; her body was embalmed and deposited in the mausoleum of Augustus. Tacitus rather caustically remarks that her body "was pickled by being stuffed with perfumes, after the custom of foreign rulers" (*Annals* 16.6). Poppaea might have appreciated such efforts at preservation, since she liked to bathe in donkey's milk to keep her skin youthful (Pliny *Natural History* 11.238).

A range of cosmetics was named after Poppaea; Juvenal unappealingly calls them the *pinguia Poppaeana* "the Poppaean greasy things" (*Satires* 6.462). Perhaps lion fat was an ingredient; Pliny says it is good for the complexion (*Natural History* 28.89).

It should surprise no one that even funeral pyres are painted nowadays (Pliny *Natural History* 35.49).

When a very young man came smelling of perfume to thank him for a military commission, Vespasian tossed his head in disgust and revoked the appointment, censuring him in a very stern voice: "I wish you had smelled of garlic" (Suetonius *Life of Vespasian* 8).

❁

The Germans have no use for amber and are amazed when they receive payment in exchange for it (Tacitus *Germania* 45).

❁

Not even the Romans' taste for decadent luxury has yet found a use for amber . . . but it is so prized that even a tiny amber statuette costs more than living and healthy slaves (Pliny *Natural History* 37.30, 49).

❁

Roman enthusiasm for amber seems not to have been dimmed by the widespread belief that it was formed from the urine of lynxes (Pliny *Natural History* 37.34).

❁

Rich people do not enjoy being rich as much as they enjoy being congratulated on being rich (Lucian *The Wisdom of Nigrinus* 23).

❁

nihil aliud est ebrietas quam voluntaria insania
Drunkenness is nothing but voluntary
madness.
Seneca *Letters* 83.18

· XVIII ·

BUILDINGS

felix illud saeculum ante architectos fuit!
How happy life was before there were any architects!
Seneca *Letters* 90.9

The vast majority of the population of Rome lived in apartment buildings of several stories (*insulae*, literally "islands"; hence the Italian *isolato*, meaning a "block" on a street). *Insulae* were notoriously dingy, cramped, and vulnerable to outbreaks of fire. A 4th-century A.D. catalog of the regions of the city records 46,602 *insulae*, but only 1,797 freestanding homes (*domus*).

The Pyramid of Cestius was erected about 12 B.C. for Gaius Cestius, a member of one of the great priestly colleges. It is an extreme manifestation of the Romans' fascination with Egypt, stimulated particularly by Cleopatra and Isis worship.

There are thirteen ancient obelisks in Rome, eight brought from Egypt by Augustus and later emperors, five carved in Rome itself. The obelisk at the top of the Spanish Steps is inscribed with hieroglyphics copied inaccurately in Roman times from those on the obelisk now in the Piazza del Popolo.

The smallest obelisk in Rome, carved in the reign of Apries, fourth pharaoh of the twenty-sixth dynasty (ruled 580–570 B.C.), was brought to Rome by Diocletian. In the 17th century, it was placed by Bernini on Ercole Ferrata's Pulcino ("chick") in the Piazza di Santa Maria sopra Minerva, beside the Pantheon.

Although the cognomen *Dives* ("Wealthy") had been in the family since the late 3rd century B.C., the Triumvir Marcus Licinius Crassus owed much of his fabulous wealth to his own unscrupulous property speculation. When a fire broke out, he would rush to the scene with his private fire brigade, but he would not order it to fight the fire until the owner of the property, growing ever more frantic, had agreed to sell it to him for a fraction of its worth (Plutarch *Life of Crassus* 2).

Augustus formed the *cohortes vigilum* ("the units of watchmen") in A.D. 6, as Rome's first public police force and fire brigade. The *vigiles* were expected to patrol the streets while the populace was at the games, to prevent burglaries.

Literary sources and archaeological investigations both attest the filthy conditions of urban life. Analysis of the polar ice caps shows that lead and copper pollution, caused by smelting, was at a high level in the Roman period.

The words "street" and "stratum" are related, for Roman roads were constructed in layers.

On the person who lives in a building from which anything is thrown down or poured onto a place where people commonly pass by or stand I will impose a fine of twice the cost of the damage inflicted or caused (Justinian's *Digest* 9.3.1). That whole section of the *Digest* is devoted to offenses concerning the *pouring or throwing of things from buildings.*

Every householder must keep the public street in front of his house in good repair and clear gutters and ensure that wagons are not prevented from having access. Those in rented accommodation should see to this themselves if the owner does not do so, and deduct the cost from their rent. They should ensure that nothing is left outside workshops. Exceptions are made

A street in Pompeii, equipped with stepping-stones to enable pedestrians to avoid the worst of the filth.

for launderers hanging out clothes and for carpenters placing wheels outside, but they must not prevent wagons from passing along. They must not allow fighting in the streets, or emptying of chamber pots, or throwing out of dead animals and hides (Justinian's *Digest* 43.10).

❋

You could seem remiss and heedless of sudden disaster if you went out to dinner without making your will. There are as many dangers as there are open windows watching as you pass by. So pray as you go along that the windows will be content to empty big chamber pots over you (Juvenal *Satires* 3.272–77).

◎

Roman roads were not, as is often assumed, inexorably straight; they were as direct as natural barriers would permit. For example, Lincoln (Lindum) is fifty-five miles from York (Eboracum) as the crow flies but, since the Roman road deviated inland to avoid swampy terrain, it was seventy-two miles long.

Noting on milestones the distance one has traveled takes away much of the fatigue of a journey (Quintilian *Education of the Orator* 4.5.22). More than four thousand Roman milestones still survive, at least two from a region as remote as southern Scotland.

Plutarch gives the 2nd century B.C. social reformer Gaius Gracchus the credit for setting up the first milestones (*Life of Gaius Gracchus* 7). In fact, the inscription on the earliest surviving Roman milestone dates it more than a century earlier, naming Publius Claudius Pulcher (consul in 249 B.C., who had the sacred chickens thrown overboard; see p. 131) and Gaius Furius Pacilus (consul in 251 B.C.) as the magistrates responsible for the roadworks.

Plutarch also credits Gracchus with being the first to place smaller stone blocks along the roadside at frequent intervals to enable riders to mount their horses without assistance. This was an important benefit, given that stirrups were unknown to the Romans. They were probably a Chinese invention, and were first brought westward by the Avars in the 6th century A.D.

The urban poor used to have window-boxes, which gave them a glimpse of the countryside every day, but now the countless violent burglaries have forced them to shutter their windows (Pliny *Natural History* 19.59).

In the old days, people washed their arms and legs every day, but bathed only on market days [every eight days] (Seneca *Epistles* 86). At the end of the Republican period, there were one hundred and seventy public baths in Rome, a number that vastly increased in the early imperial period (Pliny *Natural History* 36.121). Rome had almost a thousand public baths by the end of the 4th century A.D. Evidence is surprisingly scanty, but it seems that men and women normally went to the public baths at different times of the day.

One of the consuls recently came to the Campanian town of Teanum Sidicinum. His wife said she wanted to bathe in the men's baths. The responsibility for driving the bathers out of the baths was given to the chief magistrate of the town, Marcus Marius. The consul's wife complained to her husband that the baths had not been made available to her quickly enough and that they were not clean enough. A stake was therefore set up in the Forum, and Marcus Marius, the most distinguished man in the community, was led to it. Then his clothes were ripped off, and he was beaten with rods (Aulus Gellius *Attic Nights* 10.3, quoting from a speech by Gaius Gracchus in the 2nd century B.C.).

Darnel seeds cause immediate dizziness if eaten in bread. They say that bath-managers in the provinces of Greece and Asia throw them on to the coals if they want to get rid of a crowd of bathers (Pliny *Natural History* 18.156).

Frontinus, curator of the water supply of Rome at the end of the 1st century A.D., complains, *We have detected fields, shops, lodgings, and brothels equipped with constant running water* (*On the Water-Supply of Rome* 2.76). It has been estimated that the aqueducts supplied Rome with about three hundred gallons of water per person per day, about five or six times the amount provided in many modern cities. Even today, the water supply in Rome is wonderfully prodigal.

Some districts in the center of Rome were more favored by the rich than others, but living space in the city was not generally divided along class lines. The *palazzo* of an aristocrat might be surrounded by commercial properties; indeed, many noble houses had their ground floor rented out as shops.

The man-made hill Monte Testaccio (Pottery Mountain), by the Tiber south of the Aventine, is now more than one hundred feet high and well over half a mile in circumference, but it was probably once considerably more substantial. It is composed almost entirely of fragments of amphoras and other such earthenware containers, discarded after being used to import olive oil from southern Spain. There are at least fifty million amphoras, with a capacity of six billion liters. The dump seems to have been in use for more than three hundred years. The earliest datable amphora found there is from A.D. 144, but the lower strata contain earlier material.

The simple early life of the Romans was commemorated by a Hut of Romulus (*casa Romuli*) on both the Palatine and Capitoline hills. One of these thatched huts burned down in 38 B.C. while a religious rite was being performed, and again in 12 B.C. when a crow dropped a piece of burning meat that it had snatched from an altar. This latter event was taken to portend the death of Augustus's close associate Agrippa, who had defeated Antony and Cleopatra at Actium (Cassius Dio *Roman History* 48.43, 54.29).

The panels on perhaps only the lowest four of the eighteen marble drums that constitute Trajan's Column could be studied in detail at ground level, yet there is no reduction in the artistry or in the importance of the propaganda farther up. Similarly, Pliny observes that some of the Pantheon's finest sculptures are on the pediment, but that they are not well known because they are so high up (*Natural History* 36.38).

Tacitus gives us the most detailed surviving description of the Great Fire of Rome, which he may have witnessed as a boy:

> *It broke out, whether by accident or through arson ordered by Nero, in shops near the Circus Maximus on the night of July 19, A.D. 64, and raged out of control through the narrow streets for six days, fanned by high winds. No one tried to fight it, some people even threw torches to make it worse, claiming to be acting on orders but perhaps simply wishing to be left free to loot. Nero returned from Antium* [35 miles away] *only when his palace on the Palatine was engulfed. He provided food and shelter for the homeless, but was rumored to have sung of the destruction of Troy while Rome burned. Of the fourteen districts of Rome, three were utterly destroyed, seven had just a few twisted and charred ruins left, and only four remained unscathed* (*Annals* 15.39).

Some people noted that this fire started on July 19, the same day as the Gauls had burned the city. Others were more elaborate, calculating that the time elapsed between the two fires was 418 years, 418 months, and 418 days (Tacitus *Annals* 15.41).

We were walking up the Cispian Hill [north of the Esquiline] *when we saw a multistoried apartment block in flames, with the whole neighborhood already ablaze. One of us said, "Rents from city properties are high, but the risks are even higher. If any way could be found to prevent the constant fires in Rome, I'd sell my country properties and buy in the city"* (Aulus Gellius *Attic Nights* 15.1).

The officer of the watch must be vigilant all night, patrolling with his boots on and equipped with hooks and axes. He must warn all householders not to allow fires to break out through carelessness. He should also ensure that each house has a supply of water handy in an upstairs room (Justinian's *Digest* 1.15.3.3).

Vinegar was kept in large jars to be used for extinguishing fires (Justinian's *Digest* 33.7.18, 33.9.5). Presumably, a certain care was needed in applying it: when Hannibal's path across the Alps was blocked by a massive boulder, he is said to have exploded it by kindling a fire under it and then dousing it with vinegar (Livy *History of Rome* 21.37). It is open to reasonable doubt whether he would have had the foresight to haul sufficient vinegar up the Alpine passes. The Romans once took a Greek city after traitors inside the city weakened a strong brick tower by soaking it repeatedly with vinegar (Cassius Dio *Roman History* 36.18).

A fire hydrant near the Circus Maximus, where the Great Fire is said to have begun. Note the acronym SPQR for *Senatus Populusque Romanus* ("The Senate and the Roman People").

Pliny notes that the Tiber floods more at Rome than anywhere else in its one-hundred-fifty-mile course (*Natural History* 3.55). During the rule of Augustus alone it is known to have burst its banks and flooded the lower-lying regions of the city at least six times (in 27, 23, 22, and 13 B.C., and A.D. 5 and 12). Such devastation continued until the river was channeled at the end of the 19th century, even though the technology to build efficient flood barriers had certainly been developed in antiquity, and just such a project was planned by Julius Caesar.

Seismological studies and written records suggest that, as well as innumerable less significant tremors, Rome has suffered widespread or severe earthquake damage about once a century over the last two thousand years.

The obliteration of many of the great monuments of ancient Rome was accomplished not by barbarian hordes (who lacked the technology and motivation to be efficiently destructive) or by acts of nature (such as fires, floods, and earthquakes), but by the inhabitants themselves:

- Theodoric the Great, the Ostrogoth ruler of Italy from 493 to 526, was almost illiterate [see p. 31]. A letter written on his behalf by Cassiodorus, his polymath courtier, instructs the prefect of Rome to use marble blocks fallen from public buildings to enhance the beauty of the city.
- One of the worst offenders was the Byzantine emperor Constans II: on a twelve-day

Three columns from the temple of Vespasian and Titus in the Forum are still standing ([R]ESTITVER[VNT] "They restored"). There is a similarly distressing inscription in the theater at Sabratha in Libya; when Italian archaeologists set it back in place in the 1930s, the only word that could be restored was LACVNAM, the rest being modern concrete. In textual criticism, *lacuna* is the technical term used to denote that a section of the text is missing.

visit to Rome in A.D. 663 (the first such visit by an emperor for two hundred years), he arranged for the metal to be stripped from prominent buildings, even removing the clamps used to keep them from falling into ruin.

- Almost none of the marble used in building St. Peter's was quarried for the purpose; it was plundered from existing buildings. A single contractor removed 2,522 cartloads of marble from the Colosseum in 1452.
- The Farnese Palace, the most magnificent of the *palazzi* in Rome, owes much to the Colosseum and the theater of Marcellus: it is said that Pope Paul III, born Alessandro Farnese, gave his nephew permission to take as much stone from the Colosseum as he could in a twelve-hour period, so the nephew set four thousand hired laborers to work furiously for a day.
- Pope Urban VIII, born Maffeo Barberini, was one of the great patrons of late Renaissance art, and he did more than anyone else in the 17th century to make Rome what it is today. He weakened the roof of the Pantheon by removing its bronze girders to make eighty cannons for Castel Sant'Angelo ["It is more important to defend the pope than to keep rain from the Pantheon"] and to supply materials for Bernini's *baldacchino* in St. Peter's. Hence the well-merited pasquinade *quod non fecerunt barbari, fecerunt Barberini* ("What the barbarians did not do, the Barberini did").
- Architectural vandalism has also thrived in more modern times. In 1932–33, the Fascist government plowed straight through the Forum area, to allow spectacular military parades along the Via del Impero from the Colosseum to the Piazza Venezia. The Piazza Venezia itself is dominated by the massive monument to Vittorio Emanuele II, the first king of Italy (1861–78); it is admired by few and utterly throws the Capitol out of perspective.

ruinis imminentibus musculi praemigrant
Little mice move out of buildings when they are about to collapse.
Pliny *Natural History* 8.103

· XIX ·

POMPEII AND HERCULANEUM

Campaniae ora . . . felix illa ac beata amoenitas, ut palam sit gaudentis opus esse naturae

The coast of Campania, so bounteous, blessed, and beautiful that it is obviously the work of Nature in a good mood!

Pliny *Natural History* 3.40

There are almost three thousand municipal election notices on walls in Pompeii. Several canvass for one Marcus Cerrinius Vatia (*Select Latin Inscriptions* 6418*a*, *b*, *c*). Some others were less supportive:

- *The petty thieves ask you to elect Vatia as city magistrate.*
- *Macerio and those who sleep a lot ask you to elect Vatia as city magistrate.*
- *All the late drinkers ask you to elect Marcus Cerrinius Vatia as city magistrate.*

  (*Corpus of Latin Inscriptions* 4.575, 576, 581)

Election notices were painted up on walls in busy streets to catch the voters' attention. The artists apparently worked at night: presumably as a joke, one notice adds in small letters the instruction "Lantern-carrier, hold on to the ladder!" (*Corpus of Latin Inscriptions* 4.7621).

A remarkably high proportion of the graffiti found in Pompeii is in verse. The opening half-line of the *Aeneid*, *Arma virumque cano* ("I sing of arms and the man") occurs seventeen times. There is a variation on this outside the premises of a launderer with the splendidly voweled name Fabius Ululutremulus ("Owltrembler"). It reads *fullones ululamque cano, non arma virumque* ("I sing of launderers and their owl, not of arms and the man") (*Corpus of Latin Inscriptions* 4.9131). To fear something more than a launderer fears an owl was proverbial: owls were an omen of death, and those in mourning wore dark clothing, which did not need to be cleaned often.

ADMIROR PARIES TE NON CECIDISSE RUINIS
QUI TOT SCRIPTORUM TAEDIA SUSTINEAS

Versions of the elegiac couplet *Wall, I am amazed you haven't fallen down in ruins, since you bear the tedious scribblings of so many writers* (*Corpus of Latin Inscriptions* 4.2487 *etc.*) are found in four separate locations in Pompeii.

Ferdinand I, the Bourbon king of the Two Sicilies, had little appreciation of the true value of the material being dug up in the excavations at Pompeii and Herculaneum. He exchanged eighteen of the priceless Herculaneum papyri, first found in 1785, for eighteen kangaroos for his mistress's theme park, which specialized in animals from Australia, a continent that had only recently been discovered.

At about this same period, according to a less well-documented story, a Danish scholar, Niels Iversen Schow, was offered fifty rolls of Greek texts by a group of peasants in Egypt; he bought just one, and the peasants burned the rest to enjoy the smell they gave off. Since papyrus sheets were held together by a gum exuded by the plant itself, or by a paste of flour, water, and vinegar (Pliny *Natural History* 13.82), this should not be regarded as an early instance of glue sniffing.

Quoting an Italian proverb, the great German archaeologist J. J. Winckelmann complained memorably, but quite unfairly, that the director of excavations at Herculaneum knew as much about antiquities as the moon knows about lobsters.

Winckelmann also complained that only fifty workmen, including Algerian and Tunisian slaves, were employed in the excavations at Pompeii. A few years later, Goethe wished that the task of excavating Herculaneum had been entrusted to German miners and not left to looters and vandals (*Italian Journey* 1786–1788).

Winckelmann observed that Pompeii is so remote that few visitors except Englishmen have the determination to make their way there.

The French novelist Stendhal met three English naval officers going into the Portici Museum at Herculaneum just as he was leaving it. Even though he galloped back to Naples, they caught up with him at the outskirts of the city and assured him that the paintings were absolutely terrific, just about the most marvelous sight in the universe. He calculated that they could not have spent more than three or four minutes in the twenty-two-room museum (*Rome, Naples and Florence* 1817). The psychosomatic condition of dizziness and tachycardia associated with exposure to high art is known nowadays as the "Stendhal syndrome."

Mark Twain noted that, after catching his foot in one of the ruts "worn five and even ten inches deep into the thick flagstones by the chariot-wheels of generations of swindled tax-payers . . . the sadness that came over me when I saw the first poor skeleton, with ashes and lava sticking to it, was tempered by the reflection that maybe that party was the Street Commissioner" (*The Innocents Abroad* 1875).

The eruption of Mt. Vesuvius that devastated Pompeii and Herculaneum had a force estimated at about five hundred times that of the

Plaster casts of a mother and child trapped in the falling ash in the eruption of Vesuvius.

atomic bomb dropped on Hiroshima. Although it is not known how many people were killed in the eruption, it is generally assumed that the recovered remains of about fifteen hundred represent only a small percentage of the victims.

The most recent severe eruption of Vesuvius was in 1944, when several villages and an entire American B-25 bomber group were destroyed or damaged. The present lull is the longest in almost five hundred years. The region is much more densely populated than it was in the 1st century, and many experts regard the current plans for evacuation as wholly inadequate.

cuncta iacent flammis et tristi mersa favilla:
nec superi vellent hoc licuisse sibi
Everything round Vesuvius lies submerged in
flames and mournful ashes;
not even the gods above would wish to have
so much power.
Martial *Epigrams* 4.44.7–8

· XX ·

TOILETS

hic qui vobis non posse videtur muscam excitare tam facile homines occidebat quam canis adsidet
This fellow, who looks as if he wouldn't bother a fly, used to kill people as easily as a dog squats.
Seneca *Apocolocyntosis* 10, the divine Augustus speaking in heaven against the deification of Emperor Claudius

The Romans were justly proud of their extensive system of aqueducts. Frontinus boasts, *Could you compare with all these many massive and serviceable aqueducts the useless pyramids or the famous but idle works of the Greeks?* (*On the Water-Supply of Rome* 1.16). Much of the water from the aqueducts was used to keep the public toilets clean, maintaining a constant flow through these facilities directly to the sewers and on to the Tiber.

According to the *notitia regionum*, an early-4th-century A.D. catalog of the city's buildings and landmarks, Rome then had 144 public *latrinae*.

The standard of engineering in Roman *latrinae* was not achieved again in Europe until the 19th century.

Just as aqueducts provided an abundant water supply, so a certain degree of sanitation was ensured by the system of sewers, especially the *Cloaca Maxima* (Main Drain). Begun in the city's earliest times, it was much admired in antiquity, and is still, to a very limited degree, operational today.

Until recently, not much research was done on ancient toilets. Archaeologists were often reluctant to identify them for what they are. Likewise, in antiquity, Vitruvius and Frontinus were very reticent about waste disposal in their influential treatises on architecture and aqueducts, respectively.

Almost all the private houses excavated in Herculaneum and Pompeii had toilet facilities, often in the kitchen or under the stairs; there is little evidence for doors to these cubbyholes.

At the animal-fighting recently, one of the Germans who was getting ready for the show withdrew to relieve himself—that was the only privacy he had, away from the guard. There he choked himself to death by ramming down his throat the stick with a sponge attached that is provided for personal hygiene (Seneca *Letter* 70). Remnants of sponges have been discovered in a Roman sewer at York in northern England.

Apollinaris medicus Titi Imp. hic cacavit bene ("Apollinaris, physician to the emperor Titus, had a fine shit here") (*Corpus of Latin Inscriptions* 4.10619, a graffito in the Casa della Gemma in Herculaneum).

I do not think that silver chamber pots are included with heirlooms, since they are not part of the silver collection (Justinian's *Digest* 34.2.27.5). This legal ruling presumably exists because chamber pots were often made of silver. Even gold ones are mentioned occasionally; most notoriously, Mark Antony was criticized for using one (Pliny *Natural History* 33.50).

The Emperor Augustus Caesar, son of a god, Pontifex Maximus, designated consul for the twelfth time, and tribune of the people for the eighteenth time, sends greetings to the officials, the council, and the people of Cnidus. So begins a letter sent by Augustus in 6 B.C. to a not particularly important Greek community, attempting to settle a dispute over the apparently accidental death of someone who tried to break into a house and was hit by a chamber pot that slipped from the hand of a slave trying to empty its contents down over him (*Select Greek Inscriptions*[3] 2.780).

A papyrus letter records the dramatic details of a similar incident brought to the royal court in Egypt in the pre-Roman period:

> *Greetings to King Ptolemy. I have been wronged by a woman named Psenobastis from Pysa. I went to Pysa on business. She leaned out of an upper-story window and drenched me by emptying a chamber pot into the street. When I complained angrily, she pulled at my cloak, exposing my chest, and spat in my face. I can provide witnesses to prove that I have been subjected to this unjust attack* (*Lille Papyri* 2.24).

I have wet the bed; I confess, I have done wrong, innkeeper. If you ask, Why?, there was no chamber pot (*Corpus of Latin Inscriptions* 4.4957, a technically quite accomplished elegiac couplet).

At lines 1026–29 of the fourth book of his *On the Nature of Things*, one of the greatest poems ever written in Latin, Lucretius gives a high-style description of bed-wetting:

> *When they are bound up by sleep, people who are normally immaculate often believe that they are raising up their clothing by a basin or a shallow pot; they pour out the liquid filtered from their whole body, and the oriental bedding with its magnificent splendor is soaked.*

During the rule of Tiberius, the frenzy for bringing charges of treason was so widespread that it did more harm to the Roman state than did the whole Civil War. Note was taken of drunken conversations and of candid witticisms: nothing was safe, every opportunity for cruelty was exploited. A senior politician named Paullus was at dinner, wearing a ring with a picture of Tiberius engraved on it. It would be silly of me to try to find a polite way of saying that he picked up a chamber pot. The notorious informer Maro noticed this. But a slave of the man for whom the trap was being set took the ring from his drunken master's finger. Calling on the other guests to witness that the emperor's portrait had been brought into contact with something disgusting, Maro was beginning to draw up the charge when the slave showed the ring on his own finger (Seneca *On Benefits* 3.26).

When Titus criticized him for devising a tax on urinals, Vespasian put a coin from the first payment from this nationalized industry under his son's nose and asked him if he was offended by the smell. When Titus said he was not, he observed, "But it comes from urine" (Suetonius *Life of Vespasian* 23). The *vespasienne* (an abbreviation of *colonne vespasienne*, not to be confused with Trajan's Column) was a type of urinal, once a common sight on French sidewalks.

Chamber pots were not all unisex; a *matella*, for example, was for gentlemen, a *scaphium* for ladies. Only men could use the large pots set up on the street, the urine from which was collected and sold to launderers as a cleaning agent. A lead pipe leads directly to a laundry from the urinal in the Baths of Mithras at Ostia.

Thais smells worse than a greedy launderer's old jar that has just broken in the middle of the street (Martial *Epigrams* 6.93.1–2).

Given that the Romans were both acutely class-conscious and also generally intolerant of public nudity, the institution of the large-scale open-plan *latrinae publicae* is rather surprising. Although there is some evidence that the rich and important went about accompanied by slaves carrying their chamber pots, it is reasonable to wonder how the upper classes visiting the public conveniences could avoid finding themselves in much more intimate contact with the masses than would be conceivable in any other circumstances. Likewise, very little is known about the segregation of men and women in these public facilities.

Latrinae with twenty-five seats are commonplace. Some could accommodate as many as eighty people at the same time. A sixty-seat *latrina* for the palace slaves has been preserved in the *Domus Flavia*, the palace of Vespasian and his sons, on the Palatine. It was once identified, despite its obvious function, as the machinery chamber for a hydraulic lift.

It is ironic that gravestones should end up being recycled as toilet seats in *latrinae* at Ostia, given that standard inscriptions on gravestones implore or threaten those who might disturb the sanctity of the grave:

- *Anyone who pisses or shits here, may the gods above and the gods below be angry with him.*

Latrinae publicae at Ostia.

- *Stranger, my bones beg you not to piss at my grave. If you want to be nicer, have a shit. This is the grave of Urtica* ("Nettle"). *Go away, shitter! It's not safe to expose your ass here.*
  (*Corpus of Latin Inscriptions* 6.13740, 4.8899)

I'll see to it in my will that no one does me wrong. For I'm going to have one of my freedmen guard my tomb, to prevent people from rushing to shit there (Trimalchio at Petronius *Satyricon* 71). The warning *cacator, cave malum* ("Shitter, watch out!") occurs several times in Pompeii.

The Second Triumvirate closed up the spot where Caesar was slaughtered, and later they had it remodeled as a toilet (Cassius Dio *Roman History* 47.19).

Public toilets had a social function quite alien to modern life. Martial teases an acquaintance for sitting around there all day in the hope of cadging an invitation to dinner (*Epigrams* 11.77).

The Seven Wise Men of early Greece were famous for such pithily profound sayings as *Know yourself, Nothing in excess, Call no one happy before he is dead.* The Room of the Seven Wise Men, however, in one of the baths at Ostia, is not so edifying. It seems to have been used as a bar, and the partially preserved paintings on the walls portray the Seven Wise Men with a pearl of lavatory wisdom attributed in Latin to each of them. The three fully legible inscriptions are:

- *Solon massaged his stomach to shit well.*
- *Thales advised those who are constipated to strain.*
- *The crafty Chilon taught how to fart with stealth.*

In a severely damaged part of the painting below the Wise Men, several men are sitting in a row, apparently in a communal toilet; one of them is saying, *My friend, shit well and let the doctors suck you* [i.e., a good digestion will keep you healthy and save you from rapacious doctors' exorbitant fees].

Manneken Pis: The Drunken Hercules.

Even in Greek cities, most open-plan *latrinae* can be dated to the Roman period. There was no call for such facilities in old-time Sparta: Plutarch twice records that, on seeing several people sitting on a row of toilets, a Spartan exclaimed, *I hope I never sit anywhere where I won't be able to stand up to give my seat to someone older than myself* (*Life of Lycurgus* 20, *Sayings of the Spartans* 12).

Both the younger Seneca and his nephew, the poet Lucan, directed bathroom humor against emperors:

- In his parodic account of the deification of the stuttering emperor Claudius, Seneca says of him: *After he had made rather a loud noise from that part of his body with which he expressed himself more readily, his last words among mortals were "Oh, dear me, I think I've made a mess of myself"* [vae me, puto, concacavi me]. *I don't know if he actually did so, but he certainly made a mess of everything else* [*omnia certe concacavit*] (*Apocolocyntosis* 4).
- *Nero insulted Lucan by leaving while he was giving a recital of his poetry, and Lucan retaliated in ways that are still notorious. Once, when he was in a public lavatory and relieved his bowels with a particularly*

Bust of Vespasian.

loud noise, he recited a half-line by Nero, "You'd think it had thundered under the earth," and all those who were sitting there with him stampeded out (Suetonius *Life of Lucan* 2).

❁

Trimalchio clicked his fingers, and a eunuch held out a chamber pot for him. When he had relieved his bladder, he called for water to wash his hands and then dried his fingers on the slave's hair (Petronius *Satyricon* 27).

❁

Vespasian had rather strained facial features. He once challenged someone to say something funny at his expense, and the joker replied rather wittily, "I will, once you've finished relieving yourself" (Suetonius *Life of Vespasian* 20).

❁

The heretic Arius suffered a stomach upset and went into a public toilet in Alexandria. When he did not come back out, those who were with him went in to look for him and found him dead. The seat on which he died was never used again, in recognition of his having thus been punished there for his impiety (Sozomenus *History of the Church* 2.29–30).

❁

si latet ars prodest
It helps if your art is hidden.
Ovid *The Art of Love* 2.313

· XXI ·

NOT FOR THE PURITANICAL

procul hinc, procul este, severi!
Away from here, far away, anyone who is prudish!
Ovid *Amores* 2.1.3

The following epigram was written by Octavian when he was besieging Mark Antony's wife and brother in Perugia in 41 B.C., and it is preserved by Martial in *Epigrams* 11.20 as an example of the *simplicitas Romana* ("Roman directness") of the future emperor's language:

> *Fulvia has determined that I must fuck her as a punishment because her husband Antony is fucking the eastern queen Glaphyra. What, me fuck Fulvia? Suppose the informer Manius begged me to bugger him? Would I do it? Not while I have any sense. "Either fuck me or let's fight," says Fulvia. My cock is dearer to me than life itself—sound the charge!*

The Latin word for a slingshot is *glans*, which literally means "acorn" and can also refer to the head of the penis. Many slingshots, relics of Octavian's siege of Perugia, have inscriptions which exploit this ambiguity:

- *I'm heading for Fulvia's cunt.*
- *I'm heading for Octavian's ass.*
- *Greetings, Octavius; you suck.*
- *Bald Lucius Antonius and you too, Fulvia, spread your ass.*
  (*Corpus of Latin Inscriptions* 11.6721.5, 7, 9*a*, 14)

HIC HABITAT FELICITAS ("Happiness dwells here") (*Corpus of Latin Inscriptions* 4.1454). This notice and the illustration were originally located in the center of the arch above a baker's oven in Pompeii, to ward off evil spirits (see p. 79). They were removed in the early 19th century, along with dozens of artifacts scarcely offensive to the most delicate sensibilities nowadays, to the "Cabinet of Obscene Objects" in the Archeological Museum in Naples. The same inscription, followed by *nil intret mali* "Let no evil come in," but without the illustration, has been found in a mosaic at the entrance to a house in the Mozartplatz in Salzburg. Many small rings survive embossed with a phallic symbol, to be worn by children as protective charms.

In a rather sprightly discussion of accidental obscenities, Cicero (*Letters to his Friends* 9.22) notes, for example, that:

- The harmless combination *cum nos* ("when we") sounds like *cunnus* ("cunt"), as does the name of Socrates' lyre teacher, Connos.
- The word *bini* ("two each") sounds like *βινεῖ* (*binei*, "he fucks").
- An ex-consul's question in the Senate, *hanc culpam maiorem an illam dicam?* ("Am I to call this fault greater or that one?") contains an embarrassing echo of *landica*, a rather coarse term for "clitoris."
- *Testes* ("witnesses") is perfectly respectable in a court of law, but not quite so respectable elsewhere.

Ovid daydreams of being transformed into a ring that he is sending as a gift to his mistress, a metamorphosis which would enable him to be with her all the time. He imagines her wearing him on her finger in the bath, *sed, puto, te nuda, mea membra libidine surgent* ("But, I suppose, when you are naked, my limbs will rise with lust" (*Amores* 2.15.25). *Mea membra* ("my limbs") is not just politely coy but also an outstanding example of the curious convention in Latin poetry of using the plural when the singular is intended.

Graffiti from a Pompeian brothel:

- *I have fucked many girls here.*
- *Phoebus the perfume maker fucked very well here.*
- *Hermeros fucked here on June 15 with Phileterus and Caphisus.*
- *When I came here, I fucked, then I went home* (possibly a parody of Caesar's *veni, vidi, vici* ["I came, I saw, I conquered"]).
- *Myrtis, you suck well* (scores of graffiti on this topic have been found on walls in Pompeii).
  (*Corpus of Latin Inscriptions* 4.2175, 4.2184, 4.2192, 4.2246, 4.2273)

Some poetic gems by Catullus:

- *I'll bugger you and make you suck me, Aurelius, you soft chap, and mincing Furius, for supposing that I'm indecent, just because my poetry is a bit spicy. A poet should himself be respectable, but his verses don't need to be* (16.1–6).
- *Please, my dear sweet Ipsitilla, my precious one, my lovely girl, order me to come to you at lunchtime. If you do invite me, it would be helpful if no one bars the door and you don't go out. Stay at home and get ready for nine nonstop fucks. So, if you are interested, invite me right away, for I'm lying here well fed and on my back, banging away at my tunic and the blanket* (32).
- *My Lesbia, that Lesbia, Caelius, that Lesbia whom Catullus loved more than himself and his whole world, now at crossroads and in alleyways she's peeling the descendants of great-minded Remus* (58). The crucial verb,

the magnificently unpleasant sounding *glubit*, means literally "strip the bark from a tree"; its precise sense here is debated by scholars.

Ithyphallic (a discreetly impressive Greek term meaning "with an erect penis") statues of the god Priapus were set up in market gardens to threaten intruders. A collection of some eighty epigrams, the *Priapea*, all probably written by the same author sometime in the 1st century A.D., is dominated by remorseless variations on a single theme, the sexual punishments that Priapus will inflict on thieves. Poem 22 is no better or worse than most of the rest of the collection: "*If a woman or a man or a boy commits a crime against me, the woman would provide her cunt for me, the man his mouth, the boy his buttocks.*"

Three epigrams by Martial, whose poetry is perhaps to be valued more for the insights it gives into contemporary life in Rome than for its literary merits:

- *When your slave's cock and your ass are sore, Naevolus, I'm no clairvoyant, but I know what you're doing* (3.71).
- *You say that lawyers and poets have bad breath, but a fellator's breath is worse* (11.30).
- *Lesbia swears she has never been fucked for free. It's true; she's used to paying when she wants to be fucked* (11.62).

In cataloguing the sexual habits of the dreadful Hostius Quadra, Seneca notes that his bedroom was equipped with strategically placed magnifying mirrors (*Natural Questions* 1.17). The poet Horace also had such mirrors in his bedroom (Suetonius *Life of Horace* 3).

Just listen to what Claudius endured. As soon as his wife Messalina sensed that he was asleep, the Augustan whore dared to put on her hooded nighttime cloak, preferring a mere mattress to her bedroom on the Palatine. Leaving the palace accompanied by just one maid, and with a blonde wig hiding her dark hair, she went to her personal cell in the snug brothel. Then, naked, with gilded nipples, under the name Lycisca [Greek for "little she-wolf"], *she worked as a prostitute, flaunting the belly that bore*

Priapus weighing his penis against a purse of gold.

you, noble Britannicus [Claudius's heir-designate, poisoned by Nero] (Juvenal *Satires* 6.115–124).

Messalina, Claudius's wife, chose to have a competition with the most notorious prostitute, and defeated her by having sexual intercourse with twenty-five men in a night and a day (Pliny *Natural History* 10.172).

Petronius added a codicil to his will cataloguing Nero's sexual partners and detailing the particular perversions they engaged in. After sealing it with his signet ring, he broke the ring so that it could not be used to forge documents that might incriminate anyone else (Tacitus *Annals* 16.19; it would be interesting to know how Petronius came by such information).

erubuit posuitque meum Lucretia librum,
sed coram Bruto; Brute, recede: leget
The proverbially pure Lucretia blushed and
put my book down—
at least when her husband Brutus was there;
back off, Brutus: she'll read it.
Martial *Epigrams* 11.16.9–10

• XXII •

TEMPUS FUGIT

quid est ergo tempus? si nemo ex me quaerat,
scio; si quaerenti explicare velim, nescio
So, what is time? As long as no one asks me,
I know; but, if I were to try to explain it to
someone who asked me, I don't know.
St. Augustine *Confessions* 11.14.17

The only measurements of time mentioned in the Twelve Tables *are sunrise and sunset. Some years later, noon was added. One of the consuls' attendants announced noon and sunset when, watching from the Senate house, he saw the sun in particular positions. This functioned only on sunny days* (Pliny *Natural History* 7.212).

The first public sundial in Rome was set up in the mid-3rd century B.C., brought back as plunder from the Sicilian city of Catania during the First Punic War. Even though the lines on its face were known not to correspond to the hours, the Romans used it for ninety-nine years (Pliny *Natural History* 7.214). The error in calibration would have been of more than 4 degrees (Catania 37.31° N, Rome 41.53° N).

May the gods damn the man who first invented hours, and first set up a sundial here, and chopped my day into little pieces! When I was a boy, my stomach was my sundial, far better and more reliable than all these modern ones. It told me when to eat (if I had anything to eat). Nowadays, people don't eat, even when they have things to eat, unless it pleases the sun. So the town is full of sundials, and most people creep along, shriveled up with hunger (quoted from a lost comedy by Plautus at Aulus Gellius *Attic Nights* 3.3.5).

The following inscriptions, from medieval and more modern times, but written in classical Latin, are found on sundials in various parts of Europe:

ab hoc momento pendet aeternitas	Eternity hangs on this moment
ad occasum tendimus omnes	We are all on our way to sunset
da mihi solem, dabo tibi horam	Give me sun, I will give you the hour
dum quaeris, hora fugit	While you seek it, the hour flees
horam dum petis, ultimam para	While you seek the hour, prepare for your last
horas non numero nisi serenas	I count only the cloudless hours
lux mea lex	The light is my law
nulla sine sole umbra	Without the sun there is no shadow
sol me, vos umbra regit	The sun controls me, my shadow controls you
sol rex regum	The sun is the king of kings

The Romans originally used a lunar calendar (*mensis*, the Latin word for "month," is related to the English word "moon"). The seasons would have quickly fallen out of harmony with the calendar, a disturbing state of affairs for an agricultural people, who needed to observe their religious festivals connected with sowing, harvesting, and so on at the appropriate time. Presumably months were liberally intercalated (i.e., added) as necessary. These intercalated months were added in February, before the start of agricultural and military activity, and before magistrates took up their posts in March.

Spring, with the onset of a new year's undertakings, is a more natural beginning than midwinter. Astrology is still today based on a cycle beginning in spring; the sequence of horoscopes given in a newspaper, for example, starts with Aries (March 21–April 19) because the sun is in or about to enter Aries at the vernal equinox (March 19–21).

As *pontifex maximus*, head of the priestly college in charge of the calendar of Rome's religious year, Julius Caesar decreed that ten days should be added to every year, with an extra day at the end of February every fourth year. The Julian system came into effect on January 1, 45 B.C., after a year with 445 days had readjusted the calendar to the seasons.

The Julian system loses touch with the seasons much more slowly than Rome's earlier calendar, and remained in force until the reforms of Pope Gregory XIII in 1582. Like Julius Caesar, Pope Gregory was the *pontifex maximus*.

The Gregorian reforms were only gradually adopted by the various European countries; Greece held out until 1923. The Julian system is still used by the Russian Orthodox Church and largely also by the Greek Orthodox Church.

The Romans reckoned years either AUC (*ab urbe condita*), that is, from the supposed founding of Rome in 753 B.C. or, more usually, by reference to the consuls then in office. For example, the birth of the poet Ovid in 43 B.C. took place AUC 711 or in the consulship of Hirtius and Pansa, *consulibus Aulo Hirtio et Gaio Vibio Pansa*.

The consular method may seem clumsy if we apply it to our own times and culture: Who was president of the United States in 1851, king of England in 1651? These are much easier questions, since they require only one answer each, and kings and presidents do not change every year.

The reckoning of the year in relation to the birth of Jesus Christ (i.e., *Anno Domini*, "In the Year of our Lord") was first introduced in A.D. 525 by a monk named Dionysius Exiguus ("Diminutive Denis"). In devising this system, Dionysius was the first person in the Roman world known to use the number zero, which was introduced via Arab scholarship from India. The symbol o for zero is commonly supposed to be derived from οὐδέν (*ouden*), the first letter of the Greek word for "nothing" (literally, "not even one").

⊕

Epitaphs sometimes record not just the years, months, and days that a person lived, but even the number of hours. On the other hand, the calculation is often much vaguer, simply *P M* (a standard abbreviation for *PLUS MINUS*, "more or less") and the number of years. For example:

- *Here lies Leburna, the manager of a company of actors, who lived more or less a hundred years. I died quite a few times* [*sc.*, in stage roles], *but never like this. I wish good health to you who are in the world above.*
- *Otacilia Narcisa set up this memorial to her very dear husband, Julius Timotheus, who lived a guiltless life of more or less twenty-eight years, but was captured by brigands along with our seven foster children.* (*Corpus of Latin Inscriptions* 3.3980, 6.20307)

❋

facilius inter philosophos quam inter horologia conveniet
Philosophers will more readily be in agreement than will clocks.
Seneca *Apocolocyntosis* 2

• XXIII •

KINGS, CONSULS, AND EMPERORS

historiae per se tenent lectores; habent enim novarum rerum varias expectationes
History holds readers' attention by its very nature, for it raises expectations of all sorts of surprises.
Vitruvius *Architecture* 5 Preface

The Byzantine historian Procopius claimed that the ship that brought Aeneas to Italy from Troy more than a millennium and a half earlier was still well preserved and on display in a boatyard on the Tiber in the center of Rome (*The Wars of Justinian* 4.22). He regarded it as a remarkable testimony to the Romans' concern for the conservation of their heritage. Procopius's statement, however, is not only unparalleled but also conspicuously at odds with Vergil's description of the transformation of Aeneas's ships into sea nymphs (*Aeneid* 9.77ff.).

In November 2007, Italian archaeologists announced that they had found a sizable grotto under Augustus's residence on the Palatine. Speculating that it was the cave which the Romans of the Classical period revered as the den of the she-wolf that raised Romulus and Remus, they called it "one of the greatest discoveries of all time."

In the early Regal period, it was agreed that Rome's war with the neighboring city of Alba Longa should be decided by a fight

Aeneas leaving Troy.

between a set of triplets from each side: the Roman Horatii against the Alban Curiatii. Two of the Horatii were killed, whereas the other was unscathed; the Curiatii all suffered wounds of varying severity. The Roman ran away, pursued by the Curiatii, each as quickly as his wound would allow. Having separated his opponents by this pretence of cowardice, the surviving Horatius was able to dispose of them in single combat (Livy *History of Rome* 1.24). Livy notes that the story is so ancient that not all his sources agree that the Horatii were Romans and the Curiatii Albans, rather than vice versa.

❁

Some people said that the destruction of Carthage and the enslavement of Greece meant that Rome's power was secure, but Nasica, a leading Roman politician, said that this made the situation especially dangerous, for the Romans no longer had anyone left to be afraid of or to make them behave decently (Plutarch *How to Profit from One's Enemies* 3).

Sulla ruled Rome with vicious severity in the early years of the 1st century B.C. He was said to have been an excellent singer (Macrobius *Saturnalia* 3.14.10), and to have had only one testicle, a deficiency that did not preclude him from military service (Justinian's *Digest* 49 *ad init.*).

Make sure that your election campaign is one long parade, magnificent and splendid, appealing to popular taste, presenting a grand and dignified spectacle. If at all possible, you should also arrange for some scandal to be stirred up against your competitors, involving either criminal behavior or sex or bribery, depending on their character (*A Little Handbook on Running for Office* 13, attributed to Quintus Cicero, giving advice to his brother on conducting his campaign for the consulship).

The enclosure in which the citizens were mustered prior to casting their vote was known as the *ovile*, which literally means "sheep pen."

The end of the Republic was a particularly violent period. Looking back at that era, the 4th-century historian Ammianus Marcellinus observed that *anyone wishing to know all the different atrocities committed so repeatedly would also be misguided enough to think of investigating the number of grains of sand or the weight of mountains* (14.34).

JULIUS CAESAR

Julius Caesar could ride at a gallop with both hands behind his back, a considerable feat given that the Romans had no stirrups.

Early in his career, when he was a provincial administrator in southern Spain, Julius Caesar saw a statue of Alexander the Great in Cadiz and was upset that he himself had done nothing significant yet, whereas Alexander, by the same age, had conquered the world (Suetonius *Life of Julius Caesar* 7). This anecdote recalls Alexander's own frustration that his father, Philip II of Macedon, had subjugated much of Greece and was leaving him so little to conquer.

Julius Caesar could dictate letters to two or more scribes while mounted on horseback (Plutarch *Life of Julius Caesar* 17). According to Pliny, he was an even greater dictator, being able to keep seven scribes busy at once (*Natural History* 7.91). James Garfield, the twentieth president of the United States, rather outdid such multitasking, being able to write a translation from English to Latin with one hand while simultaneously writing a translation of the same passage in Greek with the other.

Cato the Younger interrupted a speech that he was giving in the Senate to challenge Julius Caesar to read aloud a letter which he had just been handed. He suspected that it contained evidence of Caesar's complicity in the Catilinarian conspiracy, but it turned out to be a racy love letter from Cato's half-sister (Plutarch *Life of Brutus* 5, *Life of Cato the Younger* 24).

When I look at his immaculately arranged hair and see him scratching his head with one finger [conventionally a sign of effeminacy], *I cannot think that he would ever conceive so great a crime as the overthrow of the Roman constitution* (Plutarch *Life of Julius Caesar* 4, quoting Cicero's opinion of Caesar). Licinius Calvus, a friend of Catullus, wrote an epigram pillorying Pompey for just such a combination of effeminacy and thirst for power (*fragment* 18).

When Pomponius was flaunting a face wound which he boasted that he had received fighting for Caesar, Caesar remarked, "You should never look back when you're running away" (Quintilian *Education of the Orator* 6.3.75).

Although discipline in the Roman army was very strict, it was traditional for soldiers marching in a triumphal parade to sing songs bantering their victorious commander. It is generally supposed that the purpose of such ritual obscenity was to ward off ill fortune. The best surviving example of this type of banter is the song which Julius

Caesar's soldiers sang during his triumph in 46 B.C.: *Citizens, keep watch over your wives; we are bringing the bald adulterer* (Suetonius *Life of Julius Caesar* 51).

On the last day of his triumph, Caesar was escorted home by practically the whole population, with a troop of elephants carrying torches for him (Cassius Dio *Roman History* 43.22).

When someone was making accusations against Mark Antony and Dolabella [a political adventurer who came to a bad end], *Julius Caesar said he was not afraid of those fat and long-haired fellows, but rather of those pale and thin ones, indicating Brutus and Cassius* (Plutarch *Life of Antony* 11).

When members of the Senate came to report to Julius Caesar that they had decided to award particular honors to him, he did not stand up as a mark of respect for their authority. This omission was one of the main reasons that the conspirators determined to assassinate him. The gods may have inspired him with folly, or he may simply have been distracted, but some people who wished to justify his behavior claimed that he had not moved because he was suffering from diarrhea; this was not very convincing, since he got up soon after and walked home (Cassius Dio *Roman History* 44.8).

In a conversation about the best way to die that arose at dinner on the day before he was killed, Caesar said he would prefer a sudden and unexpected death (Suetonius *Life of Julius Caesar* 87).

ANTONY AND CLEOPATRA

When Octavian was returning to Rome elated by his victory at Actium, among those who rushed to congratulate him was a fellow holding a raven, which he had taught to say ave, Caesar victor imperator! *"Hail, Caesar, victorious commander!" Caesar* [Octavian] *admired the well-trained bird and bought it for twenty thousand* sestertii. *A companion of*

A coin issued jointly by Antony and Cleopatra.

the bird's trainer, who had gained nothing from this generous deal, told Caesar that the trainer had another raven as well, and demanded that he be made to fetch it. When it was fetched, the bird uttered the words which it had learned, ave, victor imperator Antoni! *"Hail, Antony, victorious commander!"* (Macrobius *Saturnalia* 2.4.29).

Before Cleopatra, the Ptolemaic rulers of Egypt did not try to learn the Egyptian language; some of them could not even speak the Macedonian dialect of Greek. She, however, was able to speak without an interpreter to Egyptians, Ethiopians, Troglodytes, Jews, Arabs, Syrians, Medes, and Parthians. Plutarch says that Cleopatra, though not outstandingly beautiful, had a remarkably pleasant voice, with a tongue like a many-stringed musical instrument, able to turn to any language (*Life of Antony* 27).

Mark Antony's father was generous to a fault. He had little money of his own, nearly all the wealth in the family belonging to his wife. When a friend asked him for money, he had a slave bring him water in a silver bowl, and pretended he was going to shave. Then he sent the slave away and slipped the bowl to his friend. His wife discovered the loss and declared angrily that she was going to find out who stole the bowl by torturing the slaves one by one. So Antonius was forced to admit what he had done (Plutarch *Life of Antony* 1).

Once, when the greatest orator in Rome was speaking, Antony saw Cleopatra passing through the Forum. He jumped from his chair and left the court, hanging on to her litter as she went along (Plutarch *Life of Antony* 58).

Antony was disgruntled that he was catching nothing, because Cleopatra was with him. He ordered the fishermen to swim beneath the boat and secretly attach to his hook fish which had been caught earlier. He pulled fish in two or three times, but Cleopatra spotted what he was doing. She pretended to admire his catch, and told her friends to come and watch the next day. A large number of people got into the fishing boats and Antony cast his line. Cleopatra told one of her attendants to swim to Antony's hook before his own diver reached it and attach to it a pickled fish from the Black Sea (Plutarch *Life of Antony* 29).

When Octavian complained of Antony's liaison with Cleopatra, Antony responded with a letter cataloguing women with whom Octavian had committed adultery (Suetonius *Life of Augustus* 69).

Antony's life in Alexandria was offensive to traditional Roman ways. The Greek inscription on a base of a statue of him, set up in 34 B.C., describes him as "Great [μέγας (*megas*), perhaps 'Big' would be a better translation], inimitable in the deeds of Aphrodite, a god" (*Selected Eastern Greek Inscriptions* 195).

A papyrus document dated February 23, 33 B.C. (*Berlin P* 25 239 Ägyptisches Museum und Papyrussammlung), gives a tax exemption in the exportation of wheat from Egypt and the importation of wine. The beneficiary is Publius Canidius, who would command Antony's land forces at Actium two and a half years later. The ordinance is of particular interest because it is endorsed with the single Greek word γινέσθω (*ginestho*, "let it be so"), quite possibly written by Cleopatra herself. [We can only wonder how an

A 1st-century A.D. lamp making fun of Cleopatra.

important document from the court at Alexandria came to be used as a mummy wrapper in a little town far up the Nile.] Antony reciprocated by giving Cleopatra a monopoly on the exportation of murex shells, the source of purple dye, from the port of Tyre.

Defeat at the Battle of Actium ended Antony's hopes of power in Rome, but, through his marriage to Octavian's sister Octavia, he was the grandfather of Claudius, great-grandfather of Caligula, and great-great-grandfather of Nero. Similarly, Marcus Livius Drusus Claudianus, an ardent Republican who committed suicide with Brutus after fighting on the side of Caesar's assassins at Philippi, was the father of Livia, Augustus's wife, and a direct ancestor of Tiberius, Caligula, Claudius, and Nero.

At the foot of the Prima Porta statue of Augustus, in which the emperor is portrayed in an imposing military style, is Cupid riding a dolphin. As Venus's other son, Cupid was half-brother to Aeneas, from whom the Julian clan claimed descent.

AUGUSTUS (RULED 31 B.C.–A.D. 14)

Much as tourists nowadays throw coins into the Trevi Fountain to ensure that they will return to Rome, people of all classes used to throw coins into the mysterious Curtian Lake in the Forum on a particular day every year to ensure Augustus's continued good health (Suetonius *Life of Augustus* 57).

Augustus liked his friends to be open and direct in their dealings with him. A man named Artemidorus once had himself brought into the emperor's presence in a covered litter, as if he were a woman, and then he jumped out with a sword in his hand shouting, "Aren't you afraid someone may come in like this and kill you?" So far from being angry, Augustus thanked him for pointing out the danger (Cassius Dio *Roman History* 56.43).

For months after the massacre in the Teutoburg Forest in A.D. 9, Augustus was said to have gone about in mourning, banging his head against doors and yelling, "Quinctilius Varus, give me back my legions!" (Suetonius *Life of Augustus* 23). Augustus himself had founded those three legions, which constituted a significant proportion of Rome's military strength. (At the time of Augustus's death there were twenty-five legions.)

Largely because of Augustus's repeatedly frustrated efforts to engineer an appropriate succession, the Julio-Claudian dynasty is labyrinthine in its ramifications:

- Tiberius was devoted to his wife, Vipsania Agrippina, daughter of Augustus's friend Vipsanius Agrippa, who was the second husband of Augustus's daughter, Julia. When Agrippa died, Augustus forced Tiberius to divorce Vipsania and marry Julia. Tiberius thus married his own former mother-in-law and his former wife's stepmother, and Augustus's wife, Livia, became Julia's mother-in-law as well as her stepmother.
- Caligula was a great-grandson of Augustus and, by different lines of descent, also of Livia and of Mark Antony.

Augustus's domestic problems were not limited to the question of the succession: the two Julias (his daughter and granddaughter) and Agrippa Postumus (his last surviving grandson) all led lives that typified the sort of decadence he wished to suppress. He used to refer to them as his three boils (*vomicae*) or tumors (*carcinomata*), and when he heard that a freedwoman called Phoebe had hanged herself because of her involvement in the adulterous behavior of his daughter Julia, he cried out that he would rather have been Phoebe's father than Julia's (Suetonius *Life of Augustus* 65).

Writing in the 4th century, Macrobius has preserved, at *Saturnalia* 2.5, some remarks reflecting the difficult relationship that Augustus had with Julia, his only child:

- *Augustus said to his friends that he had to tolerate two spoiled daughters, Rome and Julia.*
- *When Livia and Julia attended a gladiatorial show together, the difference in their entourage excited notice: Livia was surrounded by serious and dignified men, but Julia was besieged by a herd of extravagant young men. Augustus wrote to Julia, pointing out the contrast. She wrote back wittily, "The men with me will be old when I am."*
- *Julia began to go gray prematurely, and used to have her gray hairs plucked out secretly. Augustus once came to see her unannounced and noticed gray hairs on her hairdressers' clothing. He didn't say anything then, but later he asked Julia if she preferred to be gray haired or bald. When she replied that she would rather be gray haired, he asked, "Then why are your hairdressers making you bald so quickly?"*
- *When she had listened to a serious-minded friend's advice that she would do better to model her behavior on Augustus's frugal way of life, she replied, "He forgets that he is Caesar, but I remember that I am Caesar's daughter."*
- *When some people who were aware of her loose morality expressed surprise that her children looked so like her husband, Agrippa, she replied, "I never take passengers on board till the ship is loaded."*

Four slaves dressing their mistress's hair.

Augustus is said to have had eyes so fiery that no one could meet his gaze. When he asked a Roman knight why he turned his face away, the knight replied, "Because I cannot bear the lightning flash in your eyes" (Servius's commentary on Vergil *Aeneid* 8.680).

When someone was hesitant about delivering a petition to him, and kept putting his hand out and drawing it back, Augustus asked him, "Do you think you are giving a penny to an elephant?" (Macrobius *Saturnalia* 2.4.3).

Statues of Augustus and representations of him on coins suggest that he had a more elegant personal appearance than did most emperors. Suetonius reports, however, that he cared so little for such matters that he would have two or three barbers working hurriedly together to cut his hair or shave him, and that he would read or write something during the process (*Life of Augustus* 79).

Augustus was so outraged by the activities of a robber in Spain nicknamed Corocotta that he offered a reward of a million sestertii *to anyone who could bring him in alive, but when Corocotta came to him voluntarily, not only did he not punish him, he actually gave him the reward* (Cassius Dio *Roman History* 56.43). [The corocotta was a mythical beast, a cross between a hyaena and a lioness, capable of imitating the human voice (Pliny *Natural History* 8.107).]

A man who looked very like Augustus came to Rome. Augustus had him summoned and asked him, "Was your mother ever in Rome?" The man said no, but added, "But my father often was" (Macrobius *Saturnalia* 2.4.20).

Among Augustus's rather homely sayings recorded by Suetonius are σποῦδε βραδέως (*spoude bradeos*, "Make haste slowly") and *celerius quam asparagi coquuntur* ("Quicker than cooking asparagus") (*Life of Augustus* 25, 87).

Many of the leading figures in the civil wars of the 1st century B.C. died violent deaths, but Augustus died peacefully in his bed just thirty-five days before his seventy-sixth birthday and had lived to see the birth of his first great-great-grandson (Pliny *Natural History* 7.58).

TIBERIUS (RULED A.D. 14–37)

Tiberius's cruel nature was evident even when he was still a boy. Theodorus of Gadara, his rhetoric teacher, seems to have been the first person shrewd enough to see this, and he hit on a very neat comparison: more than once when he was criticizing Tiberius he called him πηλὸς αἵματι πεφυραμένος (*pelos haimati pephuramenos*, "mud steeped in blood") (Suetonius *Life of Tiberius* 57).

Alas for the Roman people, which will be ground by such slow-moving jaws (Suetonius *Life of Tiberius* 21, Augustus, on the prospect of Tiberius succeeding him).

In A.D. 15, the year after Augustus's death, *a funeral procession was going through the Forum when someone bent over and whispered in the corpse's ear. When asked what he had whispered, he said that he was sending a message to Augustus that the poor citizens had not yet received the small sum of money that he had left each of them in his will. Tiberius had him executed immediately, saying that he could take the message personally, but soon after he did pay out the bequest* (Cassius Dio *Roman History* 57.14).

Tiberius greatly admired Lysippus's statue of the Apoxyomenos [a young man scraping olive oil from his body after exercise], *which Agrippa had dedicated in front of his baths. Although he was restrained in the early years of his rule, he could not resist this statue and had it transferred to his bedroom, setting up another statue in its place. But the populace made such an uproar at the theater demanding its return that he put it back* (Pliny *Natural History* 34.62).

Sextus Marius, who had become rich and important through his friendship with Tiberius, had a dispute with a neighbor. He invited him to be his guest for two days, on the first of which he completely demolished the neighbor's villa; on the second, he rebuilt it on a more expansive scale. Marius told the bewildered man that he was responsible, commenting that it showed that he was powerful enough both to defend his own interests and to repay favors (Cassius Dio *Roman History* 58.22).

Tiberius's left hand was stronger and more supple than his right, with knuckles so powerful that he could bore a hole in a firm and fresh apple with his finger or inflict a wound on the head of a boy or even of a young man with a single flick of his finger (Suetonius *Life of Tiberius* 68).

Tiberius left Rome in A.D. 27 and never returned to the city. He spent most of his declining years in decadent luxury on the island of Capri in the Bay of Naples. *Within a few days of his arrival on Capri, a fisherman suddenly came up to him when he was alone and offered him a large mullet. Tiberius ordered him to have his face rubbed with the fish, for he was alarmed that the fellow had managed to reach him by climbing up from the back of the island over a rough and trackless area. In his agony, the fisherman cried out that he was glad that he had not given the emperor the huge lobster that he had also caught. Tiberius had his face torn to shreds with the lobster* (Suetonius *Life of Tiberius* 60).

Artabanus, the king of Parthia, wrote Tiberius a letter criticizing him for the murders he had committed, for his sloth, and for his decadence, and advising him to give redress to the citizens' deep and wholly justified hatred of him by committing suicide (Suetonius *Life of Tiberius* 66).

Tiberius spared the life of Lucius Caesianus, who had not only been a close friend of the disgraced and executed Sejanus but had also made fun of the emperor's baldness by having the entertainment at the *Floralia* provided exclusively by bald men and then having five thousand boys with shaved heads hold torches for the crowds as they left the theater (Cassius Dio *Roman History* 58.19).

Because Lucius Piso was able to keep up with him in a drinking bout for two days and nights, Tiberius appointed him to the post of guardian of the city (Pliny *Natural History* 14.145). Such was his reputation for drinking that his name *Tiberius Claudius Nero* was perverted to *Biberius Caldius Mero* ("Drinker of hot undiluted wine") (Suetonius *Life of Tiberius* 42). This is rather wittier than the rabble's cry when he died—*Tiberium in Tiberim!* ("[Throw] Tiberius into the Tiber!") (Suetonius *Life of Tiberius* 75), given that the name *Tiberius* means "the man from the Tiber."

Corpses of other emperors, but not of Tiberius, did get thrown into the Tiber: Vitellius (A.D. 69) and Elagabulus (222), and possibly Commodus (192). Both of the Gracchi brothers had suffered the same indignity, Tiberius in 133 B.C. and Gaius in 121. Maxentius was pushed into the Tiber and drowned when his troops were fleeing Constantine's army in the Battle of the Milvian Bridge (A.D. 312).

Initially, when people protested against his cruel behavior, Tiberius pretended to suppose that they were merely angry and resentful at the severity of his moral reforms, and said repeatedly, oderint, dum probent (*"Let them hate me, provided that they approve my decisions"*) [a variation on a phrase in Accius's tragedy *Atreus*, see also below.] *Later, he proved their assessment of his cruelty to be only too correct* (Suetonius *Life of Tiberius* 59).

CALIGULA (RULED A.D. 37–41)

Caligula rarely allowed anyone to be executed other than by numerous little wounds. His instructions were always the same and quickly became notorious: "Strike him in such a way that he can feel himself dying." Once, when confusion over names led to the wrong man being executed, he said that the dead man had deserved that same punishment. He was always quoting that famous line from tragedy oderint, dum metuant (*"Let them hate me, provided that they fear me"*) (Suetonius *Life of Caligula* 30).

When Caligula asked someone who had spent years in exile how he had passed his time, the man gave the flattering reply, "I always prayed for Tiberius's death and your accession." Thinking that those whom he himself had exiled must be praying for his death, he sent men to the islands to kill them all (Suetonius *Life of Caligula* 28).

Caligula used to complain openly about the times he lived in as not having been made remarkable by any widespread disasters. Augustus's rule was notable for Varus's debacle [the Teutoburg massacre; see p. 19], *Tiberius's for the collapse of the amphitheater at Fidenae* [where as many as fifty thousand people were killed], *whereas his own rule was threatened with oblivion because of its prosperity. He repeatedly prayed for a military disaster, a famine, a plague, fires, or an earthquake* (Suetonius *Life of Caligula* 31).

By the end, Caligula had developed a passion for handling money; he would often walk barefoot over huge heaps of gold coins poured out in a large open space, and sometimes he even lay down and wallowed in them (Suetonius *Life of Caligula* 42).

A plebeian called Publius Afranius Potitus, in a fit of misjudged groveling, swore to give up his life if Caligula recovered from an illness, and a knight called Atanius Secundus declared that he would fight as a gladiator. They hoped to gain a financial reward but lost their lives, for Caligula recovered and forced them to keep their promises (Cassius Dio *Roman History* 59.8).

The assassins intercepted Caligula in a narrow passage and killed him. When he had fallen, none of them held back; they all inflicted savage wounds on his corpse, with some even tasting his flesh. His wife and daughter were quickly killed also. So it was that Caligula, after doing so many dreadful things for three years, nine months, and twenty-eight days, found through actual experience that he was not a god (Cassius Dio *Roman History* 59.29).

After Caligula's death a huge chest full of various poisons was discovered. Claudius had it thrown into the sea, but it is said that the sea was polluted and many fish died, being washed up on the nearby beaches by the tide (Suetonius *Life of Caligula* 49).

CLAUDIUS (RULED A.D. 41–54)

Before becoming emperor, Claudius was often the target of insults. *If he came late to a dinner, he had to prowl clumsily around the couches to get a place. Whenever he dozed off after dinner (as happened quite regularly), olive and date pits would be thrown at him. Sometimes practical jokers teased him by waking him up with a blow from a stick or a whip. They would also put his slippers on his hands while he was snoring so that he would rub his eyes with them when he was suddenly awakened* (Suetonius *Life of Claudius* 8).

Frightened by the report of Caligula's murder, Claudius slunk off to a nearby terrace and hid behind the curtains that covered the door. A private soldier who happened to be wandering about noticed his feet as he lurked there and wanted to find out who he was. When he recognized Claudius, he dragged him out and saluted him as emperor as he groveled on his knees in terror (Suetonius *Life of Claudius* 10).

Quite a number of dice that have survived from Roman times are "loaded."

Gambling was legal only during the festival of the *Saturnalia* in December, but this restriction was not observed. Claudius enjoyed gambling with dice and even published a book on the subject. He often played while being carried along, with his vehicle and playing board specially adapted so that the board would not be upset (Suetonius *Life of Claudius* 33). According to Seneca's satirical account of Claudius's deification, he was condemned to play in the Underworld for all eternity with a bottomless dice shaker (*Apocolocyntosis* ["Turning into a Pumpkin"] 14). The future emperor Vitellius won his friendship through a shared interest in gambling.

In Seneca's *Apocolocyntosis*, Augustus uses his maiden speech in the Olympian Council to protest that, if the gods allow Claudius to be a god, no one will believe that *they* are gods.

NERO (RULED A.D. 54–68)

Nero omitted none of the exercises by which singers preserve or improve their voice: lying on his back with lead sheets on his chest, taking enemas and emetics, abstaining from apples and any other foods thought to be damaging to the voice (Suetonius *Life of Nero* 20).

Nero used to prowl the bars and streets of Rome at night looking for trouble. He would beat up people he met on their way home from dinner and drop their bodies into sewers if they put up a fight. He himself was beaten almost to death by a senator whose wife he had molested (Suetonius *Life of Nero* 26).

Nero once gave ten million sestertii *to Doryphorus, his secretary in charge of petitions. His mother Agrippina had the money piled in a heap, in the hope that he would change his mind when he saw it all together, but Nero doubled it, remarking, "I didn't realize I'd given him so little"* (Cassius Dio *Roman History* 61.6).

When the head of Rubellius Plautus, a rival for the throne, was brought to him, Nero glanced at it and said, "I didn't realize he had such a big nose," as if he were implying that he would have spared him had he known (Cassius Dio *Roman History* 62.14).

Nero poisoned Britannicus. Since the poison gave his skin a telltale bluish tinge, he smeared the corpse with chalk. As Britannicus's body was being carried through the Forum, the chalk was washed off by heavy rain (Cassius Dio *Roman History* 61.7).

Among other measures he considered taking when he heard that Galba and his troops had revolted, Nero thought of poisoning the whole Senate at a banquet and setting fire to Rome after releasing wild beasts so that the people would have difficulty saving their lives (Suetonius *Life of Nero* 43).

After his death, demons were about to turn Nero into a viper, in punishment for the murder of his mother. Suddenly, however, a bright light appeared, and a voice ordered them to change him into a less nasty sort of animal, the sort of creature that sings beside marshes and lakes (Plutarch *On the Slowness of Divine Vengeance* 32).

THE YEAR OF THE FOUR EMPERORS, A.D. 68–69

I am undertaking to write an account of a period rich in disasters, dreadful in its battles, torn apart by civil unrest, and vicious even in peace, with four emperors perishing by the sword (Tacitus *Histories* 1.2, on the upheaval that led from Nero, through the brief reigns of Galba, Otho and Vitellius, to more stable times under Vespasian).

In 150 B.C., a direct ancestor of Galba systematically massacred men, women, and children in an attempt to exterminate the Lusitanians (the people of the region that is now Portugal).

When Galba's father, a hunchback, was pleading a cause in Augustus's court, he kept saying, "Set me straight, if you find any fault in me"; Augustus retorted, "I can advise you, but I can't set you straight" (Macrobius *Saturnalia* 2.4.8).

When Galba was taken as a boy to pay his respects to Augustus, the emperor squeezed his cheek and said to him in Greek, "My child, you also will have a little nibble at the power I wield." Tiberius spared his life only when he was assured that Galba would be an old man before he came to power (Suetonius *Life of Galba* 4).

Augustus had a seal ring with his own image. Emperors after him used this same seal, except for Galba, who used one with a dog looking out from the prow of a ship (Cassius Dio *Roman History* 51.3). That ring was an heirloom, but Galba had a dog so devoted to him that it died trying to keep his murderers from decapitating him, defending its dead master just as soldiers defend their fallen comrades (Aelian *On Animals* 7.10).

Vitellius's father had been consul three times, censor, and overseer of the empire while Claudius was in Britain. He was also a notorious flatterer:

- *He asked Messalina* [Claudius's third wife] *to allow him to remove her shoes, and when he took off her right shoe he kept it inside his toga, often stroking and kissing it.*
- *He worshipped golden images of Narcissus and Pallas* [Claudius's powerful freedmen] *among his household gods.*

- *He was the one who said to Claudius, who was putting on the Secular games* [which were meant to be held once a century], *"May you do this often."* (Suetonius *Life of Vitellius* 2)

Vitellius was unusually tall, with a ruddy complexion caused mostly by drinking, a fat paunch, and a slight weakness in one thigh from being hit by a four-horse chariot driven by Caligula (Suetonius *Life of Vitellius* 17).

When Vitellius visited the battlefield at Bedriacum where his army had defeated Otho, he had the audacity to try to encourage some of his retinue, who were appalled by the decomposing corpses, by saying that a dead enemy smelled very good, but a dead fellow citizen even better (Suetonius *Life of Vitellius* 10).

In intervals between fighting in the second Battle of Bedriacum, the soldiers of Vitellius shared their food and drink with their opponents, the army of Vespasian (Cassius Dio *Roman History* 64.13).

Vitellius uses more perfume to wash with than I use water. I suppose that if someone struck him with a sword, more perfume would flow than blood (Vespasian, reported by Philostratus at *Life of Apollonius* 29).

Your life was idle and your death was ghastly. Vitellius, you did not deserve to be made Caesar. This is how the Fates amuse themselves. Your rule was a brief shadow, for unworthy men often attain the prize of rule, but only the worthy retain it (Ausonius *The Caesars*). By the time Ausonius wrote this epigram in the late 4th century A.D., its general sentiment applied to the majority of the emperors.

THE FLAVIAN EMPERORS

Vespasian (ruled A.D. 69–79), Titus (ruled A.D. 79–81), Domitian (ruled A.D. 81–96)

Roman tax collectors tended to be ruthlessly extortionate. Vespasian's father was honored with statues erected to commemorate his fairness in collecting taxes (Suetonius *Life of Vespasian* 1).

Vespasian is believed to have habitually promoted his most rapacious officials to the highest posts so that he could condemn them when they had made themselves richer. It was widely said that he used these men like sponges, soaking them when they were dry and squeezing them when they were wet (Suetonius *Life of Vespasian* 16).

He had no ambition for outward splendor. On the day of his triumph parade [celebrating the destruction of Jerusalem in A.D. 70], *he was exhausted by the slow and boring procession and could not refrain from saying, "It serves me right! What a foolish old man I was to want a triumph, as if it was something I owed to my ancestors or ever desired for myself"* (Suetonius *Life of Vespasian* 12).

A stray dog once picked up a human hand at a crossroad, brought it into the room where Vespasian was having breakfast, and dropped it on the table (Suetonius *Life of Vespasian* 5). Having been the magistrate responsible for the cleanliness of Rome's streets during the reign of Caligula, Vespasian no doubt took a dim view of the incident.

When he suspected that his muleteer had jumped down to shoe the mules so as to give someone involved in a lawsuit time to approach him and beg a favor, he asked the muleteer how much he was getting for the shoeing, and he split the profit with him (Suetonius *Life of Vespasian* 23).

Vespasian was notoriously parsimonious. It is therefore paradoxical that he should have built Rome's most splendid and abiding monument, the Colosseum. He was criticized for his miserliness by an old cowherd, who asked him to free him from slavery when he became emperor but was told he had to pay for it; the old man shouted out "A fox changes his fur, but not his nature" (Suetonius *Life of Vespasian* 16).

At Vespasian's funeral, the leading mime actor wore his funeral mask and, as is customary, imitated the dead man's words and gestures. He asked the imperial officials how much the funeral and the procession cost; when they replied "A hundred thousand sestertii,*" he exclaimed, "Just give me a thousand and throw me in the Tiber"* (Suetonius *Life of Vespasian* 19).

Vespasian is said to have commented ironically on the practice of deifying emperors at their demise by saying on his deathbed, "Oh dear, I suppose I'm turning into a god" (*vae, puto, deus fio*) (Suetonius *Life of Vespasian* 23). Suetonius goes on to report that his actual dying words were "An emperor should die on his feet" (*imperatorem stantem oportet mori*), but that he collapsed as he tried to stand up.

It is partly fortuitous, but partly also an indication of the precarious nature of the imperial system, that in the first two hundred years of the empire, Vespasian was the only emperor to be succeeded by his own son (in his case, by both of his sons, Titus and Domitian).

At the beginning of his rule, Domitian used to spend hours alone doing nothing but catch flies and stab them with a very sharp stylus. Someone once asked if there was anyone in with Domitian and got the witty reply, "Not even a fly" (Suetonius *Life of Domitian* 3).

Sometimes Domitian had a slave stand far off with the palm of his right hand open, and shot arrows with such accuracy that they all passed between his fingers without harming him (Suetonius *Life of Domitian* 19).

Since Claudius's brief appearance at the front in Britain, no ruling emperor had gone on campaign. Domitian went once to Germany and three times to the Danube. He seems to have had some skill as a military commander, though the best success of his rule was won for him by Agricola at Mons Graupius, a still unknown location in Scotland, probably late in A.D. 83. [The famous criticism of Roman imperialism *ubi solitudinem faciunt, pacem appellant* ("Where they make a desert, they call it peace") is attributed by Tacitus, Agricola's son-in-law, to the British leader Calgacus, in his speech to his troops before this battle (*Agricola* 30).]

They say that Domitian dreamed that a golden hump had grown on his back, which he took as a sure sign that the state would be happier and more prosperous when he was gone. This turned out to be the case thanks to the restraint and modesty of the emperors who followed him (Suetonius *Life of Domitian* 23).

Domitian became more neurotic every day. He had the walls of the portico where he exercised fitted with shiny marble, the reflection from which allowed him to see what was going on behind his back. Moreover, he gave an audience to prisoners only if he was alone with them and holding their chains in his hand. . . . He used to say that emperors lived a very wretched life, for no one believed they had discovered a conspiracy until they had actually been murdered (Suetonius *Life of Domitian* 14, 21). Domitian was murdered on September 18, A.D. 96.

LATER EMPERORS

During his campaign against the Dacians, local tribesmen warned Trajan to turn back, sending him a message in Latin inscribed on a mushroom (Cassius Dio *Roman History* 68.8). Some scholars maintain that this incident is represented on one of the panels on Trajan's Column.

When an earthquake struck Antioch [in A.D. 115], *a superhuman being rescued Trajan, leading him out through his bedroom window with only minor injuries. Since the tremors continued for several days, Trajan lived out of doors in the Circus* (Cassius Dio *Roman History* 69.25).

Trajan was enrolled among the gods, and was given the exceptional honor of burial within the city. His bones were placed under his column in a golden urn, in the Forum which he built (Eutropius *Breviarium* 8.5). The urn is no longer there, and the statue of Trajan which once surmounted the column was replaced in the 16th century by one of St. Peter.

Hadrian once encountered a veteran who had served under his command rubbing his back against the wall in the public baths. The old soldier said he was doing so because he had no slave to do it for him, so Hadrian gave him slaves and money for their upkeep. On a later occasion, he saw several old men rubbing themselves against the wall, so he ordered them to scrape each other in turn (*Historia Augusta* Life of Hadrian 17).

Given the history of imperial assassination and the need which some emperors felt to set themselves apart from their subjects, this bantering exchange between Florus (whose precise identity is uncertain) and Hadrian is pleasantly surprising (*Historia Augusta* Life of Hadrian 16):

Florus:	
Ego nolo Caesar esse,	I do not wish to be Caesar,
ambulare per Sygambros,	to stroll among the Sygambri,
latitare per Britannos,	to lurk among the Britons,
Scythicas pati pruinas.	to endure the Scythian frosts.
Hadrian:	
Ego nolo Florus esse,	I do not wish to be Florus,
ambulare per tabernas,	to stroll among the taverns,
latitare per popinas,	to lurk among the snack bars,
culices pati rutundos.	to endure the plump gnats.

Lucius Verus, who was co-emperor with Marcus Aurelius from A.D. 161 to 169, was said to have sprinkled gold dust in his hair to emphasize its natural blonde color (*Historia Augusta* Life of Verus 10).

It has been estimated that, at its height in the 2nd century A.D., the Roman Empire was administered by some ten thousand bureaucrats—about 2 percent of the modern equivalent in the European Union. Even so, there was a considerable degree of micromanagement at the highest level:

- *In a single day, Claudius made twenty proclamations. One was that, since the grape harvest was abundant, wine jars should be covered carefully with pitch; another announced that yew juice was the best antidote for adder poison. . . . It is said that, after hearing about someone who almost died because of his modest restraint, Claudius even considered publishing an edict excusing the passing of gas during dinner* (Suetonius *Life of Claudius* 16, 32).
- Trajan exchanged letters with the younger Pliny, then the governor of the province of Bithynia in northern Turkey, about the sewer system in the unimportant town of Amastris (*Letters* 10.98, 99).
- Septimius Severus adjudicated in a dispute involving pig breeding when he held court in Alexandria in A.D. 200 (*Oxyrhynchus Papyri* 42.3019).

Commodus (ruled A.D. 180–192) was the first emperor to be born to a ruling emperor, on August 31, 161, six months after his father, Marcus Aurelius, had succeeded Antoninus Pius.

When he was eleven years old, Commodus gave an early sign of his sadistic tendencies. His bathwater was too cold, so he ordered the bath attendant to be thrown into the furnace. The slave instructed to do so burned a sheepskin in the furnace, so that the stench would make Commodus believe that the order had been obeyed (*Historia Augusta* Life of Commodus 1).

To escape persecution by Commodus, Sextus Condianus drank the blood of a hare, then deliberately fell from his horse. He vomited up the blood, as if fatally wounded, and was taken to his bedroom. A sheep was placed in a coffin and burned, while he himself disappeared. Nevertheless, a large number of heads, each supposedly his, were brought to Rome for identification and reward. It was never known if any of them was actually his (Cassius Dio *Roman History* 73.6).

Commodus was strangled in his bath by a wrestler named Narcissus. It would be good to know whether his erstwhile bath attendant lived long enough to learn this. If he had been strangled a day later, there would have been six claimants to power in A.D. 193, as there were in 238.

Three years after his murder in the bath, Commodus was declared a god by his successor, Septimius Severus.

Born to the Purple

- The reign of Clodius Albinus (A.D. 196–197) was presaged by the birth of a white bull calf with purple horns (*Historia Augusta* Life of Clodius Albinus 5).
- Geta's reign (A.D. 211) was presaged by a hen's laying a purple egg and by the birth of a lamb with purple wool on its forehead (*Historia Augusta* Life of Geta 3).
- Diadumenianus's reign (A.D. 217–218) was presaged by the birth of twelve purple lambs (*Historia Augusta* Life of Diadumenianus 4).
- Alexander Severus's reign (A.D. 222–235) was presaged by a pigeon's laying a purple egg and by his own mother's dream of giving birth to a little purple snake (*Historia Augusta* Life of Alexander Severus 13).
- Aurelian's reign (A.D. 270–275) was presaged by the birth of a huge calf, white except for a purple blotch on each side, one forming the word "Hail! [*ave*]," and the other in the shape of a crown (*Historia Augusta* Life of Aurelian 4).

Geta (ruled A.D. 211, jointly with his brother Caracalla, who killed him in their mother's arms) liked to have his cooks prepare dinners at which the name of every dish started with the same letter (*Historia Augusta* Life of Geta 5).

A Roman bathtub. The low siting of the swimming birds may suggest that baths were not normally filled very full.

After murdering Geta, Caracalla had his name and image removed from public records. The 174 inscriptions that survive originally included Geta's name, but the name is intact in only thirty-seven. Many of these thirty-seven are on water pipes, presumably buried before Caracalla's edict. On this wooden tondo, showing Caracalla and their parents, Septimius Severus and Julia Domna, the space once occupied by Geta's face was rubbed with manure said to be still slightly fragrant. (I have not been able to check this point.) Although "Geta" was a traditional name for slaves in comedies, Caracalla banned dramatists from using it (Cassius Dio *Roman History* 78.12).

Damnatio memoriae Getae.

⊕

Elagabalus's four-year reign ended in A.D. 222, when he was brutally assassinated at the age of about twenty. The following is a very small selection of the less vicious eccentricities attributed to him by the *Historia Augusta*:

- *At the start of his consulship, instead of throwing silver and gold coins or sweets or tiny animals to the people, he threw them fat cattle, camels, donkeys, and deer to tear apart, saying that it was the imperial thing to do.*
- *He drove a chariot drawn by four elephants on the Vatican hill, destroying tombs that stood in his path.*
- *He also had his chariot pulled by dogs, stags, lions, tigers, or even naked women.*
- *He would invite to dinner eight men who were all bald, or all one-eyed, or all gouty, or all deaf, or all black, or all remarkably tall, or all fat.* (Eight was the conventional number of guests at a formal dinner; they would recline with their host on three couches.)
- *He would give his fellow diners air cushions rather than real cushions, and then let the air out, so that they suddenly found themselves under the table.*

- *He would have his guests served food made of wax, wood, ivory, pottery, or stone, while he himself ate real food.*
- *He would often make his companions drunk and then shut them in bedrooms with lions, leopards, or bears which had been rendered harmless.*
- *At banquets, he used to give out spoons with prizes written on them, one reading "ten camels," another "ten flies," another "ten pounds of gold," another "ten pounds of lead," another "ten ostriches," another "ten hen's eggs."*
- *He did the same when he put on games, with prizes such as ten bears, or ten dormice, or ten lettuces, or ten pounds of gold; he invited the performers also to take part, with prizes such as a dead dog, or a pound of beef, or a hundred gold, silver, or copper coins.*

❁

Emperors liked to be portrayed in military postures, but the first ruling emperor known to have taken part in a battle was Maximinus Thrax (ruled A.D. 235–238). According to the frequently implausible *Historia Augusta*, he often drank seven gallons of wine in a day and ate forty or sixty pounds of meat, but he never ate vegetables and was eight feet, six inches tall (*Lives of The Two Maximini* 4, 6). The Roman foot measured 11.65 modern inches. Even so, Maximinus would have stood out in a crowd: forensic examination of skeletons from Pompeii show that the average height was five feet, five and a half inches for men, and five feet, one inch for women.

◎

The half-century from Maximinus to the accession of Diocletian in 284 was a period of unusual instability, with dozens of emperors and usurpers. A remarkable number of them perished at the hands of their own troops, but none suffered a fate as noteworthy as that of Valerian, co-emperor with his son Gallienus from 253 to 260: he fell into the hands of Shapur I of Persia, who used him as a mounting block when he got on his horse. It is alleged that when Valerian died, the skin was removed from his body and put on show in a temple. (The Byzantine emperor Romanos IV is similarly said to have been skinned, in 1071.) Shapur II, an equally successful king in wars with the Romans, ruled his whole life, from 310 to 379, having had the strange distinction of being appointed king before his actual birth.

Numerian ruled for a little more than a year, in A.D. 283–284. While campaigning against the Persians, he traveled in a closed litter to protect his eyes from the elements. He was killed by his father-in-law, Flavius Aper, who kept the corpse in the litter for several days to give himself time to consolidate his power. Eventually, however, the soldiers were alerted by the smell emanating from the litter. (*Historia Augusta* Lives of Carus, Carinus and Numerian 12).

An Iranian cameo, dramatizing the capture of Valerian by a rather implausible equestrian maneuver.

Diocletian ruled from A.D. 284 until 305, when he felt strong enough to abdicate, compelling his co-ruler Maximian to do the same. He lived on as a private citizen for about seven years in his magnificent palace near Split in Croatia, where he prided himself on growing large cabbages (Summary of Aurelius Victor *On the Caesars* 39).

In 2006, an intricately worked staff was discovered near the Palatine along with a rich trove of military regalia. Some scholars believe it to be Maxentius's imperial scepter, hurriedly hidden by his supporters after his defeat by Constantine at the Battle of the Milvian Bridge in A.D. 312.

Constantine the Great (ruled A.D. 307–337) had a checkered and very significant career:

- He was the son of an innkeeper's daughter.
- He was proclaimed emperor in the remote province of Britain.
- He fully legalized Christianity by the Edict of Milan in 313.
- In 321, he ordained that Sunday should be a day of rest.
- He had one of his own sons executed.

- He removed the center of power from Rome to Constantinople.
- Although he was at least nominally a Christian, being baptized just before he died, he was posthumously deified (as were several subsequent emperors who also professed Christianity).

❂

On September 4, A.D. 476, at the age of thirteen or fourteen, the last ruler of the Western empire, Romulus Augustus, was deposed by Odoacer, a Germanic chieftain. It is an ironic coincidence that he should be named after Rome's founder and the first and greatest of its emperors. The diminutive *Augustulus*, by which he is now universally known, alludes to his youth and political insignificance. He was also referred to by the Greek diminutive *Momyllus* ("little disgrace"). The Eastern empire continued until the capture of Constantinople by the Turks in 1453.

❂

Ohe, iam satis est, ohe, libelle!	Whoa, that's enough now, whoa, little book!
iam pervenimus usque ad umbilicos.	We've come now right to the end.
Tu procedere adhuc et ire quaeris,	You're keen to keep going on further,
nec summa potes in schida teneri,	And you can't be held back on the last page,
sic tamquam tibi res peracta non sit	As if you hadn't finished the task
quae prima quoque pagina peracta est.	That was finished already on the first page.
iam lector queriturque deficitque,	Now your reader is grumbling and giving up,
iam librarius hoc et ipse dicit	Now even the scribe himself is saying
"Ohe, iam satis est, ohe, libelle!"	"Whoa, that's enough now, whoa, little book!"

Martial *Epigrams* 4.89

GLOSSARY

THIS GLOSSARY defines briefly some of the people, places, events, and institutions referred to most often and most prominently in the book. It is not comprehensive. Further information is readily available in reference sources such as the *Oxford Classical Dictionary* (Oxford University Press, 3rd ed., 1996).

Actium: in 31 B.C., Octavian defeated Antony and Cleopatra at Actium in western Greece, thereby gaining control of the Roman world.

Aeneas: prince of Troy and son of the goddess Venus; the legendary founder of the Roman people.

Agrippa (Marcus Vipsanius Agrippa, c. 63–12 B.C.): a close personal friend of Augustus and leader of the victorious forces at Actium.

Ammianus Marcellinus (c. A.D. 325–after 391): the last great Roman historian, who wrote an account of the three centuries following the accession of Nerva; only the eighteen books dealing with A.D. 353–378 have survived.

Antony (Marcus Antonius, 83–30 B.C.): Julius Caesar's lieutenant, Cleopatra's lover, and Octavian's rival for power.

Appian (c. A.D. 95–c. 165): author of a history of Rome in Greek.

Augustine (Aurelius Augustinus, A.D. 354–430): author of *The City of God*, *Confessions*, and more than a hundred other works.

Augustus (63 B.C.–A.D. 14; until 27 B.C., referred to as Octavian): the first and most influential Roman emperor (ruled 31 B.C.–A.D. 14).

Aulus Gellius (c. A.D. 125–after 180): author of the *Attic Nights*, a collection of quotations and discussions on wide-ranging and miscellaneous topics.

Brutus (Marcus Junius Brutus, 85–42 B.C.): co-leader with Cassius of the assassins of Julius Caesar.

Caesar (Gaius Julius Caesar, 102 or 100–44 B.C.): the greatest Roman of them all.

Caligula (Gaius Julius Caesar Augustus Germanicus, A.D. 12–41, more formally known as Gaius): the third emperor (ruled A.D. 37–41).

Campus Martius: the Plain of Mars, about six hundred acres in extent, the site of the Circus Maximus.

Cannae: in 216 B.C., the Romans were defeated catastrophically by Hannibal at Cannae in southern Italy.

Capitoline: with the Palatine, the most important of Rome's hills.

Carrhae: in 53 B.C., Crassus's army was destroyed by the Parthians at Carrhae in northern Syria.

Carthage: located on the outskirts of modern Tunis, Rome's great rival for supremacy in the western Mediterranean, destroyed in 146 B.C.

Cassius (Gaius Cassius Longinus, before 85–42 B.C.): co-leader with Brutus of the assassins of Julius Caesar.

Cassius Dio (c. A.D. 160–c. 230): author of a history of Rome in Greek.

Catiline (Lucius Sergius Catilina, 108–62 B.C.): leader of a conspiracy in 63 B.C. to overthrow the government.

Cato (Marcus Porcius Cato, 234–149 B.C.): an iconic advocate of the traditionally simple Roman way of life, the *mos maiorum* ("the custom of the ancestors"); his like-named great-grandson (95–46 B.C.) had a similar conservative attitude to politics and life in general.

Catullus (Gaius Valerius Catullus, c. 84–c. 54 B.C.): the most influential poet in the last generation of the Republic.

Celsus (Aulus Cornelius Celsus, 25 B.C.–A.D. 50): the author of an encyclopedia, of which only the books on medicine survive.

Censor: every five years, two censors were appointed to review the citizenship register and supervise public morality.

Cicero (Marcus Tullius Cicero, 106–43 B.C.): the greatest of all Roman orators, and a leading politician in the late Republic.

Civil wars: for almost a century before Octavian gained decisive control at Actium, Rome was riven by civil wars.

Claudius (Tiberius Claudius Nero Drusus Germanicus, 10 B.C.–A.D. 54): the fourth emperor (ruled A.D. 41–54).

Cleopatra: Cleopatra VII, the last Greek ruler of Egypt, the lover of Julius Caesar and of Mark Antony, with whom she was defeated by Octavian at Actium.

Commodus (Lucius Aurelius Commodus Antoninus, 161–192 A.D.): son of Marcus Aurelius and mad emperor par excellence (ruled A.D. 180–192).

Consul: after the expulsion of the last king, two consuls were elected annually to supreme authority, their dual command being an effective means of ensuring that no individual could again seize power as king.

Corpus of Latin Inscriptions: the definitive storehouse of Latin inscriptions, arranged by regions of the empire. *Select Latin Inscriptions* is a compilation of some of the most significant inscriptions in a more accessible format.

Crassus (Marcus Licinius Crassus; c. 115–53 B.C.): a leading politician at the end of the Republic, who formed the First Triumvirate with Pompey and Caesar, and was killed at Carrhae.

Dacians: the people who inhabited present-day Romania, subjugated by Trajan in the early 2nd century A.D.

***The Deeds of the God Augustus* (*Res Gestae Divi Augusti*)**: Augustus's record of his achievements, displayed prominently throughout the empire late in his reign.

Dictator: at times of crisis, a dictator was appointed with sole power, overriding the authority of the consuls.

Diodorus Siculus (c. 90–c. 27 B.C.): the author of a universal history in Greek.

Dionysius of Halicarnassus (c. 60–after 7 B.C.): the Greek author of a history of Rome down to the First Punic War, and of various treatises on rhetoric.

Domitian (Titus Flavius Domitianus, A.D. 51–96): the eleventh emperor (ruled A.D. 81–96).

Etruscans: a non-Indo-European people living north of Rome who were among Rome's most powerful neighbors in the early centuries.

Frontinus (Sextus Julius Frontinus, c. A.D. 40–103): the author of treatises on Rome's aqueducts and military stratagems.

Fronto (Marcus Cornelius Fronto, c. A.D. 100–170): Fronto's reputation rests predominantly on a badly preserved collection of letters which he exchanged with his imperial pupils Marcus Aurelius and Lucius Verus.

Galba (Servius Sulpicius Galba, 3 B.C.–A.D. 69): the sixth emperor (ruled A.D. 68–69).

Galen (Claudius Galenus, c. A.D. 129–after 200): the most influential of ancient doctors, endearingly opinionated.

Gallus (Gaius Cornelius Gallus, c. 70–26 B.C.): a leading poet of the late Republic, and first Roman governor of Egypt.

Gauls: the people of modern France and surrounding regions.

Gracchi (Tiberius and Gaius Sempronius Gracchus, 163–133 and 154–121 B.C.): social reformers who both fell foul of the Senate.

Hadrian (Publius Aelius Traianus Hadrianus, A.D. 76–138): the fourteenth emperor (ruled A.D. 117–138).

Hannibal: the great Carthaginian commander in the Second Punic War (218–201 B.C.).

Herculaneum: after Pompeii, the most important town destroyed by the eruption of Mt. Vesuvius in A.D. 79.

Historia Augusta: the *Augustan History* is a thoroughly unreliable collection of biographies of 2nd- and 3rd-century emperors and usurpers, of uncertain date and authorship. The citations from it should be regarded with particular skepticism.

Horace (Quintus Horatius Flaccus, 65–8 B.C.): a leading poet of the Augustan age.

Josephus (Titus Flavius Josephus, A.D. 37–after 100): author of the *Jewish Wars* and *Jewish Antiquities*.

Justinian (Flavius Petrus Sabbatius Justinianus, A.D. 482/483–565): ruler of the eastern empire (ruled 527–565), who commissioned the compilation of the *corpus iuris civilis*, the most significant and influential Roman legal texts.

Juvenal (Decius Junius Juvenalis, late 1st century A.D.): a viciously mordant satirist.

Knights/equites: the second-highest stratum in Roman society after the senatorial class.

Lepidus (Marcus Aemilius Lepidus, ?–13/12 B.C.): the least significant member of the Second Triumvirate.

Livia: the wife of Augustus.

Livy (Titus Livius, ?59 B.C.–?A.D. 17): the author of a voluminous *History of Rome* from the beginning to the Principate of Augustus, about a quarter of which has survived.

Macrobius (Ambrosius Theodosius Macrobius, late 4th/early 5th centuries A.D.): a grammarian and philosopher, author of, most notably, the *Saturnalia*, a wide-ranging dialogue on many subjects, especially literary criticism of Vergil.

Maecenas (Gaius Cilnius? Maecenas, 70–8 B.C.): a close friend and political advisor to Augustus and patron to Vergil and Horace.

Marcus Aurelius (Marcus Aurelius Antoninus Augustus, A.D. 121–180): Stoic philosopher and emperor (ruled A.D. 161–180).

Marius (Gaius Marius, c. 157–86 B.C.): a leading military and political figure in the late 2nd and early 1st centuries B.C.

Martial (Gaius Valerius Martialis, c. A.D. 40–c. 101): a prolific writer of epigrams.

Master of the Cavalry/*magister equitum*: the second-in-command to a dictator.

Mithridates (134–63 B.C.): Mithridates VI (ruled 120–63 B.C.) of Pontus in modern Turkey, Rome's most dangerous foreign enemy in the 1st century B.C.

Nero (Lucius Domitius Ahenobarbus, A.D. 37–68): the fifth emperor (ruled A.D. 54–68).

Nerva (Marcus Cocceius Nerva, A.D. 30–98): the twelfth emperor (ruled A.D. 96–98).

Numa Pompilius: Rome's second king.

Octavian: see Augustus.

Otho (Marcus Salvius Otho, A.D. 32–69): the seventh emperor (ruled A.D. 69).

Ovid (Publius Ovidius Naso, 43 B.C.–A.D. 18?): author of the *Metamorphoses* and many other immortal poems.

Palatine: with the Capitoline, the most important of Rome's hills.

Parthia: the Parthian empire, which extended over much of the area from the Mediterranean to India and was a serious threat to Rome's eastern possessions.

Patricians: the Roman aristocracy.

Petronius (? Petronius Arbiter, probably Neronian): the author of the *Satyricon*, a satirical novel.

Plebeians/*plebs*: the lower class of Roman citizens.

Pliny the Elder (Gaius Plinius Secundus, A.D. 23–79): author of the *Natural History*, an endlessly fascinating encyclopedia, conveying (by Pliny's computation) twenty thousand facts.

Pliny the Younger (Gaius Plinius Caecilius Secundus, A.D. ?62–?113): nephew and adopted son of Pliny the Elder, whom he declined to accompany across the Bay of Naples for a closer view of the eruption of Mt. Vesuvius, preferring to read Livy instead; he survived to write copious volumes of letters, mostly edited for publication, and a panegyric of the emperor Trajan.

Plutarch (c. A.D. 45–127): as well as biographies of prominent Greeks and Romans, he also wrote the *Moralia*, essays on a wide range of philosophical, religious, and literary topics.

Polybius (c. 203–120 B.C.): author of the *Histories*, an account in Greek of Rome's expansion in 220–146 B.C.

Pompeii: the most important town destroyed by the eruption of Mt. Vesuvius in A.D. 79.

Pompey (Gnaeus Pompeius Magnus, 106–48 B.C.): a leading military and political figure at the end of the Republic, who formed the First Triumvirate with Crassus and Caesar, and was killed in the aftermath of his defeat by Caesar at Pharsalus.

Pontifex maximus: the most important of Rome's priests.

Praetor: after the consuls, the praetors were the most important Roman magistrates.

Principate: when Octavian/Augustus gained power, he adopted the title *princeps* ("leading man") as a means of understating his absolute authority.

Proscriptions: during political unrest, the names of citizens were posted by the faction in power; the victims were then hunted down, a bounty was paid to their killers, and the rest of their property was confiscated by the state. The most notorious proscriptions were conducted by Sulla in the late 80s B.C. and by the Second Triumvirate after the assassination of Caesar.

Punic Wars (264–241, 218–201, 149–146 B.C.): the three wars fought by Rome against the Carthaginians (whose origin in Phoenicia in the eastern Mediterranean is reflected in the term "Punic").

Pyrrhus (319/8–272 B.C.): king of Epirus in western Greece, who invaded Italy in 280 to fight the Romans.

Quintilian (Marcus Fabius Quintilianus, c. A.D. 35–c. 100): author of *The Education of the Orator*, a highly influential treatise on rhetoric.

Republic: the period from the expulsion of the last king at the end of the 6th century B.C. until the establishment of the Principate under Augustus.

Romulus: Rome's legendary first king, the son of Mars and the vestal virgin Rhea Silvia.

Sallust (Gaius Sallustius Crispus, 86–34 B.C.): a moralizing historian of rather dubious morality.

Samnites: a warlike people in central Italy. For several centuries, they were a serious threat to Rome's power, until they were all but annihilated by Sulla in the Social War.

Scipio: (Publius Cornelius Scipio Africanus the Elder, 236–183 B.C.): defeated Hannibal at Zama in 202.

Senate: the Senate, membership of which required a very substantial property qualification, ran the state throughout almost all the Republican era.

Seneca the Elder (?Lucius Annaeus Seneca, ?54 B.C.–?A.D. 40): author of the *Controversiae* and *Suasoriae*, memoirs of his time in the schools of rhetoric in the Augustan period.

Seneca the Younger (Lucius Annaeus Seneca, ?4 B.C.–A.D. 65): son of the above, politician, philosopher, dramatist, and advisor to Nero.

***Sestertii*:** the *sestertius* was a coin valued at 2.5 *asses*, and 0.25 of a *denarius*. In the early imperial period, a legionary usually earned nine hundred *sestertii* annually, and one million *sestertii* was the property qualification for the Senate.

Social War (91–87 B.C.): the Romans' Italian allies (*socii*) revolted when denied citizenship, which was granted to them as a result of the war.

Strabo (?64 B.C.–A.D. ?24): author of a voluminous treatise in Greek, the *Geography*.

Suetonius (Gaius Suetonius Tranquillus, c. A.D. 70–after 130): author of biographies of Julius Caesar and the first eleven emperors, as well as of poets, rhetoricians, teachers.

Sulla (Lucius Cornelius Sulla Felix, c. 138–78 B.C.): a prominent military and political leader who ruled Rome in the early years of the 1st century B.C.

Tacitus (?Publius Cornelius Tacitus, c. A.D. 56–c. 117): the greatest Roman historian.

Teutoburg Forest: the marshy woodland where, in A.D. 9, German tribesmen massacred three Roman legions, thousands more auxiliary troops, and an unknown number of camp followers.

Tiberius (Tiberius Claudius Nero, 42 B.C.–A.D. 37): the second emperor (ruled A.D. 14–37).

Titus (Titus Flavius Vespasianus, A.D. 39–81): the tenth emperor (ruled A.D. 79–81).

Trajan (Marcus Ulpius Nerva Traianus, A.D. 53–117): the thirteenth emperor (ruled A.D. 98–117).

Tribes: for voting purposes, the citizen body was divided into tribes, which numbered thirty five by the end of the Republic.

Triumph: after an important military success, a general was permitted to parade through Rome with his army, his plunder, and his captives.

Triumvirate (literally, "a group of three men"): in the late 60s B.C., Pompey, Crassus, and Caesar formed the First Triumvirate to run the state in their own interests; after Caesar's assassination, Antony, Octavian, and Lepidus formed the Second Triumvirate.

Twelve Tables: as a step toward making the administration of justice fairer, the laws were posted in the Forum in the middle of the 5th century B.C.

Valerius Maximus (flourished in the Tiberian period): the author of a moralizing collection of *Famous Deeds and Sayings*.

Varro (Marcus Terentius Varro, 116–27 B.C.): a voluminous author on many topics, whose only works to survive complete or in substantial part are his *On Farming* and *On the Latin Language*.

Varus (Publius Quinctilius Varus, 46 B.C.–A.D. 9): the general responsible for the massacre in the Teutoburg Forest.

Vegetius (Publius Flavius Vegetius Renatus, of unknown date in the Late Empire): author of *On Military Affairs* and *On Veterinary Medicine*.

Velleius Paterculus (Marcus or Gaius Velleius Paterculus, c. 39 B.C.–c. A.D. 19): author of a history of Rome.

Vergil (Publius Vergilius Maro, 70–19 B.C.): the greatest Roman poet.

Vespasian (Titus Flavius Vespasianus, A.D. 9–79): the ninth emperor (ruled A.D. 69–79).

Vestal virgins: a college of six priestesses responsible for safeguarding the sacred fire of the goddess Vesta.

Vitellius (Aulus Vitellius Germanicus, A.D. 15–69): the eighth emperor (ruled A.D. 69).

Vitruvius (?Marcus Vitruvius ?Pollio, before 70–c. 25 B.C.): author of a highly influential treatise on architecture.

Zama: Scipio Africanus brought the Second Punic War to an end by defeating Hannibal at Zama (in modern Tunisia) in 202 B.C.

THE COIN IMAGES

ALL IMAGES of coins on the first pages of chapters are reproduced courtesy of Classical Numismatic Group, Inc., www.cngcoins.com.

⊕

Chapter I: Janus, the two-headed god of doors (*ianuae*) and new beginnings (as in January). Minted c. 225–212 B.C.

Chapter II: The vestal virgin Tarpeia agreed to let the Sabine troops into Rome in return for what they wore on their left arms. She meant their gold bracelets, but they buried her under their shields.

Chapter III: A coin minted in commemoration of Julius the God (DIVI IVLI) in 40 B.C. The curved object is the head of a *lituus*, a staff carried by the augurs, who predicted the future by observing the flight of birds.

Chapter IV: AVGVSTVS CAESAR. Minted c. 18 B.C.

Chapter V: MARS VICTOR on a coin of Elegabalus. Minted in A.D. 219.

Chapter VI: Mark Antony. Minted in 36 B.C.

Chapter VII: A high-ranking magistrate escorted by *lictors*, officials who carried an axe in a bundle of rods (the *fasces*), a symbol of his power to inflict corporal or capital punishment. Minted c. 54 B.C by Marcus Junius Brutus, the assassin of Julius Caesar.

Chapter VIII: A curvilinear Celtic horse. Minted in Britain about the time of the Roman invasion in A.D. 43.

Chapter IX: Marcus Aurelius, the nearest Rome came to the Platonic "philosopher king" and father of Commodus, who imagined himself to be a reincarnation of Hercules.

Chapter X: Minted in 46 B.C, by Julius Caesar as AVGVR and PONT(ifex) M(aximus).

Chapter XI: The late Republican moneyer, Quintus Pomponius Musa, minted ten coin-types, nine with a different Muse, and one portraying Hercules Musagetes, Hercules the Leader of the Muses.

Chapter XII: Phraataces, king of Parthia. Minted in 2 B.C.–A.D. 4.

Chapter XIII: A denarius minted by Tiberius, of the type popularly known as the "tribute penny," the coin to which Jesus referred when he said that we should "render unto Caesar the things which are Caesar's" (Matthew 22.21, Mark 12.17, Luke 20.25).

Chapter XIV: Minted by Julius Caesar soon after he crossed the Rubicon in January of 49 B.C. Some said that an earlier member of his family had won the cognomen by singlehandedly killing an elephant in battle (*casai* being Moorish or *caesa* Punic for "elephant").

Chapter XV: Jupiter, with his scepter and thunderbolt, riding in a chariot driven by Victory. Minted c. 225–212 B.C.

Chapter XVI: A(ulus) VITELLIVS GERM(anicus) IMP(erator) AVG(ustus) TR(ibunus) P(lebis). The disgraceful gourmet Vitellius, who ruled for eight months in A.D. 69.

Chapter XVII: Nero. As the flabby features show, this coin was minted when his reign was drawing to its close.

Chapter XVIII: An unusually unflattering portrayal of Hadrian. The inscription is in Greek, for the coin was minted for use in the eastern provinces of the empire.

Chapter XIX: TI(berius) CLAVD(ius) CAESAR AVG(ustus) P(ontifex) M(aximus) TR(ibunus) P(lebis) VI IMP(erator) XI. Minted by Claudius in A.D. 46–47.

Chapter XX: The Medusa. Minted in 47 B.C. Greek mythological figures are not uncommon on Roman coins.

Chapter XXI: Minted by Caligula just before his assassination in A.D. 41. The inscription honors him as the great-grandson of the god Augustus, as Pontifex Maximus, as Tribune of the People, and as Father of the Fatherland.

Chapter XXII: Vespasian, one of the best emperors, if not the most handsome.

Chapter XXIII: Maximinus I. The coin does no justice to his massive physique (see p. 230).

ILLUSTRATION CREDITS

© Vanni/Art Resource: pp. 2, 24, 210
© Kathleen Cohen: pp. 4, 11, 60 (top), 76, 90 (top), 144, 145, 192, 228
© The Trustees of the British Museum/Art Resource: pp. 5, 155, 208
© Réunion des Musées Nationaux/Art Resource: pp. 7, 86, 102
© Scala/Art Resource: pp. 14, 79, 88, 109, 129, 140, 148, 197, 204, 219
© Canyonlights/Susan S. Peirce, all rights reserved: pp. 23, 156
© Rheinisches Landesmuseum Trier: p. 29
© Gilles Mermet/Art Resource: pp. 30, 61, 80, 160
© Alinari/Art Resource: pp. 39, 131, 153, 166
© The Trustees of the British Museum: pp. 42, 115, 209
© Erich Lessing/Art Resource: pp. 48, 60 (bottom), 69, 74, 112, 122, 126, 143, 152, 162, 163, 191, 194, 213, 231
© Jo Winston: pp. 53, 172, 178, 189
© A. M. Rosati/Art Resource: p. 72
Used with permission from Brett Holman, p. 90 (bottom)
© Scala/Ministero per i Beni e le Attivitá culturali/Art Resource, pp. 146, 184
© Oldrich Barak, 2009; used under license from Shutterstock.com, p. 174
© Douglas Clapp, p. 179
© Bildarchiv Preussischer Kulturbesitz/Art Resource, p. 229